KICK
YOUR OWN ASS

KICK
YOUR OWN ASS

The **WILL, SKILL,** *and* **DRILL**

of **SELLING** *More*

Than You Ever Thought Possible

ROBERT EARLY JOHNSON

WILEY

JOHN WILEY & SONS, INC.

Published by John Wiley & Sons, Inc., Hoboken, New Jersey.
Published simultaneously in Canada.

For general information on our other products and services or for technical support, please contact our Customer Care Department within the United States at (800) 762-2974, outside the United States at (317) 572-3993, or fax (317) 572-4002.

Wiley also publishes its books in a variety of electronic formats. Some content that appears in print may not be available in electronic books. For more information about Wiley products, visit our web site at www.wiley.com.

Library of Congress Cataloging-in-Publication Data:

Johnson, Robert E., 1962-
  Kick your own ass : the will, skill, and drill of selling more than you ever thought possible / Robert E. Johnson.
    p. cm.
  Includes index.
  ISBN 978-0-470-59884-9 (cloth)
  1. Selling.   I. Title.
  HF5438.25.J6538 2010
  658.85—dc22   2009054221

Printed in the United States of America

10 9 8 7 6 5 4 3 2 1

CONTENTS

ACKNOWLEDGMENTS

Everything I know about selling I learned from someone else. My friend Ed Kless often quotes Charles Murray's book *Human Accomplishment*, which states that only 4,002 people ever had original ideas, and everyone else is simply borrowing. I don't have any idea if this is true, but the subject matter discussed in *this* book certainly meets the "borrowing" criteria. Over my 25-year career in sales, I have read hundreds of books, attended classes, and worked with some of the best and brightest trainers and practitioners in the business. I have learned something of value from every one. To those unnamed and unrecognized who have helped to shape my understanding and beliefs around the concepts of what it takes to succeed in sales, I offer my profound thanks and deepest gratitude. My career to date has been a blast, and I feel truly lucky to have the chance to work in a career where I get paid to help people change the arc of their potential, and improve the quality of their lives.

When referring to specific content in the book, I have attempted when possible to recognize the author or creator. If I have failed to provide adequate recognition, it is through my own ignorance, and no attempt to take credit for what is not of my own making. In particular, I have benefited greatly from the works of Zig Ziglar and Mahan Khalsa. If you haven't yet read their works, I encourage you to do so. As you read this text, it will be impossible to miss the influence of these two very gifted writers, thought leaders and sales practitioners.

For years, my dream of writing a book lived only in my thoughts as I ran along University Boulevard in Jacksonville, Florida. It wasn't until others badgered me into believing that I could and should pursue writing one that it actually grew out of the "impossible dream" phase and into the "I could actually do this" phase. However, bringing the dream of writing a book to the reality of writing a book is a long and interesting journey, and one that isn't traveled alone. In other words, I had a ton of help.

To my friend and running buddy Steve Shaull, for not cutting me an inch of slack. Ever.

To Bob Sandelands, the best salesperson I know, for kicking my ass into committing to a date to complete a book in 2009—which set the laws of expectation and attraction in motion, and without which, the book simply would never have happened.

To my particular friend Tom Hume, a marketing genius, for sending me Sophfronia Scott's book, *Business by the Book,* which actually led me to work with her to create an outline and a plan for getting published.

To Sophfronia Scott, author of *Business by the Book* and president of *The Done For You Writing & Publishing Company,* for helping to develop the concept that would become *Kick Your Own Ass,* her encouragement and assistance in pursuing a publishing agreement with John Wiley & Sons, Inc. Hiring a coach was a giant step forward, and she is terrific.

To my professional colleague Ron Baker, thought leader and author of numerous books on the subject of value pricing, for his willingness to create an introduction on my behalf.

To Sage, my employer and a great company with which to work, for providing me the opportunity to focus my greatest strengths for the most good, and for their support of this effort.

By the way, if you, or someone you know, are in the market to radically improve your business performance, look us up at www.sagenorthamerica .com. We have accounting and CRM solutions for nearly every business— even yours. (Hey, I can't resist plugging my company. I'm in sales. It's what we do.)

To Tom Miller, for his remarkable ability to listen without judging, his even-keeled approach to problem solving, and his commitment to helping our partners succeed. Also, for his love of good food in out-of-the-way locations.

To Ed Kless, who continuously challenges my thinking and prods me into achieving better results.

To Taylor Macdonald, for his friendship and his insight in seeing something in me that I didn't know existed, and encouraging me to pursue it.

A very special thanks to Dr. Phillip R. Yates, Ph.D. for his tremendous contribution to the project, specifically the content in Chapter 6, "The Will Killers." His insight, wisdom, and knowledge of the core issues that prevent us from changing our life's trajectory were instrumental. Furthermore, his practical experience and the skills and processes that he utilizes to help his clients change the arc of their potential, thus improving the quality of their lives, provided the groundwork for creating the model for change discussed in the book. His open willingness to work, share, and brainstorm how to help salespeople overcome their core issues was simply invaluable.

To Bob Kreisberg, president of OPUS Productivity, for his contributions to Chapter 5, "Debunking the 'Sales Personality' Myth," and for providing a free personality profile to the readers of this book.

To Professional DynaMetric Programs®, Inc. for the use of their proprietary content in Chapter 5, and for working collectively with OPUS Productivity to provide our readers a free personality profile.

A special thanks to my close friend Greg Kirshe, president of United Solutions, for his steadfast friendship over many years and for his willingness to read early drafts of the book, providing thoughtful feedback while not laughing too hard.

To the thousands of students I have had the privilege of training over the years. Thanks for sharing your successes as a result of attending our programs.

To Richard Narramore, my editor at John Wiley & Sons, Inc., for taking on the project. To Christine Moore, Lydia Dimitriadis, Peter Knox, and Lauren Freestone, for their help in making the book terrific.

To you. Thanks for buying this book. I hope that in it you will find answers to your questions on how to improve your career in sales, and that it will become part of your process of changing the arc of your potential.

To our children: Jana, Hilary, Seth, Chelsea, and Riley. Thanks for the joy you have brought into our lives.

To my mother, Mary Early Johnson, a beautiful and tender soul—artist, librarian, collector of stuff, and superb pie maker—for not killing me when I was a child and likely deserved it. And for her blind faith that her children are capable of achieving anything they choose to pursue.

Finally, I thank my best friend and wife Anita Pryor, whom I love and admire. And, without whom, my life would still be a complete mess. She not only implanted the belief that I could and should write a book, she thoughtfully and carefully edited my writing, and helped shape the thoughts and concepts into a coherent structure, which included the use of complete sentences. A beautiful person, a terrific wife and mother, and a brilliant and successful lawyer—she is an inspiration to me.

FOREWORD

In September of 1970, and recently graduated from the University of Maryland, I had the good fortune of becoming a sales representative for the Federal Systems division of Sperry Univac, selling mainframe computers to the federal government in Washington, D.C. I did not know it at the time, but this was the beginning of my 40-year career in selling and providing automated technology solutions to customers.

Over the course of that career, I have been exposed to arguably the best sales training available in the world. In addition to Sperry, my career had stops at Xerox and as an independent computer value-added reseller (VAR) authorized for Apple, IBM, and Compaq. The professional solution sales training I received from Xerox and IBM are still recognized as global "best-of-breed" training, to say nothing of the training from Apple and Compaq.

In the summer of 1976, I took a huge leap of faith and started my own business, which was a computer service bureau providing automated services to regional CPA firms. It was here that I somehow got connected with the software that made accounting actually happen on computers. From that moment, my life took a strange and wonderful turn. If you weren't around the market in the late 1970s or early 1980s, let me say this: It was different then. In 1977, I set up my first payroll processing business, and in the process became one of Apple Computer's first actual independent resellers in Cumberland, Maryland. Before long, I had a thriving business, full of the challenges of managing payroll, employees, and taking care of customers. The one thing that absolutely came out of left field was how hard selling was even though I had had extensive professional sales training.

As my business grew, the demands for acquiring new customers grew along with it. This exposed the inherent difficulties of actually being a salesperson. In my mind, I wasn't a very good salesperson even though I had had all of that training. I was a business owner. Then it hit me: Selling is what drives business, and I needed to spend more time selling and be better at it. In addition, I needed to train my sales staff to be more effective. That need to improve sales performance exposed me to many sales training books, training programs, and methodologies. Most, while very good at teaching the basics of selling prospecting, objection handling, and closing—didn't actually help improve our performance. The reason, at the time, was difficult to diagnose. I believed we had 'bad salespeople,' who weren't cut out for sales. Then I realized, salespeople had to feel good about their product and knowledge, and they had to feel good about what they were selling. They needed a way to overcome their fear and self-doubt, and, they needed a plan. In short, sales training didn't work for us for the same reason it probably hasn't worked for you; it only addresses part of the problem. Simply put, most salespeople and small business owners struggle to sell. Most put off the parts they dislike or are afraid of. The result is they never seem to have the time to sell. For many salespeople and small businesses, it is a failure to reach their true potential.

After several years, I sold my business, eventually landing at Great Plains Software and then Microsoft, and for nearly 20 years, I helped small businesses do one thing: Improve their sales performance. The challenges I faced in running my business were the exact same challenges the thousands of companies I've worked with faced. Recently, I left Microsoft and joined Sage, and this is where I became acquainted with Rob Johnson, the author of this book. In fact, he is part of my leadership team.

Rob's role at Sage, as head of Channel Programs, is to create and deliver programs for our more than 3,000 partner organizations to improve their business performance. A former sales professional himself, Rob understands the sales process, and the challenges small businesses face. He truly understands what it takes to succeed. He has helped thousands of our salespeople and our Sage business partners improve their performance. He can help you improve your performance as well. I know it. I've seen it.

The promise of this book is that you can sell more than you thought possible, that selling isn't only for a certain personality type, and that anyone who truly wishes to improve their performance can with honesty and hard work. And Rob delivers on his promise. The foundation of his sales methodology is developing trust-based relationships and the skill of listening. Salespeople who adopt this methodology become very excited about what they do, because their goal is to help their customers become more successful. To them, selling isn't something you do to a prospect; it's what you do for a prospect. This no-nonsense approach is based on the golden rule. And it works. I know it can work for you, too.

I truly hope you enjoy this book, and that Rob's messages in the book will be a catalyst in changing the trajectory of your performance.

—Tom Miller

INTRODUCTION

Welcome to *Kick Your Own Ass: The Will, Skill, and Drill of Selling More Than You Thought Possible*. You are about to embark on a journey. As such, it is helpful to have an idea of where you are headed, and the general route of travel. The intent here is to provide you a brief overview of the journey.

Perhaps a word about the title of the book, *Kick Your Own Ass*, would be appropriate. It is my strongly held belief that each of us is responsible for our success and happiness—as we define it. Too many of us spend our lives blaming others for our misfortune and lost potential. What a shame! The sooner you take responsibility for your success, the quicker you will change the arc of your potential, and achieve more than you ever thought possible. As we brainstormed possible titles, once we landed on *Kick Your Own Ass*, we simply couldn't think of another title that accurately communicated the intent of the book. We knew the risk that some could be offended by the use of the word "ass." If you are offended, please accept my apology. Further, please accept my preemptive umbrella apology for all the instances of the word "ass" you are about to read in the following text. I got on a roll.

Off we go. In Section I, "This Is Harder Than It Looks," two big things happen: first, we introduce the key concepts and importance of Will, Skill, and Drill (see definitions below); second, we learn the importance of knowledge as the foundation to a successful career.

Definitions:

- The *will* is the required mental preparedness: the drive to persevere and to face and overcome fear, procrastination, constant adversity, and rejection. Your will sets you in motion, and can stop your momentum. This quality is the toughest to diagnose and handle since so much of our internal struggle is masked by excuses and our positive external voice.

- The *skill* is the vast foundation of knowledge of a product, industry, competition, and selling skills. It is the mastery of these four basic areas that enables you to successfully guide prospects through a sales process.

- The *drill* is the process of setting goals, creating strategic and tactical plans, planning territory, and executing the key leading indicator activities that create sustained superior results on a daily basis. The "drill to sell" is possible only by first engaging the "will and skill to sell."

In Section II, "Engage Your Will," we look at the impact your personality has on your career and the influence within the sales process. We explore the fact that any personality type can be a successful salesperson, if they engage energy and drive. Subsequently, we look at the *will killers*; the core issues which can derail careers and prevent one from reaching their true potential. And finally, we explore the potential process; a five-step program to change the arc of your potential, including a look at 8 key tools to keep you engaged in managing your will throughout your career.

In Section III, "Essential Skills," we look at the core communication and process skills necessary to execute a sales career. This isn't meant to be all the skills, indeed many are omitted, but rather the foundational skill elements. First we look at understanding the fundamentals of persuasion, and the importance of buyer awareness. Then, we'll examine creating a sales process, developing a prospecting system, creating trust, learning to listen and communicate, developing a value proposition, engineering a decision, and managing questions and objections.

In Section IV, "The Drill: Succeed Every Day," we take a look at the basics of developing a simple sales plan that includes analyzing your selling metrics. From there, we examine the development of a daily, weekly, and monthly action plan, along with a step-by-step process for creating one. Last, we look at the key areas necessary to continue changing the arc of your potential.

Throughout the book are questions. The intent is to create an opportunity to reflect and consider. Additionally, Chapters 7 and 16 are action chapters. They are designed to help you create plans. To make it easier for you to answer the questions and complete the projects, without having to write in the actual book, we created a downloadable workbook, which can be found on our web site www.willskilldrill.com.

My hope is, of course, that you will be entertained, informed, and inspired to try a few new ideas that will be instrumental in helping you change the arc of your potential, and create more success and happiness in your life, as you define it. Strap in. Let's get going.

This Is Harder
Than It Looks

The Arc of Your Potential

New Year's resolutions have been made, and broken, for centuries. They are handed down to us as a gift from the Romans. The idea of reflecting upon the previous year and looking toward the upcoming one with self-improvement goals in mind came from the Romans' worship of Janus, the god of two faces—one that looked back, and one that looked forward. It's also from Janus that we get the name for the month of January—which is about as long as most people actually keep a resolution. Research shows that around 40 percent of Americans set them annually, and, while survey data is inconclusive, some very creditable research shows that only about 10 percent of those who set NYRs actually keep them past January—of the same year. It's generally accepted that almost no one actually keeps a New Year's resolutions for an entire year. Simply observe a gym parking lot on January 2, and again on February 2. There is a startling abundance of parking spots in early February.

It is helpful to pause at the end of the year, reflect on your accomplishments, and develop a set of objectives for the upcoming year, and writing these goals down greatly improves your chances of achieving them. But resolving to lose 50 pounds, keep a journal, stop smoking, read 100 books, eat better, and be nice to the children every day without the assistance of a plan or a technique isn't helpful; it's actually harmful.

NEW YEAR'S RESOLUTIONS ARE STUPID.

An Uphill Run

Early in January 2004, I was eating lunch with my running buddy Steve Shaull, a former collegiate speed-merchant who demoralized opponents by trashing them on hills in cross-country races and marathons. We were at our regular burger joint, "The Loop," in Jacksonville, Florida: elevation, eight feet above sea level. We were discussing New Year's resolutions, which Steve never set, declaring them to be stupid and inane. I myself only opted for ridiculous ones, such as my vow in 2002 to no longer slow down for yellow lights. (Coincidentally, my 2003 resolution was to not get another ticket for an entire year—thus retaining my legal ability to drive.)

In a Ditch

Steve and I felt that this year would be different, though. While we still felt that creating a resolution was idiotic, we were in a position where we actually *needed* to do so. We were, perhaps, in the worst shape of our lives. Steve—beat up and down from years of running hard while ignoring pain—would always say, "The acceptance of pain is simply a matter of attitude." He knew that his best athletic years were behind him, and that he had gained over 40 pounds since his competitive running days. While we were still running three to five times per week, we both weighed at least 200 pounds, and our exercise regimen was far from routine and disciplined. Clearly, our calories-burned to calories-consumed ratio was out of whack. We were in a rut, and we knew we needed a major jolt to escape the otherwise inevitable slide into the frailties of middle age.

As we ate our cheeseburgers and fries (how's that for irony?), we expressed our complete dissatisfaction with our current sorry state of affairs. Without a major shift in our lives, we were on a trajectory that neither of us liked very much. We were accepting our reality; we were fat and out of shape. Steve suggested, and I agreed, that what we needed was a truly unrealistic and outlandish goal; something so completely outrageous and monumentally dumb that it would move us from fat and lazy to lean and mean. The question was what. We knew that a standard road race would never do it. Steve agreed to do the research and we would reconvene back at The Loop in a week.

Later in the week, I received the following e-mail from Steve:

We are running the Pikes Peak Ascent, August 21st, 2004.

Steve had chosen the hardest half-marathon in the United States of America.

Pikes Peak Ascent Is the Way Up

The Pikes Peak Ascent half-marathon begins in Manitou Springs, Colorado, at an elevation of 6,295 feet above sea level—6,287 feet higher than The Loop. The small town sits in the shadow of Pikes Peak near Colorado Springs. From there, the race goes up the Barr trail, a three-foot-wide dirt path that winds 13.2 miles up the mountain to the summit of Pikes Peak with an elevation of 14,110 feet above sea level—one of the highest peaks in North America. For those of you who care about these things, the course offers a 7,815-foot elevation increase over 13.2 miles, averaging an 11 percent grade. It's *super fun*.

The Pikes Peak Ascent is run on a Saturday; and the following day's Pikes Peak Marathon goes up and then back down the Barr trail. Each race has been run annually each August since 1966. According to local lore, the Ascent race actually began in 1956 when three smokers challenged 10 nonsmokers to a race up the trail. The smokers lost. Imagine that! As a former smoker, I question what they were actually smoking to have come up with such a ridiculous idea.

The annual event draws exactly 1,800 runners, nearly all of whom are nonsmokers from Colorado. The National Park Service limits the number to 1,800 to avoid overcrowding the trail. Typically, the race fills up in 48 hours. There are a disturbing number of runners who run both races, back to back.

Pain Is *Inevitable*; Serious Injury Is *Likely*

A number of factors can ruin a Pikes Peak Ascent experience. For example, if you become dehydrated you will become a zombie and wander around the mountain aimlessly before losing consciousness. Runners who get AMS—acute mountain sickness—experience headache, dizziness, shortness of breath, fatigue, and nausea, or, in serious cases, extreme fatigue, impaired motor control, and fluid accumulation in the brain and lungs. The faster one ascends, the more likely one is to develop severe symptoms of AMS, which can begin to occur above the elevation of 7,000 feet, or about six minutes after the start of the race. A competitor who is unfortunate enough to develop both dehydration *and* AMS requires serious medical assistance; and therein lies the problem. Unlike most half-marathons, Pikes Peak Ascent doesn't make for a particularly easy rescue. Emergency personnel cannot run up and down the Barr trail in ambulances to pick up the injured and stragglers; those who become injured or ill have to be rescued on horseback.

Well, Steve had certainly filled the parameters of "outrageous" and "ridiculous" in picking our joint resolution.

GIDDYUP!

At our lunch the following week, we made a commitment to run it. Just to show how seriously I was taking this whole run-up-the-mountain thing, I ordered the chicken sandwich instead of my customary hamburger— *without mayonnaise.* Next, we discussed how it would feel to actually run up a hill that big. I had no experience running hills other than the local bridges around Jacksonville. Steve had a lot of experience, and requested that I "quit whining and man up."

QUIT WHINING AND MAN UP!

We Form a Plan

Steve and I would have to lose a lot of weight and get into serious physical shape to succeed. Steve set a goal of losing 35 pounds, which would put him near his former race weight of 165 pounds. I would shoot for 170 pounds, for a total weight loss of 35 pounds, putting me at "emaciated."

Mathematically, it could work; 35 pounds over 8 months equals about 4.5 pounds a month, or about one pound per week, which is a "no-brainer." But figuring out a way to train in Florida—essentially, a big sand-bar with an altitude of about 345 feet above sea level at its highest point— would prove to be a "brainer." We created a plan that included extensive treadmill training on an 11 percent grade, long runs of three to four hours, and extended bridge repeats over the various Jacksonville bridges.

The Plan

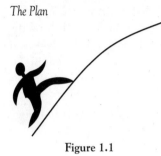

- Lose 35 to 40 lbs.
- Treadmill workouts at 11 percent grade.
- Long runs of three to four hours.
- Two hour bridge repeat workouts on Saturdays.

Figure 1.1

I Encounter Adversity

By the beginning of April, Steve was doing great. He was running faster, eating better, and had lost over 15 pounds. I had lost less than five—*a lot less than five*. The scale at the local YMCA became my worst enemy. Every time we ran together, Steve wanted to get on the scale and compare our weight. I was beginning to get really worried, and began to secretly hope he would pull something like a hamstring; nothing too serious, just debilitating. I wanted to lose weight—but exercising alone was not doing the trick. It was becoming clear that I was actually going to have to D-I-E-T—an obstacle that was nearly my undoing.

I shared my deep concern with then-girlfriend and now lovely wife Anita, and told her of my predicament. She agreed to help. On a trip to the Florida Keys later that month, we bought a diet book called *Secrets of Good-Carb Low-Carb Living* by Sandra Woodruff. While we drove south through the Everglades and into the Keys, we read the book to each other and learned how to eat better. Before our return to Jacksonville, we understood the eating habits that we needed to develop, which was a big turning point. I now had a plan I could execute, with Anita acting as my diet accountability coach.

Back in Jacksonville, Steve and I began doing our intense training to get ready for the race. Then it happened: my new healthy eating regimen helped me begin to lose weight.

NEWSFLASH: FOOD INTAKE AND WEIGHT LOSS ARE CONNECTED!

I Overcome Adversity

By race day, I weighed 167 pounds, was in the best running shape of my life—and looked like hell. Friends and coworkers thought for sure I was losing a battle to a serious illness. Steve weighed in around 162 pounds. We stood at the starting line at the end of the second-wave—behind the other 1,798 runners and at the absolute back of the line—and looked up at the peak. At that moment, our training regimen of treadmill and bridge running seemed like nothing more than a stupid, futile joke. *What on earth were we doing?*

However, once we got going and the idea of quitting began to evaporate, we made our way through the streets of Manitou Springs, past the Pikes Peak Railway, and onto the Barr trail. The actual running uphill was a blur of breathing, passing slower runners and walkers, stopping for frequent food and drink breaks, and moving ever forward and upward. Seconds became minutes. Minutes became miles. Miles became an hour. Before long, we were at the halfway point; and amazingly, neither of us was yet wandering aimlessly about the mountainside.

A Barren Moonscape

The last three miles of the race occur above the 12,000-foot tree line, where the landscape becomes barren, rocky, and boulder-strewn. As we passed the 10-mile point, runners everywhere were sitting or wandering around, no doubt suffering from one of the aforementioned maladies. Our pace slowed to a walk as we climbed over boulders. During the last 70 minutes of the race, we could hear the results announced as runners crossed the finish line above us, and we couldn't believe how long those last three miles took. I could hardly speak by the time we finished. It was 62 degrees at the start of the race, and four hours thirty-two minutes later, as we crossed the finish line at the peak, it was snowing—*in August*.

Steve and I collected our change bag filled with snack food and warm clothes and made our way to the bus for the ride down the hill. We knew we could have run it quicker; but we also knew we had *done it*. Steve could have finished the race at least an hour faster than me; the only reason I finished at all was probably that he waited. I was fighting negative internal messaging during much of the race about how I could not make it. Then I would look up, Steve would ask how I was doing, and I would yell "fine." He knew better. In the end, it wasn't so much about the time as it was the experience. The next one will be about the time.

Nice Story, Dude

I can imagine what you're saying right now: "Hey Rob, that's a nice story; but it has absolutely nothing to do with selling." But it does. This book is

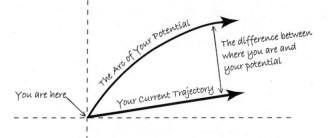

Figure 1.2   The Arc of Your Potential

about changing the arc of your potential and enhancing your life by improving your sales performance. My experience with Pikes Peak was about coming to terms with reality, visualizing something better, engaging the will to change, and developing necessary skills. It allowed me to deal with adversity, fight off fear and self-doubt, and execute the drill necessary to succeed. You'll read about how I struggled with sales as well, and used the exact same process to improve. Furthermore, I have used the principles, skills, processes, and daily drills we discuss in this book in *all* areas of my life—because many of the challenges we face in sales have very little to do with the actual sales process.

By running the race, Steve and I literally kicked our own asses, and permanently changed the arc of our potential. By making and keeping a commitment to do something big, I now knew that I could kick something *big*'s ass. I had taken control of my potential, and succeeded. I am no longer afraid of hills or of the unknown. I am now a faster, smaller runner. But these lessons transcend running and fitness; they're a part of my DNA. I am a better salesperson and trainer—and a different human being—because of this experience. By opening myself up to entirely new challenges, I now allow myself to grow in ways I could have never imagined. (See Figure 1.2.)

What Is the Arc of Your Potential?

Each of our lives is on a trajectory or path that comprises our relationships, careers, health, knowledge, giving, happiness, and spiritual walk. Trajectories are predictable and easy to calculate. Your potential is connected to your life's trajectory, and a sales career is a part of your current potential. Doing nothing will keep the arc of your sales potential static. The reality is that you cannot have what you have never had by staying where you have always stayed. You have infinite untapped potential to achieve more than you thought possible. You simply must take the first step.

I personally know this to be true; there were many times during my life when I struggled to visualize my life ever getting better. It's difficult to envision what is over the hill or around the corner during tough periods; it's hard to accept our true potential. But the person that you have the potential to become is waiting for you to get off your couch and kick your own ass—into gear. It's simply a journey of small steps in the right direction. The arc of your potential rises and falls as you move in the direction of your most dominant thought. The more positive your thoughts and expectations become, the higher your capability becomes; but the more negative you are, the less you believe you can accomplish your goals. In either case, your thoughts will manifest in your actions and in what you really *do*—or don't—achieve.

You still have your life's story to write. Whatever has happened up to this exact moment is now permanently behind you. Nothing you can do will ever bring it back or change it; what you have is this moment forward. Your potential to do greater things is as yet unproven. I am living proof that you can achieve more than you thought possible—beginning now.

IT'S TIME TO START KICKING.

You Can Change Your Trajectory

Altering the arc of your potential requires a paradigm shift in how you manage and execute your career. Simply reading a sales book—even a very good one—won't help much. One sale doesn't make you a salesperson, a golf lesson won't make you a golfer, and a single run won't make you a runner. To achieve sustained superior results in your sales career, you must work daily on the three areas of will, skill, and drill of selling. In other words, meaningful change is the result of very hard work. The purpose of this book is to help you master the few basic skills and develop a daily sales execution program that will help you sell more than you thought possible.

To change your life's trajectory and the arc of your potential, you must take a first step.

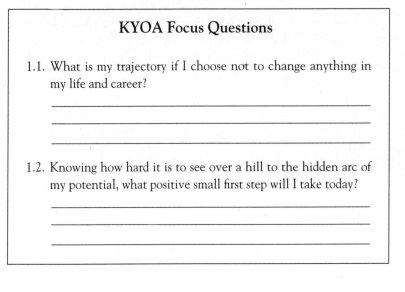

KYOA Focus Questions

1.1. What is my trajectory if I choose not to change anything in my life and career?

_____

_____

_____

1.2. Knowing how hard it is to see over a hill to the hidden arc of my potential, what positive small first step will I take today?

_____

_____

_____

Get the Most Value from This Book

Get the free workbook offered at the web site, begin filling out your profile, and join the community. The workbook will help guide you through the process of changing the arc of your potential; it is an easy way to record your thoughts and build your plan.

See www.willskilldrill.com.

My sincere hope is that you'll decide to take a step toward change. You have to change yourself. You have to kick your own ass into gear. If you do, you will see amazing results.

Over the past 10 years, I've worked with thousands of salespeople and business owners to improve their sales performance. I've seen it work in their lives, and I know it can work in yours too. Regardless of what you are facing, I know that these principles, skills, and processes can work for you, too.

Enjoy the uphill run. (See www.pikespeakmarathon.org/entry.htm.)

Chapter 1 Recap: The Arc of Your Potential

- Each of our lives is on a trajectory or path that comprises our relationships, careers, health, knowledge, giving, happiness, and spiritual walk. Trajectories are predictable and easy to calculate.

- Your potential is connected to your life's trajectory, and a sales career is a part of your current potential. You cannot have what you have never had by staying where you have always stayed.

- Achieving your goals is simply a journey of small steps in the right direction. The arc of your potential rises and falls as you move in the direction of your most dominant thought. The more positive your thoughts and expectations become, the higher your capability becomes.

- Altering the arc of your potential requires a paradigm shift in how you manage and execute your career. You must work daily on the three areas of the will, skill, and drill of selling. The purpose of this book is to help you do just that: implement a change management process, master the few basic skills, and develop a daily sales execution program that will help you improve your sales beyond belief.

Your Raise Becomes Effective When You Do

My career shift from carpenter to software salesperson was abrupt. The recession of 1983 caused a general construction slowdown for framing and trim carpenters in the normally bustling construction market of North Florida. My new position marked the beginning of a long and arduous struggle to achieve success in sales. In the beginning, I simply wasn't prepared to succeed. I lacked nearly every conceivable skill required to execute the job. How I managed to get hired with no experience, skills, or domain knowledge remains a mystery to this day.

The position was with a small software company and was my second actual sales job (we'll discuss my bizarre introduction to selling later in the book). The initial training consisted of listening to the other two salespeople "work the phones" for a few days before getting a list, a desk, a phone, and a quota. I learned later that this was—and still is—the normal training regimen for most salespeople in most companies in most industries. Perhaps this is one of the primary reasons for salespeoples' incredibly high failure rate; we simply don't prepare them to succeed.

I possessed none of the three primary elements needed for sales success—the will, skill, or daily drill. My fledgling sales career was powered solely by my desperate need to earn a living to support my family and a willingness to talk to perfect strangers. I had no idea if I would ever succeed; and was convinced at most times that I would probably fail.

PREPARE YOURSELF TO SUCCEED.

Jump on the Roller Coaster

By some miracle, I managed to learn enough of the basics of selling through osmosis to avoid termination. However, my sales performance was inconsistent, marked by frequent high and low periods. My sales charts looked eerily similar to a roller coaster. My employer actually hired a sales training firm to come in and do a two-day sales class with some of my colleagues and me. The company expected huge results, as though we were going to be magically transformed into H.H.s (Heavy Hitters) over the course of 48 hours. The sales team felt as though we had been through the filming of a fake reality show called "Sales Training Intervention." Not surprisingly, we didn't achieve the results touted by the sales training firm, and the company felt as though they had wasted their investment. The attempt to instill new skills and structure into our sales team actually created a selling Frankenstein: We began to practice a disjointed collection of skills and sales processes, which produced even worse results—scary.

This inconsistency in performance naturally increased my anxiety, which ultimately drove me to listen to recordings and read books by sales professionals. Much of the literature felt manipulative and disingenuous, presenting sales as though it were something you *did* to someone: "I sold them!" instead of something you did *for* someone: "I helped them!" While the reading was entertaining, I had a hard time connecting to it. One reason might have been that many of the authors I read were former sales superstars who decided to write a book. It was as if they had an epiphany and said: *"I was a sales superstar. I should write a book detailing all of the great techniques I used to slay the competition and slam the deals. If you read the book, you too can be a sales superstar."* Invariably, their methods and suggestions didn't work for me. For a long time, I wasn't sure I was meant to be a salesperson. And yet I rocked along, up and down, winning and losing, feeling overly confident and then feeling utterly desperate.

Hearing Voices

I don't know about you, but I hear things in my head; specifically, the sound of my own voice. Or perhaps *voices* would be more accurate. I have two primary ones—internal and external—each of which comes in two forms: negative and positive. For example, I often say something positive

External Positive Voice	Internal Positive Voice
"I love your product"	"Pretty nice product they've got"
External Negative Voice	Internal Negative Voice
"I'm not sure the product will fit our needs"	"That is a stupid product!"

Figure 2.1   Hearing Voices

using my external positive voice (*"I like your solution"*), while my internal voice is simultaneously saying something negative (*"This solution is stupid"*). That way, I get to appear to be positive and upbeat—something I value—while ripping the target at the same time. Our internal voices can chastise our external voices as if we are someone else (*"Nice going, sport."*) The primary combinations of these dialogues that we hold with ourselves are shown in Figure 2.1.

Our internal programming has a lot to do with which voice is in control of the situation at any given moment, that is, how we see ourselves in the world, and our attitude about the future. As we will discuss in Chapter 6, our internal messaging drives our external behaviors. And negative messaging—both internal and external—plays a *major* role in shaping the arc of our potential.

My Internal Voice Freaks Out

Early, I struggled with my need to make quota—and a commission check— and with my internal voice as my career developed. I learned how to close deals by telling the prospect what they wanted to hear and, while I wasn't lying, I often wasn't telling the whole truth, either. It was very difficult to stare down the end of a month without reaching quota, knowing I could probably make the sale by simply avoiding discussing the weaknesses in my product. I was able to rationalize this behavior using the *percentage of fit* mentality—the rationalization that a product will fix X percent of a prospect's problems, and that no product will fix 100 percent. I knew from experience that my product would solve *part* of the client's problems; what I didn't know was the exact percentage. Even worse was that I couldn't be sure what problems our product might *create*. I wasn't concerned with helping the client; I was merely interested in earning a commission. My internal voice was yelling at me for misleading a prospect, and my external voice was doing whatever it took to make the sale, avoid being fired, and to beat my competitors and coworkers. And I was being rewarded for winning the deals, not for helping customers solve their problems.

Your Raise Becomes Effective When You Do

During this era of struggle, my manager and I sat down to review my sales results for the previous year and look ahead at the coming year. I began to recite my well-rehearsed litany of reasons why I had missed my target, hoping that something would perhaps stick to the wall and sound to him like a rational and logical reason for missing my goal. He was very polite as I discussed the external factors like the economy and competitors, as well as the internal issues like our product's weaknesses and the waning marketing efforts that weren't producing nearly enough leads. I had charts, graphs, competitive SWOT (strengths, weaknesses, opportunities, threats) analysis, and so on. I thought I was doing a fantastic job of explaining away my less-than-desirable performance, and building a compelling argument as to why this coming year would be better. In fact, I explained, I really needed a raise to offset all the adversity I was being asked to absorb. After listening intently, my boss calmly looked me in the eye and said, "Rob, your raise becomes effective when you do."

> YOUR RAISE BECOMES EFFECTIVE WHEN YOU DO!

The Big Idiot

My internal voice—a victim of my own super salesmanship—began screaming at the top of its lungs that he was a big idiot. Simultaneously, my external voice exhaled a long "Duhhh!" while I tried to determine if my boss was joking or actually being serious. I had somehow convinced myself—and everyone around me—that *I* was not responsible for my poor results. Yet I knew deep down that this wasn't entirely the case. Somehow, my sense of self-worth had become entangled with my sales performance. When my career was going well, I felt great about myself as a person. But when I struggled professionally, I felt inadequate and unworthy; and the more inadequate and unworthy I felt, the harder it was to do the tough work of selling. It had become difficult to manage the sales process for fear of being rejected.

As you can imagine, this fear of rejection and extreme rationalization caused all sorts of tactical problems. For example, I convinced myself that it was okay to *not* return some phone calls, because I had somehow received a signal that the prospect was not going to buy. The questions that the prospect was hoping to ask would only confirm my telepathic abilities. And there were the instances when I drove past a prospect's building, deciding at the last moment *not* to call on them because of the way their building looked—*from the outside*—which gave me all the information I would need to determine that they were not qualified. And the hours I spent cleaning my desk, drawers, bookcases, and so on, while the list of prospects to call remained untouched next to the phone, were okay, because it was a terrible list anyway.

As I sat there waiting to figure out how to respond to my boss, images of procrastination, avoidance, and failure to perform were invading my brain. My internal voice broke rank with my external voice and openly admitted that he might be right; and then started screaming that *I* was the Big Idiot. So there we were. I had two options before me: I could admit that he was right and risk the unknown danger that came with it, or I could keep denying, bargaining, lessening my impact, and maintaining the illusion.

Take a Leap

In the four to six seconds after my manager informed me that my raise would become effective when I did, I had what alcoholics often call "a moment of clarity." This is when they see the real impact that alcoholism has had on their lives and the lives of those around them; and I immediately saw that my boss was right. I recalled the instances where I was frozen by fear and remembered how difficult they had been to accept. I took a six-second self-inventory, and knew that I was cornered. I uttered something incomprehensible and tried to get out that I appreciated his insight and that I believed he had a good point. I admitted to him that I had been struggling with my confidence of late, and that it had impacted my performance at work. He suggested a plan to increase my training and work more closely with him for a few months. I had taken a leap of honesty. I had in fact, kicked my own ass—and as a result, began the journey of kicking my own ass into gear. I started to take responsibility for my actions.

HAVE YOUR MOMENT OF CLARITY RIGHT NOW.

I Have Issues

My primary issue was that I blamed factors other than my own attitude and actions for my inconsistent and unacceptable performance. It was a crutch I used to make failing okay, and I had to settle for failing. I didn't possess the tools necessary for success, which prevented me from changing the arc of my potential.

I continued on the roller coaster for a period of time, but I began to intently study the subject of selling. I sought out models of success that were not dependent on old, tired selling paradigms of Hurt and Rescue.[1] Gradually, I found my selling equilibrium; and through reading, listening, and borrowing skills from many different selling models, managers, mentors, and teachers, I developed a process that made sense to me. Once I began to integrate the disciplines of will, skill, and drill, an amazing thing happened:

My performance skyrocketed.

I became *consistently good* at selling. I had developed a system for managing my career; and it was working. More importantly, I *enjoyed* helping clients solve their problems and capitalize on opportunities. Selling became something I was proud to do. Before long, I was promoted to a management position. Then, I took another position, thus beginning my corporate climb up sales organizations.

My question for you is: What is preventing you from changing the arc of *your* potential? An equally important question is: "Why is this preventing *you*"? In other words, even though I realized what had kept me from reaching my true potential, it took some effort to discover why I had connected my self-worth so strongly with my professional performance. And as the character Curly says in the movie *City Slickers*, the answer to that question "is for you to find out."

Make a Commitment to Be Your Authentic Self

If you choose to embark on this journey, I ask that you listen to your positive internal voice—your authentic self. Be the person you are meant to be. Be open to total honesty. Though this is of course easier said than done, to truly make a change in your life, it is essential that you commit to honesty. In turn, I will make this commitment to you—I will be my authentic self while creating this book. Even if it is painful, I pledge to share my authentic internal voice with you.

---

[1] A selling methodology primarily based on a persuasion technique known as Hurt and Rescue, the concept of which is that a drowning person will grab at anything; so push them in the water and then throw them a lifeline. Read more about this in Chapter 8.

This Book Could Be for You

You bought the book for a reason; and what I believe to be a very good reason. You want to improve your performance, which can—and should—increase the amount of enjoyment you derive from your chosen pursuit. It wouldn't hurt to like what you're doing while you're earning money to help put your children through college and finance things like (gulp) weddings. Or perhaps you're just starting out and would like to buy your first home, and know that you need help getting there. Regardless of your level of experience or performance, if you wish to improve the arc of your potential for yourself or those on your team—and you have a strong desire to improve—this book is for you.

Caution for the Overconfident

However, if you have mastered every aspect of the sales career, and you have no desire to improve, this book might *not* be for you. If that is the case, please give this book to the salesperson next to you. Here's a word of caution, though: the moment you decide that you have nothing left to learn is the exact moment that you *do*. Life has a funny way of demonstrating this—often with the force of a ball-peen hammer.

WATCH OUT FOR THE BALL-PEEN HAMMER.

Your Success Is Your Own Doing

You alone are responsible for your success or failure; not your manager, or product, or competitors, or economy, or lack of training, or anything else

---

KYOA Focus Questions

2.1. What is the one thing preventing me from reaching my true potential?

_____

_____

_____

2.2. What is the *why* behind this *what*?

_____

_____

_____

you can conjure up. The sooner you accept this simple rule and stop blaming others for your misfortune, the sooner you will succeed.

Chapter 2 Recap: Your Raise Becomes Effective When You Do

- I—like most people—have two primary voices, internal and external, each of which comes in two forms: negative and positive. Our internal programming has a lot to do with which voice is in control of the situation at any given moment—how we see ourselves in the world, and our attitude about the future.

- In order to change your career trajectory, you have to discern what's preventing you from changing the arc of *your* potential, and *why*. You have to listen to your positive internal voice, be your authentic self, and remain open to total honesty. Regardless of your level of experience or performance, if you wish to improve the arc of your potential for yourself or those on your team—and you have a strong desire to improve—this book is for you.

- *You alone* are responsible for your success or failure: not your manager, or product, or competitors, or economy, or lack of training, or anything else you can conjure up. The faster you accept this simplest of rules and stop blaming others for your misfortune, the sooner you will succeed.

The Will, Skill, and Drill of Selling More Than You Ever Thought Possible

Sales as a Career Choice

I am a big fan of sales and salespeople. I love the industry, the art and skill of selling, and the strategy of the deal. I love helping companies achieve their goals—which only happens if someone sells something to somebody. Selling offers one of the highest potential income opportunities. The sales profession drives commerce, and creates wealth and opportunity for nations, companies, and individuals. It offers opportunities for you to expand your horizons, and is a part of nearly every profession. Whether you're selling an idea, service, or product—selling is a big part of the process.

Kick Your Own Ass

It's your decision to make a change in your life; no other living soul can do this for you. As we will discuss in detail in the Will section, your motivation to change and grow must stem from within. Coerced or mandated change rarely works effectively, and in fact usually produces the opposite outcome. While many believe that behavior is hard-wired—supporting the adage that "a leopard can't change its spots"—I vehemently reject that premise. In fact, I am living proof that you can change your spots and potential.

YOU CAN CHANGE YOUR SPOTS—AND POTENTIAL.

It is my experience that anyone who truly tries can improve his or her sales—this means you, too. And if you truly desire to improve your performance, the income amount on your W-2 form, and the level of your personal satisfaction, you have to embark upon your journey well armed. For most people, this means knowing where and how to begin. This book will help you do just that: create and implement your personally tailored path to success.

To Struggle Is Normal

In his terrific book on selling entitled *Let's Get Real or Let's Not Play: The Demise of Dysfunctional Selling and the Advent of Helping Clients Succeed*, author Mahan Khalsa states that "Selling is the second oldest profession, often confused with the first." If this is true, then there must have been a need back then for salespeople to sell their wares; and if there were salespeople in the beginning, there was most likely a division between those who struggled to achieve their goals and those who didn't. I can imagine a cave-salesperson somewhere selling a whole lot more wheels and fire than the competition, while the underperformer was blaming his poor sales record on dinosaur attacks, evolution, floods, fires, and meteor strikes.

WATCH OUT FOR THAT METEOR!

Salespeople have always faced challenges; the issues with which I—and every salesperson before me—have had to contend are not unique to me or to you. If "normal" is defined as "being approximately average," then salespeople who struggle are normal, because *most* salespeople struggle! Some struggle more than others. The term used to describe the separation between those who struggle less and those who struggle more is called the 80/20 Rule.

Pareto's Law: The 80/20 Rule
In the 1860s an Italian economist named Vilfredo Pareto began and completed work on a project to study the distribution of land ownership in his
native Italy. Since the findings revealed that 20 percent of the population
owned 80 percent of the land, the study's results came to be called the Pareto Principle, and eventually, the 80/20 Rule. As the world underwent the
industrial revolution and salespeople became the generators of commerce,
Pareto's Law was found to apply in an increasing number of situations and
exchanges. Pareto's Law is a fact of life in the world of selling and sales force
management: 80 percent of sales are made by 20 percent of the sales force.

Break Pareto's Law
Every sales organization with which I have worked, consulted, or managed
has experienced the effects of the 80/20 rule. While I can't guarantee you
that you'll become a 20 percenter by reading this book, I can tell you
that—regardless of your current situation—you can improve your performance, sense of pride, and have more fun making more money
than you currently do. Take ownership of your success, and you will, by
kicking your own ass, kick Pareto's Law at the same time—sort of a
two-birds-with-one-stone scenario.

Why Do We Struggle to Achieve the Results We Desire?
When we look at the big picture, we can see that the reason behind our
difficulties is often the fact that we don't close enough sales to meet our
objectives. Many sales "experts" claim that the reason for this is because
we don't know how to cold call, ask for an order, or handle an objection.
While this may be true, it isn't the whole story. Simply put, we encounter
hurdles because we lack will, skill, and drill. To illustrate why we need to
possess and develop these assets—and what happens when we don't—I
will share three stories about salespeople with whom I have worked. The
first story is about problems in the skill and drill areas, and the second
concerns a will issue connected to passion. The third story is also about a
will issue regarding an unresolved psychological issue.

Story 1: How Julie Lost Track of the Process (Skill, Sales Process and Drill, and Daily Prospecting)

I recently worked with a businessperson named Julie who owns a company
that sells and implements technical applications. She has been in the

industry for many years, and while some of those years have gone better than others, her career was in a pretty big ditch when we connected. As we began working together, we focused first on understanding her current situation: how many leads were in her pipeline, an explanation of her "typical sales process," what she perceived to be her biggest challenge, and other concerns.

As we dug into the data, we began to discover that Julie had two primary issues that contributed to her poor performance. First, she had little marketing and lead generation in place, and second, she had an ineffective sales process. While those sound bad—and, in fact, are—they aren't uncommon, and they're extremely treatable. I've worked with countless small business owners and salespeople who faced similar predicaments, simply because it's so easy to lose track of the process—especially if you work in a micro organization. Julie's problem was that she had previously relied on her vendor to provide leads for her; and over time, this source began to dry up. She had never developed the necessary skill and drill of developing opportunities for herself.

Julie's sales process was ineffective because even though she had attended numerous sales training programs, she had simply forgotten how important it is to have the prospect connect with the impact or cost of not solving their issues before seeing a solution. The result was that though many prospects liked her product, they didn't like it enough to actually buy it. Julie had lost track of how important it is to follow a proven sales process; she had opted to take shortcuts in the interest of saving time. Once we understood the big issues, we built a plan to rebuild her pipeline and improve her skills and processes. Over the next several months, we began to right Julie's ship. She regained her focus, and the arc of her potential grew higher.

Story 2: Passion and the Bonsai Gardener (Will, Misplaced Passion)

Several years ago, while assisting a small New England technology company to recruit, hire, and train a salesperson, I had the opportunity to interview a young man for the position. He dressed and spoke the part, and possessed the appropriate experience and skills to meet the demands of the role. After concluding the testing and interview process, the company offered him the job. Interestingly, after he accepted, I asked him what he did for fun when he wasn't at work—and his entire persona changed before my eyes. He told me that he was an avid bonsai gardener, and that his entire life was devoted to the care and development of diminutive plants. After listening to a 30-minute history and overview of the art and science of growing tiny plants, I asked why he was not pursuing a career in the field of bonsai. He responded. "My father sold computers, and insisted that I do so as well, as it afforded him a very comfortable life."

My client and I reflected upon the situation and agreed that his pursuit of computer sales was not his passion. We moved forward with the hire with a sense of foreboding. We should have listened to our internal voices! As the late great Paul Harvey would say, "Now, for the rest of the story." Three years later, after a modest career with my client's firm, the young man's father passed away suddenly, leaving him with a reasonable inheritance. Within days, he resigned his position, pulled up stakes, and moved his wife and plants south to take over a bonsai garden operation. At last check-in, his business and beloved plants were thriving.

Our bonsai gardener was able to connect the dots of income and passion directly together. However, if your passion is watching sunsets with your family—and you haven't found a way to turn your passion into a vocation as well—don't worry! It isn't *essential* that you do; it's merely essential to connect your vocation to the way in which it allows you to pursue your passion. If you do, you'll become increasingly enthusiastic about your work. You'll find in many cases that you're able to both do your job more effectively *and* enjoy your chosen pursuits.

Story 3: Need for Approval Run Amok (Will, Unresolved Psychological Issue)

Struggle for success is not always directly related to the sales process or degree of passion one feels for their work, but instead stems from deeper psychological issues. As I discussed in Chapter 2, I struggled with the need for acceptance that was most likely due to a spectacularly dysfunctional family life during my early and adolescent years. This became evident early in my career, and required work to overcome. Personal struggles affect everyone differently, and there's no way to tell how the problems we've encountered in the past will manifest themselves in the future.

Not too long ago, I began work with a bright young medical equipment salesperson named Burt. He was highly driven, and had an easy, outgoing "sales personality" that many people found attractive. He possessed the tools and qualities that he needed to become a top performer. However, Burt's manager was becoming increasingly concerned about his sales performance, relationship with his coworkers, and some trouble he was having with clients and prospects, so he requested that I work with him.

To get started, we decided to run a phone-based prospecting workshop to improve the entire team's technique for creating new opportunities— also known as *cold calling*. The plan was to work as a group to develop strategies for connecting with companies within their target market, and begin a dialogue to schedule an initial exploratory meeting. The workshop required that the employees write scripts to use when making the calls, and then break into groups to make actual calls. Each member would then take turns making the calls while the other members observed.

And *that's* when the trouble began.

Burt initiated the cold-call by using the script to connect the target company with one of their customers. However, what came out of his mouth was entirely different from what was written on the paper. He began by telling the prospect that he had just visited their web site (a lie), and that he was really impressed by the kind of work they did (another lie). He went on to claim that he believed his company had a lot to offer them (another total lie, as well as a presumption of a solution without knowing anything about the prospect—which, in the medical field, is akin to malpractice.) Burt then boldly asked the prospect if he'd like to have a meeting.

Those of us sitting in the conference room were horrified. The prospect didn't answer, but began to ask Burt when he was on the site, how he liked it, what specifically he liked about it, and so on. Burt soldiered on and attempted to redirect the dialogue back to the potential meeting. Eventually, Burt began to realize he was in deep trouble, and the client revealed the truth: *The company actually didn't have a web site.*

The prospect proceeded to call Burt all sorts of names, declare him to be the most unprofessional salesperson he'd ever encountered, and demanded that he never call him again, before hanging up. *That* was bad, but what made it worse was Burt's reaction. He instantly blew it off, called the guy an idiot, and laughed. It was a nervous laugh, and I could sense that it was really a test to see if we were going to laugh it off with him. We weren't, and we didn't.

Not too long after "the clinic," my client and Burt parted ways. As they discovered, Burt had a problem with lying—he would lie often for no logical reason. Burt admitted that he couldn't handle confrontation or rejection, and would do anything to avoid this in interactions with others. The more we peeled the onion, the more we realized that he was consumed with creating and maintaining lies.

LOSERS LIE TO WIN SALES.

Julie, the Bonsai Gardener, and Burt's Situations Are Not Hopeless

Julie lost track of how important it is to develop a formal sales process (skill), and needed to build an opportunity pipeline (drill) to support her sales objectives. The result was poor performance. Selling is a simple process; even so, it is easy to lose track of the few important elements required to be successful. If you are struggling to achieve the results you desire, look first at your pipeline. It is likely not big enough to support your goals. In Chapter 11, we'll work on developing your pipeline. If you are losing sales to "no decision," we'll work to improve your close rate in the Skills section.

The bonsai gardener needed to connect his passion to his work. He used his creativity to nurture and develop plants rather than aiding small businesses to improve their profits and operations. His success required a career change to properly align his passion with his product and, once that happened, it was much easier for him to build the necessary skills and complete the daily execution of tasks. It might not be possible for you to do exactly this. You'll need to make a connection between your vocation and how it *allows* you to pursue your passion: This will help build passion for your vocation.

Burt the compulsive liar was dealing with some very tough challenges relating to acceptance and rejection, and needed professional help. Facing these issues helped him learn to dissociate these feelings from the sales process. As bad as it seems, his case is neither hopeless nor unique, and by taking the leap and meeting his problems head-on, he can overcome them.

NO SITUATION IS HOPELESS . . . NOT EVEN YOURS.

Most of us struggle with something that can prevent us from reaching the success we desire. Regardless of your own particular issue, you're not alone. Be confident that you can overcome whatever adversity you're facing, and change the course of your career.

The Will, Skill, and Drill of Selling

Sales success doesn't come simply from the execution of sales skills. Rather, it's an amazing journey wherein you develop the ability to manage the will, skill, and drill of selling.

- The *will* is the required mental preparedness: the drive to persevere and to face and overcome fear, procrastination, constant adversity, and rejection. Your will sets you in motion, and can also stop your momentum. This quality is the toughest to diagnose and handle since so much of our internal struggle is masked by excuses and our positive external voice.

- The *skill* is rooted in a vast foundation of knowledge of product, industry, competition, and selling skills. It is the mastery of these four basic areas that enables you to successfully guide prospects through a sales process.

- The *drill* is the process of setting goals, creating strategic and tactical plans, planning territory, and executing the key leading indicator activities that create sustained superior results on a daily basis. The "drill to sell" is possible only by engaging the "will to sell."

YOU ARE NOT A LOSER UNTIL YOU QUIT TRYING.

Chapter 3 Recap: The Will, Skill, and Drill of Selling More Than You Ever Thought Possible

- Selling is a hugely important part of our economy, as it offers one of the highest potential income opportunities. Sales drive commerce, and create wealth and opportunity for nations, companies, and individuals.

- Your motivation to change and grow must come from within. Coerced or mandated change rarely works effectively, and in fact usually produces the opposite outcome.

- A rule of thumb that describes the separation between those who struggle and those who don't is called the 80/20 Rule, or Pareto's Law. This states that, in the world of selling and sales force management, 80 percent of sales are made by 20 percent of the sales force. Simply put: We encounter hurdles because we lack will, skill, and drill.

- The *will* is the required mental preparedness needed to execute the job.

- The *skill* is the mastery of the necessary knowledge and techniques.

- The *drill* is the process of setting goals, creating strategic and tactical plans, planning territory, and executing the key activities that create sustained superior results.

- There are several reasons that salespeople struggle that relate to all three of these areas. Some have trouble establishing and following a structured process; some aren't connected to their chosen careers in meaningful way; and others may even have underlying psychological issues that inhibit their ability to execute sales.

One Golf Lesson Doesn't Make You a Golfer – Great Potential Requires Great Work to Realize

Golf Is a Lot Like Selling

The game of golf and the career of selling share many similarities. Golf clearly requires skill, which players attain and improve upon by undergoing training, coaching, and consistent practice. Golf requires will and a passion to pursue, as well as mental toughness to manage any pressure and self-doubt. Golf is a game of strategy; knowing the course, opponents, and environmental conditions are essential to winning. Achieving and maintaining competence entails constant review of the fundamentals.

Personal Golf Testimony

I took up golf in my early twenties under the advice that a good golf game is a valuable sales tool. However, I discovered firsthand that a terrible golf game is an equally terrible sales tool. I learned to play "on-the-fly" with friends and family, and rarely practiced. I only took a few lessons, other than what I learned from well-meaning playing partners: *"Keep your head down, and pivot off the back foot, and then swing like you're trying to hit an egg. That is all you need to know about golf."*

Salespeople often take this same approach to learn the ins and outs of their careers. Learning on the fly, never practicing, attending one sales expert's motivational seminar, and getting advice from "the sales dude": *"Dude, remember the ABCs—always be closing! Close early, close often! That is all you need to know about selling."*

Not surprisingly, after several years of shooting average scores in the low thousands, I elected to give up golf; really, as a gift of mercy to the entire golfing industry. It was obvious that I did not have the will to pursue the game. However, in terms of ROI, I was getting a great deal for my golf greens fees, since my "cost per shot" was well below the industry average; in fact, it was *way* below the industry average.

No Natural-Born Golfers

Like selling, success in golf is not based on heredity. There are few, if any, natural-born golfers. This is not to say that we have equal innate ability or potential: we don't. It *does*, however, mean that *great potential requires great work to realize*.

There are those people who, in any pursuit, even sales, seem to perform better than their peers. For example, my running buddy and aforementioned partner in Colorado's Pikes Peak Ascent, Steve Shaull, is now—and always will be—faster than me. He has greater lung capacity and has spent more time spent in training than I have. During his competitive years, he was willing to endure more intense pain than his opponents were in order to win.

Some golfers may have physical qualities derived from other pursuits that lend themselves especially well to a good golf swing; or perhaps their heightened sense of hand/eye coordination allows them to contact the ball so accurately mid-swing. Likewise, there are salespeople who possess greater energy and drive to honing their craft who will inevitably be more successful than others will. There *are* those people who play golf twice a year, shoot in the 80s—and demoralize their opponents into quitting. However, most who pursue golf find it to be a game of addictionlike dedication. Achieving a lower handicap drives their focus, compelling them to practice their skills constantly.

Golfers Are Easy to Spot

Golf addicts are always on the lookout for a game. They wear logo golf attire at *all* times to *all* occasions and pack their automobile trunks full with golf bags, shoes, and other golf-related collectibles and paraphernalia. When striking up conversations with me, these folks will end their introduction with a question like "What's your handicap?" I respond, "Well, I was a drug addict as a child, but mostly overcame it with therapy. What's yours?" They realize they are not speaking to someone from their planet, and begin backing away, glancing at their TAG Heuer Men's Professional Golf Watch while mumbling something about a meeting, until they reach a safe distance.

The Training Strategy of a Professional Golfer

Golf is a tough game, one in which it is nearly impossible to achieve perfection: flashes of brilliance only drive the addiction deeper. Being competitive requires that the truly dedicated participants play about three rounds a week, while undergoing constant swing coaching, and practice hitting buckets of balls at the range. Ask any pro golfer about their approach to mastering the game, and they will tell you they have four different coaches—Mental Focus, Diet, Strength, and Skills. Plus, they practice four to eight hours per day just to stay competitive. And that doesn't count actual match-play. How good could *you* become if you applied this approach to changing the arc of your sales potential?

KNOWLEDGE IS THE FOUNDATION OF GREAT POTENTIAL.

Sales Training Alone Isn't the Answer

When salespeople decide to improve their sales career, the typical go-to strategy is to seek help in the form of books, CDs of training classes, and motivational seminars—and there are plenty of these available. One could even argue there is an *overload* of available material. For example, a recent Amazon.com search on the keyword "Selling" returned 498,804 books. A similar search on "Closing" returned 505,411 books, and a Google search on "Sales Training" returned 3,140,000 hits. Yet with all of this help available, so many salespeople continue to struggle because being profitable in sales requires more than merely possessing selling skills. As we've already figured out, it involves the will, skill, and drill to sell, and the foundation of all three of these qualities is knowledge.

Knowledge Is the Key

The goal of increasing knowledge creates the opportunity for you to provide enhanced value to your prospects and customers, which will lead to an improvement in your performance. Buyers want to work with people whom they believe to be experts in solving their problems, and who they feel have their best interests in mind. While selling skills are vitally important to achieving success, these skills are a part of the required knowledge for a salesperson to reach competency. (In Section III, we will focus on the Essential sales skills every salesperson must have to succeed.)

In their book *The Trusted Advisor* (2001), authors David Meister, Charles Green, and Robert Galford coined the phrase "Trusted Advisor." They argue that achieving this status with customers and prospects opens the door to a new level of relationship between buyer and seller, and they are right. While buyer and seller rarely reach trusted advisor status in practice, it is the proper goal to endeavor to achieve.

Bern's Steakhouse Understands the Importance of Knowledge

A good example of the impact that knowledge can have on success is evident in the process that Tampa-based Bern's Steakhouse uses to train their waiters. Dinner at Bern's is an exquisite experience. Having opened its doors in 1956, the restaurant's owner, Bern Laxer, envisioned an "Art in Steaks" experience for patrons—and by all accounts, he succeeded.

Today, son David continues his father's tradition of culinary excellence. The interior—occasionally described as "gaudy ornate" in a building without windows—helps create the unique atmosphere. The restaurant has one of the largest wine cellars in the world, several dining rooms, and a separate dessert room upstairs. But what makes Bern's especially unique is the way in which the owners develop the food they serve, and how they train their wait staff to be experts.

Years ago, during a business trip to Tampa, our party ended up at Bern's for dinner. It was a memorable evening, and what made it truly great was our waiter. Bern's has as astonishingly well-trained and knowledgeable waitstaff who literally knows *everything* about everything connected to the restaurant. It was completely evident in the fact that our waiter was everything you could want in a server: funny, but not too funny or off-color; attentive, but not overbearing; quick and confident with answers to questions about the menu and the locale. He was there when we needed him, and out of sight when we didn't. Plates, silverware, and drinks seemed to come and go without our party noticing. By the end of the evening, we realized what a unique dining experience Bern's truly was—and, last but certainly not least, the food was *terrific*.

The Will, Skill, and Drill of Becoming a World-Class Waiter

Of course, none of this was an accident: Becoming a waiter at Bern's requires a long process of executing the will, skill, and drill of serving the finest food available. According to a former Bern's waiter, the steakhouse's staff-in-training spend their first two years working at the Bern's organic produce farm, in the wine cellar, and in the kitchen, learning all aspects of food prep and clean-up. The two-year apprenticeship prepares them for their four months working with dining room captains in one of the ornate dining areas. If they graduate to the next level with permission from the captains—which is *not* guaranteed—trainees are then allowed to wait tables on their own. If they pass that test, waiters are then placed on probation for one year. After their first probationary year, they take an exam, and if they pass, they become "Full-Fledged Waiters."

They Clearly Take Waiting Tables Seriously at Bern's.

Remember Pareto's 80/20 rule? Bern's "Full-Fledged Waiters" are 20 percenters. They make a very good living helping people have a great meal. They have earned this living: They have kicked their own asses to get there.

BECOME A "FULL-FLEDGED" SALESPERSON.

Make a Commitment to Become Knowledgeable

Knowledge is essential. Expert selling skills alone won't do the trick. To change the arc of your potential, become a "Full-Fledged" Salesperson and achieve true sustained superior performance, you must become a walking dictionary in your chosen field. Consider the following broad categories:

- Product
- Industry
- Competition
- Sales skills

Since your individual industry and selling situation will be unique, use this list as a frame of reference around which to build a plan.

Product

Broad and thorough product knowledge is the first test in a prospect/salesperson relationship. If you can't answer questions about the product's purpose and functionality, how trustworthy will the prospect believe you are to help develop a solution? Not very. And, since trust is essential, a lack of product knowledge is a big barrier.

I spend what some might argue is an *excessive* amount of time at the home centers around Jacksonville doing research and seeking solutions to any number of the various home-related disasters and "projects" that come up. The salespeople at those very home centers working the floor have to know how to diagnose the problem and help develop a solution, often working with prospects who have no earthly idea what they are talking about. When salespeople know their stuff, customers will buy whatever they recommend without regard for price. When they don't, the customer walks out of the store crestfallen and forlorn, faced with the reality they may have to return home to a leaking $\frac{9}{16}$-inch fetzer valve and no way to stop it. Worse, they may have to resort to calling a professional in to do the job, and suffer the embarrassment of having the pro fix the fix. In other words, it is *essential* that the salespeople know the products.

Use What You Sell

In his book *Secrets of Closing the Sale*, author Zig Ziglar talks about his early career selling cookware and working with a salesperson who was struggling to make a go of it. He tells the story of asking the man, "Do you use the cookware at home?" When the man replied, "No, I don't," Ziglar explained that the salesperson would never succeed until *he* personally owned a set of the cookware, and cooked with them himself.

Now, this may not work if you sell jets or military equipment, but you *should* know as much as possible about the products you sell. As evidenced by Ziglar's example above, any salesperson's efforts to make the sale must be centered on his or her belief in the product. How can a salesperson selling a product really argue their point and convince a prospect to buy if they aren't even willing to buy it themselves? They can't!

If you sell accounting systems, you should have some fluency in accounting principles. If you sell airplanes, you should be a pilot and have a thorough understanding of basic aerodynamics. Whenever possible, you should spend a significant amount of time learning to operate, install, repair, or implement what you sell. Using a product is the single best way to learn it. This gives you experience from which to draw, as well as a firsthand understanding of how customers use and benefit from them. I implemented this strategy after eating at Bern's, and have continued to use it hundreds of times since, for example, by encouraging software sales reps to implement and train at least two software systems in their first year of employment. It always works for them, and you should do it, too—whatever it takes.

KYOA Focus Questions

Product Knowledge Self-Analysis
Ask yourself the following questions—and answer honestly.

4.1. How well do I know the products I sell?

_____

_____

_____

4.2. What steps could I take today to improve my product knowledge?

_____

_____

_____

Industry or Specialization

It is smart to become a part of the specific industry or specialization in which you work and sell. Just as having expert product knowledge raises customers' level of trust in you, becoming an expert in their industry will enhance their faith in your ability to understand their issues. If you don't currently specialize in a highly focused area, I believe you'll benefit from considering it.

The Rotator Cuff

To illustrate why it's good to specialize in a particular industry, I'll tell you about my most recent encounter with the medical industry. Last year, while pretending to be a weight lifter who could bench-press 250 pounds, I heard a big pop emanating from the region known as my right shoulder. I immediately noticed that it was impossible for me to do anything that required the movement of my right arm. As I do with most injuries that don't involve profuse bleeding, I elected to do nothing and wait and see if it healed on its own.

Over the next several months, I managed despite the pain and altered my life to accommodate the limited ability of my right arm. (For the record, a torn rotator cuff makes it nearly impossible to do even the most basic functions, such as reaching the radio button in the pick-up truck.) Eventually, I ended up at the doctor's office—a place where I am known well enough to be greeted with "Hey, it's Rob!" I first met with my general practitioner, who referred me to an orthopedic surgeon, who was a shoulder specialist. He took one look at the shoulder and ordered several tests—including one that involved a long needle. I hate long needles.

Once the tests came back, the doc said I had torn the rotator cuff, the labrium, and that there were issues with my shoulder bone, as well. Pretty nice work. We reviewed my options for treatment, which included doing nothing, trying physical therapy, or going straight to surgery. I chose surgery—which, by the way, was successful. My recovery involved four months of daily workouts to strengthen and loosen the shoulder, which, I am told, set some sort of record. I may be a slow learner, but I am a fast healer.

Specialists Are Better

The doctor who performed my surgery is a specialist who focuses on doing a few specific types of orthopedic surgical procedures—including shoulders.

He therefore has a lot of practice doing these procedures, which in turn improves his skill and expertise and is a great comfort to his patients. The surgeon is making a very good living, creating great outcomes, and deriving high satisfaction by tightly narrowing his focus in a very specific area. He has reached the status of "trusted advisor."

The same is true for salespeople: The more highly focused you make your business, the more of an expert you will become; and the more your clients will respect and trust your suggestions.

The more you focus on improving your product and industry knowledge, the more of an expert you become.

> CUSTOMERS *AND PATIENTS* WANT TO WORK WITH SPECIALISTS.

Industry Associations

It is vital that you get involved in industry trade associations as an associate member. The full members may become your friends, and also customers. It's easy to find associations: One quick way is to visit the Internet Public Library (www.ipl.org/div/aon), which lists associations for nearly every business and industry. There are countless benefits of association membership and involvement, so if you work in a local or regional territory, make sure that you become a part of these in one way or another.

Become a Volunteer

Don't just join; *volunteer*. Volunteering connects you to members and makes you visible to others, allowing you to create and develop relationships with existing and potential customers. One of my most productive methods of prospecting came from becoming heavily involved in the local chapter of a national association. Cold-calling an association member was much easier when I could begin my introduction with a referral from a fellow member; in fact, it most always produced an initial meeting.

Don't join associations simply to get a list of members; there are much easier ways to get that. Join *only if* you plan to become actively involved. The fastest way to do so is to get to know the Executive Director, who can be of great assistance in helping you connect the dots of your skills with the needs of the association. Members really appreciate associate members (what they typically call members who are vendors) who take an active interest. We will work on prospecting in Section II, and you'll see how your industry involvement is essential to creating your own ocean of opportunities. So—best to get started now!

Industry Journals and Periodicals

Every industry group publishes journals: begin to subscribe to them and read them. Even better—submit an article to them. Most are constantly seeking new content and authors.

KYOA Focus Questions

Industry Knowledge Self-Analysis
Some industry questions you need to know how to answer are:

4.3. What are the key business challenges and/or opportunities in the industry?

_____

_____

_____

4.4. What are the key governmental issues facing the industry?

_____

_____

_____

4.5. What are the top issues facing most of the businesses in your industry?

_____

_____

_____

4.6. How does your product/service help solve the industry-based issues?

_____

_____

_____

KYOA Focus Questions

4.7. What solutions to the threats are being discussed?

_____

_____

_____

4.8. What are the natural strengths of the industry?

_____

_____

_____

4.9. What are the key industry associations?

_____

_____

_____

4.10. Which associations should you join and contribute to?

_____

_____

_____

4.11. Who are the leading companies in your industry?

_____

_____

_____

4.12. How can you contribute to the success of these organizations?

_____

_____

_____

4.13. How does your product or service help the industry?

_____

_____

_____

4.14. What are your top industry action items?

_____

_____

_____

Competition

One of the larger screw-ups of my early career involved the process of gathering competitive intelligence. The primary area of my territory was home to a locally owned software provider, a small organization of perhaps ten employees that looked, on paper, as though they would be easy to beat. Our company was far larger with more resources, and therefore, more "stuff" for the customer to love.

However, the customers in this market did *not* love our stuff. It wasn't that we weren't lovable; it was just that the other company was super fantastic at doing just what the customer needed, and they had established a huge base of adoring fans. I don't recall exact numbers, but my win average was roughly 0.00 percent. In over a year of calling on companies and presenting at least a dozen proposals, I had won exactly zero. Nada. *Ix-nay on the osing-clay*.

I'm not a very good loser, so this incessant failure was really beginning to bother me. I worked with my manager to develop a plan of attack. Our first strategy was to begin a price war. I was reminded that the adages "price overcomes all objections" and "discount early, discount often" are mostly true, *if* you are willing to execute a low-price leadership strategy. However, in this case, we created "trade-in" programs designed to significantly reduce our price point to about half of our competitors. Amazingly, it *did not work*; not *one* company took advantage of our offer.

The Big Kahuna

Our next strategy was to ship in the Big Kahuna to show the tenderfoot sales rep how to "slam a deal." I'll admit—it was fun to watch him get his ass completely kicked by a prospect who knew of roughly 100 companies that loved the other product, and who was a little put off by the Kahuna's sell-by-attacking-your-competitor approach. After that little incident, I was ordered to "do whatever is necessary" to "take them out." I *so* felt like I was in the software mafia.

The region's other rep and I held a brainstorming session on how to gain the competitive advantage against this company. We determined that we needed to know the weaknesses of their product, and once we knew that, we could highlight our strategic advantage by emphasizing their inherent product weaknesses to the prospects, explain how awful they were, and so on. But since none of their existing customers were unhappy, we had no idea how we going to get a good long look at their product.

We decided to become "owners" of a company who were seeking a new computer system, and ask the competitor in question if we could possibly use their software to "give it a good test drive." We called them and made an appointment to see a demonstration with the understanding that they would loan us a system for a day.

We were *incredible*. We went in, sat with the owner and watched his presentation, and walked out with an IBM AT (for any of you who know what that is . . . you are old!) loaded with their software. We spent the next 24 hours in a hotel creating a detailed slam sheet. This stuff *was* horrible; we couldn't fathom how we had ever lost to it.

The other rep and I returned the system to their office and told them we'd "think it over and give them a call." We went back to our office to execute phase II of our diabolical plan, and proceeded to send the slam sheet via facsimile to all of the prospects who were currently considering our two systems.

It Didn't Work!

The response was immediate—and horrific. Virtually every prospect responded to my follow-up call by explaining two things: First, they forwarded the slam sheet to the other company, who refuted every single claim. Second, they unanimously stated that they would never buy from a company who would resort to such underhanded tactics. Responding to the onslaught of unhappiness presented to his boss, the Supreme Kahuna, Mr. Big Kahuna executed the classic "plausible deniability" maneuver— and instantly threw the two of us under the bus. He emphasized to the Supreme Kahuna that he would never have agreed to such a stupid and devious idea. It was masterful to watch. My coconspirator and I were simply dumbfounded by this. It was our first introduction to The Law of Corporate Self-Preservation: All crap rolls downhill.

It did some rolling that day: We barely escaped with our employment intact. It would not be my last experience with the law of CSP, nor anything like it.

A Valuable Lesson

Later that year, while attending an industry trade show, the owner of the small software company visited our booth. He shook our hands, began laughing—and told us that he knew who we really were when we pretended to be "business owners," and had therefore purposely given us a presentation on software that was *several decades* old. As painful as this was—and it was *painful*—I am glad I learned the lesson about competition early. I kid you not: My coconspirator left the business of selling shortly thereafter, and now runs a very successful acting school.

> NEVER SELL BY PLAYING UP THE NEGATIVES OF YOUR COMPETITORS.

Negative selling *doesn't work*, so avoid it for the following reasons:

- It moves the focus away from understanding the client's issues. All the competitor has to do to win is to discredit your negative statements, which is usually easy enough to accomplish. When they do so, the boomerang effect ensues, and the two of you are concentrating almost entirely on one another instead of *the customer*.
- It is unprofessional.
- It can become unethical (see example above!).
- It goes against most personal and corporate mission statements.
- Prospects who are persuaded by negative selling are typically difficult-to-satisfy customers.
- It leaves most of us with an "icky" feeling.

This doesn't mean, of course, that prospects won't approach you and ask to hear about your competitors' weak points, or request that you comment on why *"your solution is better than theirs."* This is a very slippery slope, and one that I advise you to avoid. When I am invited by a prospect to slam a competitor, I attempt to point the conversation toward a more productive topic. Typically, a prospect will respond with a comment such as, *"Well, your competitor is sure slamming you."* If the prospect persists, I will use a Zig Ziglar/Mahan Khalsa move, and offer to walk away—

something Ziglar called the "Break Up Close," and Mahan referred to as "Take the Solution off the Table." Both techniques do essentially the same thing by attempting to redirect the dialogue in a more positive direction. For example, you can say: *"It's possible that we may not be a particularly good fit for your firm. We focus our entire effort to helping you make the best decision possible, not to examine what other companies you may be considering might lack. Knowing that, do you feel we should continue?"*

If a prospect is negative during the buying cycle, it is quite likely they may become negative clients. You may be well advised to walk away.

BODY-SLAM NEGATIVE PROSPECTS.

Bring Out the Boxing Gloves

However, avoiding negative selling doesn't mean that you shouldn't sell hard against a competitor: *You should.* If you are truly on the customer's side and there to help them make the best possible decision—and you sincerely believe that you offer them the best choice—you owe it to them to fight for it. There are fewer feelings greater than that of winning a sale after competing in a tough field, especially if you were considered the "underdog." Pulling victory out of the jaws of defeat is incredibly exhilarating: There's a huge adrenaline rush and endorphin release that comes when a customer chooses your solution. Winning a tough sale is the force that grabs most salespeople early in their careers and keeps them firmly planted in the game.

There will always be other companies and salespeople competing for your prospect's business. In most cases, potential clients are making decisions based on factors other than price. So what are those factors? Are they looking to solve a problem or take advantage of a new opportunity? Do they want to provide a better solution to their customers? Lower their risk? Improve their margins?

Differentiate yourself, so the prospect sees a clear choice: *You.*

Your key to winning in a competitive environment is to distinguish yourself and your offering so that the customer sees a clear difference and an easy choice. To do that, you need to be armed with knowledge; so ask yourself the following key focus questions.

KYOA Focus Questions

4.15. Who is your primary competitor?

_____

_____

_____

4.16. What are the strengths and weaknesses of their offerings?

_____

_____

_____

4.17. What is their sales process?

_____

_____

_____

4.18. Why do they win when they do?

_____

_____

_____

Create Your Strategic Advantage

You must create a strategic advantage to make your product and company unique. This is where knowledge of your product, your competitor's product, and a thorough understanding of your prospects' issues intersect. In most cases, outselling is really just *"outknowing"* (a word of my own invention) your competition. The more knowledge you bring to the opportunity, the more likely it is you'll be able to find areas of opportunity where you alone can provide a solution.

FBA

Sales training programs are filled with sections that study their product's features, benefits, and advantages. Often termed FBA, these programs help salespeople understand the difference between a *feature*—what something does—and a *benefit*—what that something does for the buyer and, if possible, why that feature offers a unique competitive *advantage* for the seller. This is both necessary and helpful information to know.

However, in reality, most products and services offer far more features than most prospects want or need. Simply reciting your product's FBA won't actually help your prospect make a good decision; this only works when the features and benefits are meaningful to the buyer. To develop a unique differentiator—your strategic advantage—you must begin by fully understanding the client issues.

Stupid Questions Salespeople Ask

Discovering the client issues is harder than it appears; most clients are on the defensive when perfect strangers approach them and ask *"Bill, what pain do you have?"* Or worse, *"Bill, what keeps you up at night?"* Furthermore, many prospects don't exactly know what their issues are. If they did, why would they need you? I don't believe I'll be sharing whatever *is* keeping me up at night with a salesperson.

In Section III, we'll work on developing a rational approach to building dialogue with a prospect that won't sound stupid and rehearsed—because it isn't. Developing a strategic advantage is the culmination of knowing your products, your competitors' products, and the customers' needs and wants. Once you are there, you will be tough to beat.

Compete to Beat "No Decision"

While whipping a competitor can be incredibly exciting, in many cases your primary competitor will be "no decision"; in other words, your prospect will simply choose to do nothing. "No decision" is the result of a prospect's analysis when they conclude that doing nothing is less risky and costs less than making a change. Understanding how to win over a "no decision" can, in and of itself, double your production and your paycheck.

In these cases, we're often beaten by common sense. Each of us has a value quotient we exercise when considering a purchase decision. If doing nothing seems like the cheaper, safer route, then we will choose this path.

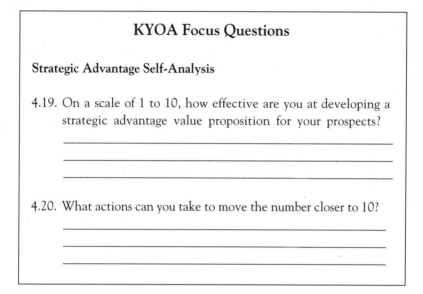

Figure 4.1   Strategic Advantage

Beating "no decision" entails competing with—and winning against—the "cost of not solving" (a concept we'll explore further in section III.) However, the foundation for achieving this is still knowing the prospect's core issues, and whether they're trying to create opportunities for gain, to remove risk, or to solve a problem.

Sales Skills

The last of our four areas of knowledge are sales skills. You have to build a solid foundation of product, industry, and competitive knowledge—as well as developing selling communication and persuasion skills—to change the arc of your potential. Great sales skills are not a replacement for the other three areas, but rather work in conjunction with them.

The Metrics of Selling

The goal of acquiring sales skills must be to improve performance, and there are two primary ways to do this: Create more opportunities to drive through the sales funnel, and improve your *effective close rate*.[1]

Larry's Selling Metrics

To explain these concepts, we'll use a made-up character and call him Larry as the subject for our discussion. If Larry closed ten sales per 100 proposals delivered in a year, his *effective close rate* sucks . . . oops, I mean, is 10 percent. Larry can improve his performance by putting more qualified opportunities—say, about 130 more proposals—through his sales funnel. If he keeps the same unimpressive close rate of 10 percent, he will close 13 sales, an improvement of 23 percent—which is pretty good. However, if Larry can improve his *effective close rate* from 10 percent to 20 percent, a marginal 10 percent improvement in effectiveness yields a 100 percent increase in performance—which is *really* good. Then, by doubling up both his improved pipeline and his effective close rate, Larry will become a 20 percenter and can buy a Mercedes Benz.

What Is Your Effective Close Rate?

Figure out your effective close rate by inputting your personal information into Figure 4.2.

Proposals delivered:	
Sales closed:	
Effective Close Rate:	
What happens to your income if you put 25% more opportunities into the funnel and improve your effective close rate by 10%?	

Figure 4.2   Effective Close Rate

[1] You will explore and create your selling metrics in detail in Chapter 16.

Larry Needs Sales Training

In fact, every salesperson does. In the fall of 2004—not long after I finished the Pikes Peak Ascent—I started a sales training program for my company called the Sage Sales Academy. SSA is a five-day course designed to provide new salespeople with a foundation of skills to prepare them for—or improve upon—a career as a salesperson. The program was originally scheduled to train 100 new salespeople in four separate sessions over a four-month period. To date, thousands of salespeople from all over the world have attended an SSA event. Based on internally developed content and taught by nonprofessional sales trainers, the program is an arc-changing experience for many of the students. So, I do believe that training can be part of the solution to improve selling skills.

Does Sales Training Work?

It *can* work; but only if students are serious and work at "improving their game." As we discussed in Chapter 2, sales training is often a last resort for underperforming salespeople, or part of initial "New Recruit" training. But without an ongoing integrated approach to skill development that includes training, coaching, and systems for management and monitoring, training alone has very limited effectiveness. Furthermore—to beat an already dead horse—sales training in lieu of product, industry, and competitive training is simply stupid. And to throw gas on the fire, nearly all training companies and programs focus their effort solely on "skill development," while the overwhelming majority of salespeople fail—or fail to reach their potential—due to *will*-related issues.

Measuring Training Effectiveness

This brings us to one of the difficulties of sales training: the difficulty of measuring its effectiveness. In 1959, Professor and past American Society of Training Directors (ASTD) president Donald Kirkpatrick published a series of articles in the *Journal of American Society of Training Directors* on the subject of evaluating training programs' effectiveness. Those articles eventually became the basis for his 1994 book titled *Evaluating Training Programs.* Kirkpatrick developed an evaluation methodology called Kirkpatrick's Four Levels of Evaluation Model, which are:

1. *Reaction of student*—what they thought and felt about the training.
2. *Learning*—the resulting increase in knowledge or capability.
3. *Behavior*—extent of behavior, capability improvement, and implementation.
4. *Results*—the effects of the trainee's performance on the business or environment.

The strength of Kirkpatrick's method is that it measures and evaluates every important aspect of the training experience. But here's the rub: It is nearly impossible to measure empirically improvement in actual results in the form of improved sales performance. For example, we routinely survey students who attend the Sales Academy after they complete the program. It scores very high marks, as the students really enjoy the experience, and can attest that they have actually learned new skills. In other words, we rock at numbers one and two on the Kirkpatrick method. However, since there are so many difficult-to-gauge factors that influence performance, it's nearly impossible to measure numbers three and four. Sales author and expert Neil Rackham's company Huthwaite International does tremendous work in measuring training effectiveness. Their research has concluded that: *Sales training effectiveness is hard to measure, and we often rely on anecdotal data to make decisions.*

Companies looking for hard ROI data to support investing in sales training are often left to believe that it doesn't work . . . and the reality is that, in many cases, it doesn't.

What You Can Do

For starters, honestly assess your level of knowledge in the four primary areas of knowledge needed: product, industry, competition, and sales skills. Once you've assessed this, develop a 12-month plan to improve your skills in each area by giving yourself something to learn every day.

Chapter 4 Recap: One Golf Lesson Doesn't Make You a Golfer— Great Potential Requires Great Work to Realize

- Golf is a lot like selling: Both require skill, will, and a passion to pursue; mental toughness to manage any pressures and self-doubt; and a clearly developed strategy.

- The foundation of the will, skill, and drill method of selling is knowledge, specifically in the areas of product, industry, competition, and sales skills.

- Every salesperson should know how to implement, use, and improve upon their products in order to explain them fully to potential customers.

- Much like patients choosing specialists for specific procedures, customers prefer salespeople who are *specialists* in their area.

- If you work in a specialization or industry with strong associations, join and become active in these. Volunteer for events, interact with other members, or offer to write articles for trade publications—anything to learn as much information as possible about your industry and get your name "out there."

- Never sell by playing up the negative aspects of your competitors. It moves the focus away from the customer and onto the competition; is unprofessional and unethical; and prospects who encourage it are typically difficult customers.

- Differentiate yourself from the competition by creating a strategic advantage. This is when you explain features, benefits, and advantages (FBA) that are meaningful to a particular customer. Client issues + Product and competitive knowledge = Strategic advantage.

- You can calculate and improve upon your Effective Close Rate by assessing the number of sales you've closed out of the total number of proposals you've given. Sales training can help you increase this percentage, but only if you are committed to "improving your game."

- Kirkpatrick's Four Levels of Evaluation Model measures the effectiveness of sales training in four key areas: Reaction of Student, Learning, Behavior, and Results. However, most sales training effectiveness is hard to measure; and we often rely on anecdotal data to make decisions. The best way to improve your effectiveness is to develop a 12-month plan to improve your skills in the areas of Product, Industry, Competition, and Sales Skills by learning something new each and every day.

Engage Your Will

Debunking the "Sales Personality" Myth

Is There a "Sales Personality?"

We know that knowledge is the foundation necessary to change the arc of your potential. Without mastering the four areas of product, industry, competition, and sales, you have little hope of improving your performance in a meaningful way. But what role—if any—does your personality play in your potential for success? That's what we're going to work on next.

Picture a "Salesperson"

What image first comes to mind when you read or hear the word "*salesperson*"?

- A glad-handing, overly friendly, joke-telling, loud-talking, plaid-golf-attire-wearing extrovert with too much cologne, who makes a little more eye contact than necessary, and whom you believe may have just tried a "sales technique" on you.

- A serious Wall-Streeter, clad in full-body armor with French cuffs and diamond cufflinks for the custom-made shirt, Italian shoes, and a $4,000 power bag, who speaks only in the latest catch-phrases and quotes the latest business books.

- A soft-spoken, shy, introverted, intellectual type, dressed from head-to-toe in Banana Republic fashions.

- A 1960s hold-over, complete with beard, pony-tail, and black turtleneck.

- A kindly, middle-aged, slightly frumpy, super-sweet individual with a friendly demeanor, helpful to a fault, who loves selling because of all the people they get to meet.

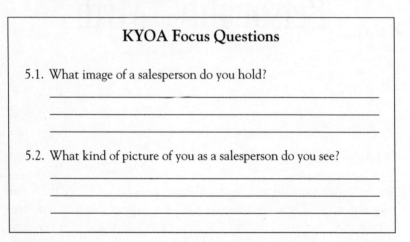

KYOA Focus Questions

5.1. What image of a salesperson do you hold?

_____

_____

_____

5.2. What kind of picture of you as a salesperson do you see?

_____

_____

_____

Different Personalities for Different Sales Roles

Although each of these personalities has vastly different characteristics, each could have a successful and enjoyable career in sales. However, there are certain personality types that tend to be a better fit among specific markets, which is why personality matching can be helpful. For example, a quiet, more technical personality type might be advantageous for selling a highly technical product to engineers, MDs, or PhDs. Thus, the myth that there is a single "sales personality" is just that: a myth. Of the basic elements needed to be successful—will, skill, and drill—having the stereotype "sales" personality isn't essential, as long as you have passion, energy, and drive.

KYOA Focus Questions

Think for a moment about how your last prospect might describe you as a salesperson. Be very detailed about how they would illustrate your passion, knowledge, personality, and physical presence.

5.3. How do your prospects see your personality?

_____

_____

_____

5.4. Are there changes you would make, if you could, regarding how your customers and prospects perceive you?

_____

_____

_____

Temperament versus Behavior

It is important to distinguish temperament and behavior—especially unwanted behavior. *Temperament* is your emotional disposition and reaction: it is the fabric of who you are. *Behavior* is your conduct, which usually depends on the situation you're in. For example, if your temperament is high in extroversion, your behavior would likely include talking. Managing the frequency, language, duration, volume, and intensity of your talking is the behavioral aspect; for example, in a classroom, disrupting the teacher would be unwanted behavior. At a party with friends, or in a business setting that calls for connecting with people, exuberant talking could be desired behavior. Every personality style has inherent temperament with potential behavior challenges. Making any radical changes to your temperament is unlikely and undesired (you are just as you were intended to be!). However, learning to manage your behavior isn't only possible, it's *essential*.

Personality Blueprinting

We're about to explore the concept of personality blueprinting—a way to define our trait patterns. Each of us has a personality. *Some of us have*

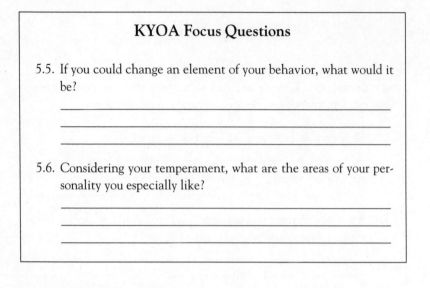

KYOA Focus Questions

5.5. If you could change an element of your behavior, what would it be?

_____

_____

_____

5.6. Considering your temperament, what are the areas of your personality you especially like?

_____

_____

_____

several. And each personality comes with types of temperament: light-hearted/outgoing/fun-loving, ambitious/driven/serious, shy/rational/observant, or any other number of combinations. While most of the psychological community believes that there is little we can do to actually change our personality and temperament, we can—and _should_—manage our behavior, especially in selling environments.

When we began the Sage Sales Academy in 2004, our primary goal was to support a short-term program to hire salespeople. One of the tools we used to assist in the hiring process was a personality profile created by PDPWorks (Professional DynaMetric Programs). Ongoing reliability and disparate impact studies are done in conjunction with the University of Colorado's Center for Applied Psychology. The profile, administered by the independent California-based firm, OPUS Productivity, provides a psychological blueprint for the candidate and the hiring firm. It gives them a detailed analysis of their score in the four basic psychological areas of Dominance, Extroversion, Patience, and Conformity. These four areas—or _quadrants_—are the foundation for understanding the basic personality. Each quadrant also contains the strengths and weaknesses of the personality type, and the challenges a salesperson will likely encounter in a sales or consulting position. Personality profiling is extremely helpful in allowing us to understand what motivates and does not motivate a given individual. It can confirm what you believe to be your natural strengths and tendencies, and where you might sell successfully. However, these blueprints are not necessarily a predictor of success, as they do not examine behaviors and psychological disorders that can derail sales careers. (We discuss these in Chapter 6.)

Blame It on Hippocrates

The PDP uses a high/low ratio of the four basic traits of Dominance, Extroversion, Patience, and Conformity. Two other very popular profiles, DISC and the Myers-Briggs testing methodologies, use techniques based upon similar traits. Many psychologists and historians give credit to the classification of personality into four basic types to the Greek physician Hippocrates, who also gets credit for being the "father of medicine." Hippocrates named the four temperaments Melancholic, Sanguine, Choleric, and Phlegmatic, after the bodily fluids that he believed influenced the personality.[1] While the theory regarding these fluids proved false, Hippocrates was right about the four basic personality types. Each of us has some blend of the four basic types: Dominance (control trait), Extroversion (social fluency), Patience (rate of motion), and Conformity (structure and detail). In the model presented, the four basic temperaments are divided into High and Low categories, for a total of eight categories. For example, we'll begin by looking at high and low dominance. Let's take a brief look into each one.

High Dominance

People with *High Dominance* qualities are hard-driving, highly competitive, innovative, aspire to lead, and conceptually analytical (which is not to say they are *actually* analytical, but to indicate that they are attracted to the *idea* of being analytical). People with high "D" traits appear to move chaotically through space and time at a frantic, dominating pace, while attempting to manage everything in sight. Think "control freak," and you've pretty well nailed it. Behavioral traits of high dominance include a propensity to challenge authority, disdain for indecisiveness, a need to be in control at any cost, and a strong inclination to stick to first impressions. They are not big decorators: High Ds tend to go for a "pile management,

---

[1] The four "humors," or fluids, are yellow bile, black bile, blood, and phlegm. Excessive yellow bile causes a choleric personality, excessive black bile causes a melancholic personality, excessive blood causes a sanguine personality, and excessive phlegm causes a phlegmatic personality.

stacks of stuff everywhere" look for office and home decor. High Ds coined the phrase *"It is better to ask forgiveness than to get permission"*—something that makes them pretty unpopular with management. Since they're instinctively driven to succeed, High Ds can be terrific salespeople. On the downside, there is the possibility that they'll leave a trail of bodies in their wake.

Low Dominance

People with *Low Dominance* characteristics are natural followers. Their leadership style is based on consensus building rather than authoritarian rule. These amiable, nonconfrontational, and good-natured creatures will go to any length to avoid a confrontation or conflict. Low Ds rarely rise to the C-level in an organization, unless they inherit it, as they are just too well-adjusted to need that much power and ego satisfaction. As you would imagine, it can be tough for low Ds to handle objections. In selling situations, Low Ds engage their passion for the product and their desire to help the customer, which they use as the great equalizer.

A long-time sales associate of mine has some strikingly Low Dominance traits. An accountant by training, he decided early in his career to work as a consultant to help companies implement and improve their computer-based accounting systems. He has developed a great reputation, is cheerful and helpful, trustworthy and reliable, and his clients love working with him. He has created a unique sales process that works with his personality.

His standard presentation takes at least two days and is generally considered a "prospect training session." It's a brilliant strategy: Prospects fear he'll never finish, and sign the agreement simply as a means of concluding the presentation. I've suggested numerous times that he show up to presentations with a sleeping bag under his arm, as I believe it would cause immediate capitulation and check-writing by the prospects. Hey—whatever works!

High Extroversion

People with *High Extroversion* characteristics have never met a stranger they didn't want to like them—*a lot*. They're the life of the party, and use understanding and persuasion as a means to accomplish objectives—which makes them the most likely "Sales Personality." Extroverts really want to make great first impressions, and feel utterly rejected if they perceive that they aren't well-liked. When combined with low self-image issues, this can make them do crazy things to attract attention and feel accepted. Extroverts are opportunists, and operate well in the abstract; however, they often need assistance with technical matters such as filling out expense reports. Extroverts are motivated by appreciation. If they don't receive it, they become defensive and unruly and will seek other outlets for acceptance. Known for being able to talk themselves out of trouble, extroverts are often good at getting *into* trouble—so this trait is essential. They're easy to spot: Extroverts care about their personal appearance and often have pictures, plaques, and diplomas posted everywhere. A typical extrovert's office will be a huge mess; many extroverts have high D traits as well. Therefore, they tend to have photographs of themselves in a variety of athletic endeavors, such as downhill skiing, scuba diving, softball playing, and the like.

But there's no perfect personality type. The trouble with being an extrovert is that nearly everyone *encourages* you to become a salesperson. Having an outgoing personality is helpful in sales, but it can also be a hindrance, especially if you're selling to anyone other than an extrovert. Selling situations often prompt extroverts to adopt the *overpromise/underdeliver* strategy, as they really want to promise what the client wants—even if it's impossible to actually deliver.

Low Extroversion

People with *Low Extroversion* characteristics are quieter than High Es—a *lot quieter*. Often referred to as "introverts," low Es enjoy being alone and don't need the same amount of attention that High Es do in order to feel happy. Low Es emotions can be hard to read. They keep their opinions to themselves, and often find public speaking difficult and small talk tedious. Low Es are not moody by nature, and don't become as discouraged as quickly as their high E counterparts by setbacks and poor performance. In selling situations, Low Es prefer working with similar personality types, and find it more difficult selling to highly extroverted and dominant personality types.

High Patience

People with *High Patience* characteristics are the great plodders. Known for their tenacity and persistence, they accomplish goals by simply trudging along. High Ps are thoughtful and helpful, and take time to understand the assigned task before launching into action. The phrase, "Ready, *shoot*, aim" does not apply to these folks. Many people with high P traits have great memories and are caring, loving individuals.

High Ps are often slow to act, preferring to avoid conflict and remain in harmony in their relationships and with nature. High Ps who have a low self-image can be plagued by procrastination, which is used primarily to avoid potential conflict or negative outcomes. They tend to avoid risk rather than seek reward, which can be a challenge in certain sales environments. However, their nurturing, persistent, and thoughtful personalities make them easy to work with—a big plus in selling.

Low Patience

People with *Low Patience* characteristics are fast-moving decision makers. They're always ready to get going, and engage in projects with enthusiasm. They're not afraid to encounter conflict in order to get things done, and are sometimes referred to as "steamrollers." They're quick-tempered if challenged, and are often also gifted with a high D trait—which can create havoc in a sales (or any other) environment. If low Ps feel that they're being held back by a slow-moving environment, boredom will set in, and they will soon seek other, faster action. If they aren't properly organized, low Ps can spin their wheels and may demonstrate very erratic behavior—something that's always challenging in a sales environment. This personality type really excels in demanding situations that require quick-on-the-feet thinkers who like to operate at a frenetic pace.

High Conformity

People with *High Conformity* characteristics are analytical in nature with a keen sense of right and wrong, and good versus bad. They prefer not to deal with conceptual ideas or work in areas of gray; high Cs tend to be formal and reserved. Often referred to as "anal retentive," high Cs are exact in their approach to work and life, and rarely make mistakes if they are properly trained. They like order, prefer to work from a checklist, and favor roles where there are preset standards for measuring success. They tend to react negatively to sudden or abrupt changes in direction, especially when they don't see the justification or value.

High Cs have a very strong sense of duty, are very thorough in whatever task or role they take on, and have a strong respect for leadership. In selling situations, high Cs do well in very technical areas selling to likeminded prospects and customers.

Low Conformity

People with *Low Conformity* characteristics have never willingly balanced their checking account. Low Cs are uninhibited, candid, and enjoy activities that veer off the beaten path. In fact, most prefer to create their own path. Low Cs have a generalist orientation to life; they would rather be a "jack of all trades" than a specialist in anything. A variety of half-completed projects usually litter their homes and lives. They desire to live with as much freedom from restraint as possible, hate to be managed (although they need it), and want minimal controls set on them.

Unusually independent, low Cs could be described as loners, unless they are also gifted with a high E trait; then they are considered a chatty outlaw. Low Cs consider laws and rules as mere suggestions, and usually resent authority. Their Wild-West-gunslinger attitude makes them naturally challenging in a sales environment, especially if they actually have to report to someone. Low Cs are creative thinkers and love operating in the abstract; they do best in challenging situations that require innovative solutions to problems.

The Author's Personality Blueprint

I imagine that you have identified with a number of the descriptions you've read on the four basic quadrants—Dominance, Extroversion, Patience, and Conformity—of personality. In 2004, as part of the preparation for launching the Sales Academy, I took my own PDP profile with OPUS Productivity for analysis, and the resulting 25-page report absolutely nailed me. I have a high E over D, with a low P over an even lower C profile. If you take a gander back through the descriptions, you'll see that this makes me outgoing and driven. It could also make me a handful. This test also scores the way in which we approach decision making; I found that I use feeling and intuition more than facts and data. The test also looks at energy levels, and I'm happy to report that I'm highly energetic (see Figure 5.1).

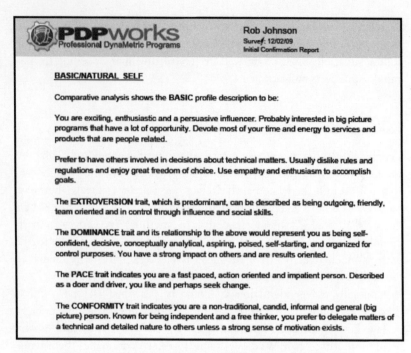

Figure 5.1   Rob's Basic/Natural Self Chart (PDPWorks)

Mr. Sales-Personality Award Winner

The personality trait-pairings of high E and D over low C and P are often described as the "sales personality." However, as you have read, each style and trait comes with its own challenges. I certainly struggled as a sales-person despite my "fitting" personality.

Trait Pairings

Thankfully, there are few of us with "pure" personality traits. Most of us are a delightful blend of flavors and styles, like coffee or wine. Studying and understanding your personality is vitally important to success, regardless of what exact blend you have. This knowledge creates awareness of your inclinations and tendencies. Awareness of your behavioral tendencies is the first step to effectively managing them. For example, if you are a high C selling to a high E, you know your behavioral tendency is to be quiet and reserved, which could make your prospect feel as though you are aloof and uninterested. In this case, you would know to turn up your personality's volume and intensity knobs. You must become adept at identifying your prospect's personality and changing your approach to suit them; it doesn't work the other way around. Failing to do so will limit you to working with potentially only 25 percent of the market: those who actually identify and match your trait pairings. To explore this further, consider the standard sales skill of building rapport, a staple of sales training classes.

Building Rapport

The personality pairing of high D over high C could be described as a "dominant control freak"; these people usually don't have a visible sense of humor (at least when sober). Therefore, spending a lot of time attempting to build rapport with this personality type is not only unproductive; it is *counter*productive. Likewise, be prepared to spend all day getting to know a high P if you're selling to them. Otherwise you could have trouble, and I often did.

Rapport-Building Guidelines

Figure 5.2 shows a brief overview of how different personality types approach the subject of rapport-building.

High D	No rapport building until after the contract is signed. Get straight to the point. Begin with the Executive Overview with no details. No funny business.
High E	Comment on the picture of the snow skiing trip on the credenza, and sit back and enjoy the show; you're going to be there a while. High Es are all about making connections and building relationships. Watch the clock, or you'll build too much rapport and actually miss the meeting.
High P	Build rapport all you want. It will not actually matter to the sale, as high Ps almost never make a decision. This would mean that they'd have to decide between two or more choices, which would put them in the position of conflict, something they avoid like the plague.
High C	No rapport necessary, *ever*. Be very detailed. Know your facts, or else. They will take whatever you say literally, so be careful.

Figure 5.2 Rapport-Building Guidelines

All Salespeople, and Personalities, Can Succeed—Even Jerry

Every single personality type can thrive in sales. For example, my friend Jerry is a quiet, analytical, and amiable guy. He hates and avoids confrontation. A plodding, detailed record-keeper, Jerry resists change and continues to use the same 3-x-5-inch index-card prospecting system that he learned during his first sales job out of college—about 40 years ago. (He may be using the same index-card box as well.) Every prospect gets a card, and every card gets a call when they come to the front of the box. Jerry makes a note recounting the details of each call on the corresponding card. Though I've tried to tell him on numerous occasions about these new-fangled devices that look like televisions with built-in typewriters that actually do a bunch of really cool things, he's having none of it. And in truth, he doesn't need it. Jerry is a super successful salesperson in his own right, and the following list explains why.

- He sells into a market which suits his personality.
- First, he has an incredible *work ethic*. He starts early and works late. He never does paperwork during the day; he does it after supper, in his home office. He completes all of his daily work before retiring for the evening.
- He manages his *mental health*. Jerry is the first to say he has issues; think *"emotional train wreck."* He struggles with anxiety, and a tendency toward depression. If he gets too far afield from a mental-health-fitness perspective, he just shuts down; his energy and drive evaporate. However, he receives treatments—including therapy and medication—that keep him generally within the lines. His self-awareness is his great equalizer; he can sense when he's in trouble, and takes action to prevent it from becoming worse.
- *He is competent.* Jerry has mastered the four areas of knowledge: product, industry, competition, and selling. He has even reached the level of becoming *a trusted resource* for his customers, keeping them in compliance with state and federal regulations.
- *He is trustworthy.* He makes and keeps all his commitments with customers.
- *He is likable.* Jerry never says the wrong thing to prospects. He has learned to adjust his personality volume and intensity when necessary to match the personalities of his more flamboyant customers.

- *He commits energy to his career.* He is the original tortoise; a steady performer, he always remains focused on the job. Among his many issues, low-blood sugar is but one. To deal with that, he keeps a supply of crackers in his car at all times to ensure he can sustain the energy he needs to get through the day.
- *He is driven.* Although his ambition is hardly visible, it's there.
- *He has a prospecting system,* albeit an archaic one, that works for him, and he executes every single day, without fail. It is painful to watch, but it *works.*

For the last five years, he has set sales records for his company. He literally redraws the arc of his potential every day of every year. Even when his life is crazy, his performance continues to improve.

Elements of a Successful Salesperson

Connected to Passion	Mentally healthy
Super work ethic	Likable
Competency in product, industry, competition, sales	Energy
Trust and intent	Drive
Personality awareness	A Daily Drill Success System

Figure 5.3   Elements of a Successful Salesperson

Drive and Energy Are Essential

Regardless of your personality, these two elements are *absolutely necessary* to change the arc of your potential.

- *Energy* is the amount of mental and physical effort you are able to bring to the task at hand; your ability to keep at something over a period of time.
- *Drive* is the internal mainspring that keeps you moving in the direction of your goal (typically difficult to see if you don't actually *set* goals).

From a personality cocktail perspective, mental health counselors, educators, and salespeople share many of the same qualities, except in the area of energy and drive. Not surprisingly, salespeople must have a very high level of energy. They're likely to fail without it, as the position requires substantial energy simply to execute the drill of the job.

The good news is that both energy and drive can be developed and improved upon through focus and work. Remember the bonsai gardener? He didn't lack either of these qualities. In fact, he was highly driven and very energetic. He just lacked the motivation to achieve sustained superior results selling computer software, because his passion lay with the care and feeding of very small plants. He could have potentially connected this passion to software sales, as it afforded him the lifestyle to enjoy his avocation; but he was fortunate enough to be able to combine sales with pleasure by actually going into the business. As a result, he was highly engaged with his drive to succeed.

CONNECT TO YOUR DRIVE TO SUCCEED.

The Source of Your Drive

The question for you to consider is: From where or what does your internal drive come? What is the thing that propels you forward and keeps you in motion? What should you do if you don't feel driven?

Often, drive springs from elements of desire and fear. For example, we know that top performers are highly driven to achieve success. However, we often don't know what drives them. For some, their drive springs from fear: the need for approval, need for security, need to feel accepted, need for respect, need for ego fulfillment, fear of humiliation, need for revenge or redemption, fear of looking stupid, fear of mortality, and so on. What separates these salespeople from others is how their fear is channeled. For example, instead of becoming complacent as a result of their fears (a common problem), they are propelled ever faster forward—feeding on their need to achieve success. Often, the results are spectacular, and occasionally spectacularly horrible. In some cases, their incessant need to achieve blurs the lines of reason. The result is we often hear of their failures in the media. For these, their drive is perhaps an attempt to fill an empty void. Their focus is turned inward. In many cases, in spite of the accumulation of great material wealth, they remain unsatisfied, unfulfilled, and unhappy.

For others, their source of drive comes from a desire to help others. They are driven to help others achieve their goals: their customers, children, spouse or significant other, coworkers, people in their community, or any other friends and relations that one can imagine. It is through their drive that they create a better world for their communities, and, as a result for themselves and their families. Their focus is outward. They pursue prosperity based on the definition of how much they can give, not how much they can get. Often, regardless of whether they ever accumulate great material wealth, they lead happy and fulfilling lives. However, many who focus their drive outward become fabulously wealthy people, as they naturally attract others to them.

Drive creates its own energy, which is essential for greater success. Energy comes from drive. Without understanding and engaging your drive, you will never have enough energy to change the arc of your

---

KYOA Focus Questions

5.7. Do you feel a sense of drive to achieve greater results?

_____

_____

_____

5.8. If yes, describe in detail the nature of the drive, recognizing that there could be more than one.

_____

_____

_____

5.9. If no, describe why you don't.

_____

_____

_____

5.10. What would you like to be your mainspring, your source of inspiration and drive?

_____

_____

_____

potential. This is why it is so important to understand the root of your drive. If you are like me, when reading the descriptions of the roots behind drive and motivation, you connect with both of the descriptions. In reality, most of us are driven by conflicting mainsprings: We need to achieve to feel accepted, and we want to help others. We are imperfect and complex beings capable of simultaneously holding contradictory positions.

No amount of external motivation—either positive or negative—can actually *make* you develop drive. You must connect your internal mainspring, your drive, to your vocational pursuit to change the arc of your potential. If you are struggling with drive, you know there are no diets, exercise programs, or sales methodology programs to help with this; those simply attempt to treat a symptom. Instead, we have to deal with the core issues behind our motivation deficiency; no amount of external encouragement will work. You can develop and expand your drive by exposing and dealing with the core issues—which we refer to as the "Will Killers"—in the following chapter. Come on, turn the page. This is getting good.

Want to Learn More About Your Own Personality Style?

As a purchaser of this book, you qualify for a FREE personalized behavioral overview from OPUS Productivity.

Featuring the same nomenclature and classifications used in this chapter, this behavioral style overview will show you how your personality style matches up to the four cornerstone behavioral traits. This insightful overview is available online and takes less than five minutes. Go to:

www.willskilldrill.com

to take advantage of your free overview, and to learn about the other OPUS Productivity services and helpful tips available to manage your selling style.

Chapter 5 Recap: Debunking the "Sales Personality" Myth

- Many of us have a preconceived notion (or several) of what a "typical salesperson" is like, but it takes different kinds of personalities to sell various products to different types of customers.

- There is a distinction between temperament—your emotional disposition and reaction, and the fabric of who you are—and behavior—your conduct, which usually depends on the situation you're in. It is important to understand both of these aspects of yourself in sales situations.

- The four basic areas or quadrants of personality—Dominance (control trait), Extroversion (social fluency), Patience (rate of motion), and Conformity (structure and detail)—are the foundation for understanding the basic personality. Each quadrant comes with strengths and challenges a salesperson will likely encounter in a sales or consulting position.

- High Dominance people are hard-driving, highly competitive, innovative, aspire to lead, and can be terrific—if sometimes too driven—as salespeople.

- Low Dominance people are amiable, nonconfrontational, and good-natured creatures who will go to any length to avoid a confrontation or conflict. They use their passion for the product and helping the customer in sales.

- High Extroversion people are the most likely "Sales Personality"; they want to be liked by everyone and often go to great lengths to garner attention. They aren't very good with detailed tasks.

- Low Introversion individuals are quieter, keep their opinions to themselves, and often find public speaking difficult. They're more apt to keep at a difficult task than other personality types are.

- High Patience people are known for their tenacity and persistence, and accomplish goals by simply trudging along. They're thoughtful and helpful, and take time to understand the assigned task before taking action.

- Low Patience personalities excel in demanding situations that require quick-on-the-feet thinkers who operate at a frenetic pace. They're often called "steamrollers," and don't shy away from conflict to get things done.

- Low Conformity people are analytical in nature with a keen sense of right and wrong. They prefer not to deal with conceptual ideas or work in areas of gray, and tend to be formal and reserved.

- High Conformity people are uninhibited, candid, and enjoy activities that veer off the beaten path. They desire as much freedom as possible and hate to be managed or controlled (even though they may need it).

- The key to building rapport with customers is to know your own personality and that of your prospects as well. Each personality type requires a different approach.

- A recipe for a super salesperson is as follows: someone who is connected to their passion; mentally healthy; has a strong, sound work ethic; is likable; exhibits competency in product, industry, competition, sales; begets trust and shows intent; has an awareness of his own and his prospects' personalities; undergoes a daily drill success system; and displays energy and drive.

- Energy—the amount of mental and physical effort you are able to bring to the task at hand—and drive—the internal mainspring that keeps you moving in the direction of your goal—are absolutely necessary for succeeding in sales. Both must come from within; no amount of external motivation will be enough to induce either quality in you.

The Will Killers

Disclaimer: I am not a psychologist, therapist, or physician, nor do I have a particular expertise in the area of psychology. I have read a number of books on various topics that fit under the umbrella terms "self-improvement" or "self-help," including many that have helped to shape the mosaic of my belief that our will to change is greater than the forces which attempt to stop us. Engaging your will is more a matter of letting go of old beliefs and paradigms than simply trying harder. I have also read a great number of books on "home-improvement," which of course, means little in this context of this book. And, of course, my library of sales-related books is in the hundreds of volumes.

This chapter is based solely on personal experience, and the experiences of others whom I've helped in dealing with core issues that hamper success. It also covers subjects related to improving performance and the quality of life. Additionally, I have had great help on my journey to the center of my equilibrium, a place I occupy with some regularity these days. Those encounters were instrumental in my understanding of the nature of issues, which was preventing me from changing the arc of my potential at the time.

—REJ

The Ultimate Will Killer: Core Issue, Manifestation, and Resulting Behavior

There are many reasons—or excuses—that we use to explain why we don't engage our drive and energy to achieve greater success. Some people do what I did, and spend inordinate amounts of time developing excuses

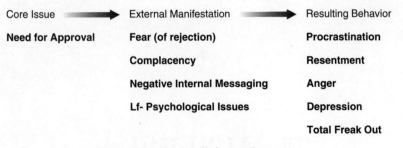

Figure 6.1   Issue-to-Behavior Overview

that sound plausible for failing to achieve their goals. Most of us face some core issue at the root of nonperformance. We experience behaviors that keep us from reaching our potential, which in many cases then become unresolved fundamental issues. In practice, a core issue is triggered by an event, which creates a manifestation. The manifestation then elicits a certain kind of reaction, which we refer to as a resulting behavior— sometimes, very bizarre resulting behavior.

For example, your core issue might be a need for approval. When activated, it manifests as a fear of rejection, which generates a resulting behavior of procrastination. The procrastination is evidenced by not making phone calls or completing tasks in a timely manner. Figure 6.1 illustrates this pattern.

Hopefully, you are totally unaffected by anything like this, and the entire idea of struggle seems foreign to you. If this is the case, you can just jump right over this entire section and go directly to Section III. However, the purpose of this chapter for the rest of you is to explore a few areas which can kill the will to sell and impact salespeople the hardest. To help, we will create a framework for indentifying why we don't accomplish as much as we could, and Chapter 7 focuses on the tools needed to overcome these challenges. The question is: What is the best method for *you* to use in attempting to resolve a given issue?

The Psychological Two-Step

Much of the work that the mental health community does is a two-step process of working with patients. They first attempt to understand core issues and then, second, they try to rebuild new neural pathways between the core issue and the manifestation, with the intent of changing the way the patient responds to stress, anxiety, and conflict. Our synapses fire in a predictable repetitive manner in response to these stressors; and the more often we repeat these responses, the more deeply grooved the neural pathways become, thereby making it harder to change. In essence, a rut is formed. Entire libraries of research and scholarly work contain explanations as to why we respond to these impulses; it's a topic of lively debate within the psychological, medical, and scientific community.

IT'S TIME TO REBUILD YOUR NEURAL PATHWAYS.

Remember the golf analogy to training and knowledge? It works here as well. Reprogramming the brain and muscles to change a golf swing is very complicated. Even minor adjustments that are easy to understand intellectually are difficult to implement. Without constant awareness, it is easy to fall back into the old swing pattern or "groove."

Changing Behavior: "Time Tellers" (Behaviorists) versus "Clock Builders" (Psychoanalysts)

Not all mental health professionals agree on a methodology for changing our behavior, or "behavior modification." Heck, not all mental health professionals agree that meaningful change in behavior is possible. However, for those that believe in change, they fall into three buckets. Some psychiatrists, whom we might refer to as the "leopard can't change its spots" crowd, believe it is impossible to make any kind of behavioral adjustment without involving pharmacology. Their belief is that behavioral malfunctions are the result of chemical imbalances, and the best one can hope for is to mask the unwanted behavior through the usage of medication. This is certainly true in certain instances. And for those affected, medications are life-changing. However, for the overwhelming majority who use medications to change their behavior, it isn't required. It's just easier. Take a pill. Mask the pain. Take another pill. Mask more pain.

Other members of the psychological community who consider themselves behaviorists—who I call "time tellers"—tend to ignore the core issue and, by using a directed therapeutic approach, prefer to bypass the core issue and work exclusively on changing the synaptic firing mechanism between the manifestation and the resulting behavior. I give them this name because they focus on solving the manifestation and resulting behavior, and would be more likely to give you the exact time when asked the question "what time is it?" For example, a behaviorist might work with a person who fears flying by dealing with the present fear, as opposed to understanding the core issue behind it. Their goal would be to gradually get their patient to the airport, to sit on a plane, to visualize flying, and to eventually fly. Detective B. A. Baracus—a fictional character played by the great Mr. T on the 1980s hit sitcom *The A-Team*—was a tough guy with a severe fear of flying. Any therapy would have worked to get him on an aircraft, as long as it included a tranquilizer gun—a fairly large tranquilizer gun.

While behaviorism is great for certain types of personalities and issues, another methodology—embraced by psychologists I called "clock builders"—utilizes an exploratory method often referred to as psychoanalysis. Often considered a Freudian derivative, psychoanalysis works by peeling the psychological onion back to childhood, where psychologists feel most of the damage that manifests itself later in life is done. Knowing the root cause for manifestations and resulting behaviors is considered an essential first step to actually overcoming it. When you ask this group what time it is, they'll likely tell you how to build a clock. They firmly believe that change begins with full awareness of the root cause; a process that can—and does—take years of patient work to unearth the root issue.

Both approaches have immense value, depending on your goals and temperament. High dominant, low conformity personality types who demonstrate the "fix me now" attitude may not have the emotional bandwidth to focus on exploratory therapy, because it can take a long time and usually doesn't provide immediate feedback and gratification. Remember Jerry, the unlikely sales superstar? He has regular psychoanalysis, and has for years. It is part of his program for maintaining his level of functionality.

Our Core Issues Impact Our Careers

The manner in which we respond to certain stressors affects how we execute our sales careers. There are an infinite number of excuses that we can give as to why we are too busy to execute a plan, initiate a call, respond to questions and objections, or ask for an order. But in reality, there are only a few actual reasons for these failures. If resolving this were as easy as me simply pointing them out and telling you to *"Stop being afraid and you'll succeed,"* then this would be a pretty short chapter. However, solving challenging problems is never that easy. We usually don't ever "get over" an issue fully; we simply acknowledge the impact it is having on our life and career and learn how to deal with it in a productive and healthy way.

Real growth comes from accepting responsibility and taking positive action. We gain tremendous self-confidence when we control our internal adversity.

KNOCK OUT YOUR CORE ISSUE.

How We Respond to Stress Is Programmed into Our Brains

We are programmed to believe that we are what our brains tell us we are, and we spend a lot of time and energy worrying about our past and about our future. It is this brain-driven focus that causes much of our anxiety in the present. In most cases, the anxiety, born out of the core issues, triggers a manifestation.

However, it doesn't have to be that way. Eckhart Tolle's 1996 book, *The Power of Now*, allowed me to realize this basic truth,

We are not our brains.

Our soul does not reside inside our brain, but rather beyond it. And our brains are wrong—very often. In fact, if you're like me, you have at one time engaged in an activity that was fully blessed by the brain, only to realize in hindsight that it was not the best of choices. The brain makes the connection between core issue, manifestation, and resulting behavior. It can therefore unmake them, as well, and change the way we process stress, anxiety, and conflict by reprogramming our minds.

YOU ARE NOT YOUR BRAIN.

Two Bulldogs

Let me give you a recent example of how our synapses fire (or misfire). I have a core issue that manifests in a fear of dogs. Not all dogs: just the big ones that chase me with the intent of killing me while I'm out for a run. I've felt this way for as long as I can remember; it has affected my running because I tend to alter courses and avoid routes that I believe have potentially vicious dogs on them. I'm not usually all that rational, either: There does not actually have to *be* a vicious dog on the route; instead, the mere possibility is enough to prompt me to change my course.

One early Sunday morning, I was taking my own dog, Jack (See? I don't dislike *all* dogs!) for a short walk after returning from a run. We passed a neighbor's house with two bulldogs, who, by the way, I had seen numerous times and who had never made me nervous. The dogs were in the court-yard behind a gate and began their good morning bark at Jack as we walked. We all realized simultaneously that the gate was unlocked. Oops. Out came the bulldogs. I was immediately gripped by fear, and out came my resulting behavior.

For the next 12 seconds, Jack, the two bulldogs, and I went on a serpentine run/chase through several yards, over hedges, up an alley, and over a porch, before I decided it would be better if Jack and I went our separate ways. At that moment, I dropped his leash, headed for the nearest escape option, where I performed a "Fosbury Flop"—a technique made famous by Oregonian high-jumper Dick Fosbury—onto the roof of a nearby parked car. As I sat there, hoping I hadn't damaged the car, my internal voices began laughing hysterically at me. I began to ponder the full impact that this fear was having on my life. I quickly realized that the dogs didn't actually want to *kill* me: they had merely wanted to sniff Jack—which they were doing actively in the middle of the street twenty feet away. I assume they thought I had just gone crazy for the car. At that point, another neighbor—completely unaware of the preceding 12 seconds of mayhem—walked by and began petting the sniffing trio. It was a triple dog love-in.

Strong Recovery

Once I saw that my life wasn't in grave danger, I nonchalantly slid off the car (as if a sober, grown man can *nonchalantly* slide off the roof of a neighbor's car) and rejoined the group, feeling like a complete idiot. I soon realized the dogs really just wanted to sniff me, too. At that moment, I took the adult way out and walked the dogs back to their home and tricked them into going back into their courtyard. I had faced down my fear; well, sort of.

FACE DOWN YOUR FEAR.

I don't know why I was so afraid of being attacked by those dogs. Perhaps it is a repressed childhood memory, or an event from another lifetime manifesting itself into this one. I'm on the journey to understand the source of this manifestation of fear and, for now, I will resist the urge to carry a weapon on runs and walks with Jack.

Figure 6.2   "Two Bulldogs" Issue

Not the Core Issue

Regardless of the core issue, my synapse fired and *triggered* the manifestation of *fear*, which resulted in my *total freak-out*: a well-worn neural highway in my brain that is illustrated in Figure 6.2.

I don't know if I'll ever fully understand the source behind this fear of mine. However, just acknowledging that there *is* an issue that is manifested through fear, and which often results in the total freak-out is a big step—and, apparently a Fosbury Flop—toward managing it.

We Don't Wear Out Treadmills

Another example of a core issue/manifestation/resulting behavior scenario is the alarming number of treadmills and other personal exercise equipment sold in the United States, that in most cases are *never* used. The treadmill can actually serve as a metaphor for how our will becomes seriously derailed. For a moment, reflect on the step-by-step process many people undergo when they desire to improve their physical condition:

- Something makes them recognize that they have a problem they would like to solve; perhaps they're out of shape, overweight, in ill health, or all three. It might also stem from an effort to improve the chances of ever going on a date.

- They research potential solutions, such as watching one of the thousands of infomercials that sell health-related equipment, or surfing the web, talking with friends, or visiting with their health professional.

- They show up at the athletic superstore.

- While at the athletic superstore, they buy the device, plus a variety of workout accessories: outfits, MP3 players, water bottles, timing devices, proper footwear, videos, floor mats, and so on.

- They load up the SUV with the amazing new exercise device and the tony new fashion-forward exercise accessories.
- They develop a plan of attack, including daily workouts, target calories, and heart rate, and a strict nutrition plan based loosely on a diet of lettuce and water.
- What happens next . . . ? Not much!

WE HATE TREADMILLS.

Overwhelming evidence suggests that few people ever *wear out* home health equipment. There is very strong anecdotal data that suggests that life-of-the-product usage amounts to less than five sessions, and even *a lot less than five*. Yet our country's physical fitness industry is booming. Here's irony for you: while the United States is one of the most out-of-shape countries on the planet, we still spend more on exercise equipment than the rest of the planet *combined*. The treadmill scenario is interesting in that "we" recognized a problem, sought help for a solution, and took positive action, only to then fail completely. People who live on Earth are really great at assessing a problem and developing a strategy and action plan to solve it—we're just not all that good at actually *implementing* it.

HEY, WEAR OUT YOUR TREADMILL, ALREADY!

Solving the Wrong Problem

From a purely psychological perspective, behavior is designed to solve a problem; so deciding to purchase a treadmill is fairly logical behavior. However, when we don't know *the actual problem we're trying to solve*, the applied behavior isn't very effective. In other words, it isn't the lack of a treadmill that keeps us out of shape; therefore, the acquisition of a treadmill won't actually help get us into shape. Hence, we stack up stuff we never use, since these weren't really the right solutions anyway.

How Long Must We Keep Unused Gym Equipment?

There must be a statute of limitations on how long we must keep unused athletic machinery around the house before we can in good conscience advertise it for sale on Craigslist or in the newspaper, or simply drag it out to the curb with a sign attached: BARELY USED. FREE TO GOOD HOME. Six years of having these devices sitting idly in rooms, obscuring the view of the television—and eventually becoming the focus of lively debates and arguments, only then to be shuffled out to the garage or basement—seems like an adequate amount of time. The device then sits there and collects dust before someone in the household demands that we *"Accept the reality that you are never getting on it and get rid of it already, for goodness sake—which I could have told you when you bought the stupid thing!"* In rare cases, these devices actually become useful in some unintended way, such as for drying laundry or as a Science Fair project parts kit.

We Have Issues

Why don't we wear out our treadmills? Why do we fail to follow most diets? Why do 20 percent of salespeople make 80 percent of the sales, leaving the other 80 percent to make only 20 percent? Why do we make resolutions and never keep them? Why do we set goals for prospecting, then do everything but prospecting? Why do we obsess over things over which we have no control? Why do we have anxiety attacks over what we dream up in our brains, or obsess about how someone *might* react, taking it so far as to actually develop resentment and anger toward them? Why are we afraid of dogs that want to lick us? We're pretty screwed up. That's why.

Many experts believe our collective inability to execute is a lack of will power and discipline. We simply need to work harder, buckle down, put the nose to the grindstone, and stop thinking about the negative stuff. Equally brilliant others believe that it's our profound inability to manage our time that blocks those 80 percenters from reaching their potential. We need only to become better planners, and then we'll do and achieve more.

Opposing Forces: The Greater Force Wins

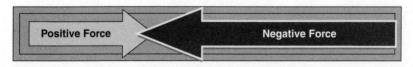

Figure 6.3   Negative Force Beating Positive Force

There is a force greater than simply a lack of discipline preventing you from achieving your true potential. For example, we attempt to overcome procrastination with time management, only to fail. We attempt to overcome being overweight by dieting. We attempt to overcome low sales performance with heroic plans to make 1,000 colds calls, only to stop after three, and so on.

When we focus on treating the behavior instead of the cause, we get a less than ideal outcome. In most cases, we're simply not prepared to "outwill" the negative forces of manifestations.

Manifestation: The Rubber Meets the Road

As discussed at the beginning of the chapter, each of us responds differently to stress, anxiety, and conflict; this is our manifestation. The manifestation isn't the core issue; it's simply what shows up on the outside. (See Figure 6.4.) If you are overweight, it's generally not because you don't know *how* to lose weight (burn more calories than you consume). The weight isn't the cause of the problem, it's the result of behavior patterns based on the manifestation of the root cause. If you are struggling in sales to make quota, it isn't likely that it's a lack of skill or market potential keeping you from succeeding.

To understand how these issues complicate your careers, we'll take a look at the five listed manifestations, beginning with fear.

Fear

Fear is the primary manifestation that prevents many salespeople from reaching their collective true potential. Fear of failing, or rejection, or

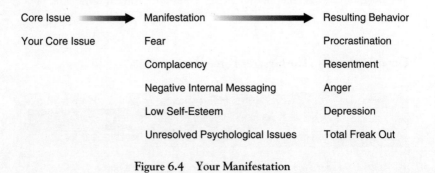

Core Issue	Manifestation	Resulting Behavior
Your Core Issue	Fear	Procrastination
	Complacency	Resentment
	Negative Internal Messaging	Anger
	Low Self-Esteem	Depression
	Unresolved Psychological Issues	Total Freak Out

Figure 6.4   Your Manifestation

insert your fear here (_____), are all bad, and are also quite real when you're experiencing them. More great ideas are set aside, sales lost, relationships terminated, opportunities avoided, and chances not taken—all because of fear.

Fear is an essential, natural, and necessary condition in human beings. Our life spans would be significantly shorter without a healthy sense of it. But at issue here is its manifestation, specifically when it prevents us from achieving our potential. Fear is pervasive; all of us are afraid of something, many of us are afraid of a lot of things, and some of us are afraid of literally everything. Not to be taken lightly or dismissed as weak self-discipline, fear-based phobias can—and do—stop us in our tracks.

KICK FEAR'S ASS.

Fear and the Self-Fulfilling Prophecy

A friend of mine began working at a small firm in the Midwest about a year ago, just before the economic downturn of 2008. He took the job as vice president of operations, where he expected to lead operations of sales and service and eventually move into an ownership position. Almost immediately after he began, the economy and stock market crashed, and the game changed. Fewer sales were taking place, and less actual operating needed to be managed. Instead, the owner needed my friend to take on a greater direct-sales position to help stimulate sales and to make it through the trough.

This is when the trouble began. My friend's expectations for the position were different than what he was actually asked to do. But instead of resigning and finding other, more suitable employment, he stayed on and resented the fact that he had to do direct selling. His attitude was obvious to his coworkers and boss, which affected his actual job performance. His boss became concerned about his lack of accomplishment and sent vibes of this dissatisfaction to my friend—which made him fear being fired. This worry began to consume him, and soon his self-fulfilling prophecy of being afraid of getting fired came true. He was fired. I'm not sure, but it looks like his core issue is connected to his belief that he is an executive who was being asked to be a salesperson. Perhaps his ego requires the title of VP of Something. However, the manifestation was likely fear, with the resulting behavior of the entire shooting match—procrastination, resentment, anger, depression, and, my favorite: the total freak-out.

The Impact of Fear-Triggered Procrastination
The most common fear-triggered resulting behavior with salespeople is procrastination, which psychologists define as the delta between our intention and our action. Most salespeople procrastinate: Why and what they put off doing is different from person to person. In many cases, it's a response to fear. Fear can often be a reaction to having no idea what they're supposed to do. To support this, many researchers now believe that procrastination is partially linked to the anticipation of an undesirable outcome.

I would occasionally procrastinate as a young sales rep when I needed to call a prospect and deliver what I perceived to be bad news. I was afraid they would react badly and not buy, and that I would be rejected. I also worried about having to remove them from my "A Prospects" list, which would expose my weak-ass pipeline. So, to avoid dealing with it, I would procrastinate. After all, I told myself, *they can't reject you if you never call them back.*

CALL THE PROSPECT BACK.

Obviously, this was severely affecting the arc of my potential. As I mentioned earlier, fear was the manifestation of other, more serious, core issues. And since my self-image was hopelessly tied to my performance, failing at my job meant that I was a failure—period. Somehow, procrastinating seemed like a good solution, as I never gave the prospect a chance to reject my offer. Needless to say, I was pretty screwed up . . . er, *unmotivated* to put myself into situations where I could fail.

My solution to this was difficult but simple: Once I recognized the issue, I developed the process of talking with one of my sales colleagues about the fact that I was very nervous about talking to the prospect about my concern. Merely discussing the situation with a friend took the stigma out of getting rejected. I asked the colleague to hang out in my office while I made the call, which made phoning my prospects much easier. It worked like a charm. No longer did I procrastinate over these issues.

"Do what you fear most, and you control fear."

—Jim Rohn

Somewhere along the way, I got my hands on a Jim Rohn motivational tape cassette that I literally wore out. (To be fair, cassette tapes were relatively easy to wear out at the time. Unlike treadmills, of course.) At some point on the tape, Rohn uttered the phrase "Do what you fear most, and you control fear." That was like magic to me. For starters, I was afraid of a lot of stuff, so this opened up a bunch of doors to experience new things.

One of those doors was the thrilling adventure of riding roller coasters, of which I had always been scared to death. My daughter Jana, an adolescent at the time, was equally petrified of this activity, so Mr. Bright Idea took Rohn's advice and decided to deal with our fear of roller coasters together. I somehow sold Jana on the idea of going to a theme park and riding a bunch of them. And I found that Jim Rohn was right. I have ridden a ton of roller coasters, and I can honestly say that, although I still don't like them, I am now able to control my bowels (but little else) while riding the devil-contraptions. Of course, Jana, Hilary, Seth, Chelsea, and Riley all now *love* riding them.

Fear is your negative internal voice acting up, and most fear is simply anxiety over the future and should be confronted head-on. I wish I had just one picture of me taken while being flung upside down in a roller coaster with my arms waving in the air, laughing and having a great time, instead of the ones with clenched jaws and eyes tightly shut.

Complacency

Many salespeople also struggle with complacency, defined as being *self-satisfied and unconcerned*. Complacent salespeople have settled into their life's trajectory; they're just rocking along, or not doing particularly good or bad in their life and career, but doing just enough to get by. This is usually a response to repeated setbacks and missed goals; they then start erroneously believing that they are not capable of doing more with their careers and lives. This isn't typical laziness, but often a sign of deeper issues.

Consider the work of Julian B. Rotter, PhD, who developed three theories related to personalities. The first, called the Social Learning Theory, states that a personality essentially represents a relationship between an individual and their environment. The second, called the Expectancy Theory, references our belief that certain behaviors will create an expected outcome. The third—the Locus of Control—works in conjunction with the Expectancy Theory, and describes our control over the expected outcomes on a continuum from internal (strong influence) to external (weak influence). Thus, those who possess a strong influence over the expected outcomes have an internal locus of control. An example of the behavior could be cold-calling to secure an appointment. Salespeople with an internal locus of control tend to secure more appointments because they *expect* to do so. Likewise, salespeople with an external locus of control tend to consider *all* the possible reasons why they will fail to secure an appointment.

If a salesperson feels helpless to change their outcomes, it could—and does—look a lot like laziness or complacency. But in reality, they may simply feel overwhelmed by their environment and expect their behaviors to result in a negative outcome, at which point sitting on the La-Z-Boy staring at the television through the treadmill looks like a pretty attractive option.

Negative Internal Messaging

Negative internal messaging, or NIM, is a biggie. In many ways, NIM—the running dialogue in our brains—can be as difficult to manage as runaway fear. As I introduced in Chapter 2, I, along with most of us, have a running dialogue of internal voices, either positive or negative, in my head. Sometimes, in response to anxiety over a future event or regret over a past event, the dialogue is negative. Other times, the internal dialogue is happy and content. There is a constant battle for superiority between positive and negative. This goes from being an annoyance to destructive when your NIM becomes predominantly negative, becomes unstoppable, and forces you to avoid situations and modify your behavior.

For example, let's assume that a sales rep needs to make a call to a client that, for whatever reason, he anticipates will end negatively, and won't result in moving the sale forward. First question: Why does his brain perceive danger with the call and trigger this response? Second question: Why does he perceive a "no decision" on the part of the prospect as "bad"?

As he prepares to dial the number, mind chatter kicks in and begins to create scenarios in which he succeeds or fails. Visualizing failure will effectively put the brakes on making the call and render him paralyzed. Even if he makes the call, the negative messaging will affect his ability to listen and communicate, and likely produce a detrimental outcome, thereby confirming his negative belief. He senses he will fail at the onset.

To make matters worse, the salesperson's mind will preemptively project a negative reaction from the prospect once he senses danger; and he will begin to resent them in response. Now, not only is he *not* making the call, he's actually created a feeling of bitterness toward his prospect—something which they have no idea is taking place. The result is avoiding potential rejection and developing an excuse that it "wasn't his fault."

Negative mind chatter is debilitating to your career and your relationships. Two primary elements of negative mind chatter are anxiety and fear about future events, and remorse and regret over past events. (Read *The Power of Now* by Eckhart Tolle.) Anxiety is prompted by something deep inside you. Sadly, many people flatten their potential and live their lives worrying about the future and feeling angry about the past. This pervasive negative mind chatter affects your personal *and* professional life.

Low Self-Esteem

The definitions for low self-esteem are so broad and all-encompassing that it could be the heading above the big five manifestations (see Figure 6.4, for example). If you have low self-esteem or a low self-image, you likely have problems with fear, complacency, damaging internal messaging, and unresolved psychological issues. You will be so entrenched in the negative expectation cycle that you'll eventually anticipate that *everything* will go wrong or turn out badly. From a strictly pragmatic sales career perspective, it isn't a huge leap to see how having a poor image of yourself and your capabilities would lower the arc of your potential.

But it isn't always that simple. It *is* possible to mistake low self-image for pessimism; and there are plenty of very successful pessimists in the world. It's a difficult attitude to manage in a career such as selling, though, and may be better suited for something else like mortuary science. (Who really wants an incredibly upbeat undertaker?)

In his book *Learned Optimism*, renowned psychologist Martin Seligman discusses in detail how to determine if you are a pessimist and, if you are, gives great advice, strategies, and exercises to move to a more optimistic view. There is evidence that optimists actually live longer lives than pessimists—a great thing if you're an optimist, and sort of a bummer if you are not. Many salespeople have their "sales personality" on the outside and a gloomy, insecure outlook on the inside. If this describes you, give Dr. Seligman's book a look-see.

Low Self-Esteem: Resentment and Unforgiveness

A common trap for people dealing with low self-esteem is an ongoing inability to forgive—and perpetual resentment toward—others. This is hugely debilitating, will wreck your career, and likely destroy your most significant relationships. We are all human beings subject to making major mistakes. Regardless of which side of the mistake we happen to sit, holding on to the blame, guilt, or anger will haunt our lives.

Two Sides of the Same Coin

For the offended, holding on to blame as a means of exacting revenge on the offender puts them in the position of having to remain angry and righteously indignant for an extended period of time—perhaps forever. While those feelings will garner sympathy from friends and loved ones for a time, anger and resentment will eventually ruin your other relationships and any chance at happiness. In most cases, the offender has moved on to a productive life. Forgiveness is an essential step for the wounded—which does not in any way mean that they must exonerate or condone the actions of the wounder, but that it is essential for them to release the anger and resentment that can otherwise destroy their own lives.

Conversely, an offender who hangs onto guilt and self-hatred simply prevents himself from ever doing anything meaningful and productive. This outlook keeps them trapped in the same negative self-image—which, in all likelihood, is what created the problem that led to the indiscretion. This cycle of guilt becomes a cycle of self-fulfilling prophecy, and a permanent cloud of remorse hinders their ability to see the true arc of their potential.

Move on, Already

Everyone on Earth makes decisions that they later regret; no one is immune. The more time we spend beating ourselves up, the longer it will take to unleash our potential. If you have offended someone, take corrective action; recognize your mistake and develop a plan to overcome it. Make amends when and where doing so won't actually hurt more than help. And move on, already.

If you are the wounded, realize that no one is perfect—including you. Recognize that the behavior was hurtful and decide to let go of it. This act will set you free to change the arc of your potential. In short: get on with it. Your time is much better spent thinking and doing so many other things.

Low self-esteem and a negative self-image are such tough mindsets to counteract that they're actually considered to be diseases in some circles. It is, at the very least, a difficult situation. If you are experiencing this, take heart in knowing that you're not the only salesperson who has it; and that by kicking your own ass, you can overcome it. And, in so doing, you'll change the arc of your potential and have a *lot* more fun.

Unresolved Psychological Issues

Every list has to have a catch-all bucket in which to throw the remainder of topics, and there are truly an infinite number of manifestations that can derail sales careers. Previously, we discussed the issue of lying. Other issues include Obsessive Compulsive Disorder (OCD), phobias, and unhealthy relationships. These issues are treatable and manageable.

Chemical Dependency

One of the most difficult and damaging unresolved psychological/physiological issues is chemical dependency. Whether food, alcohol, drugs, or something else, it strikes across the spectrum of careers and salespeople. If you are reading this and making excuses as to why your particular addiction isn't a problem, then it probably is. If you use a chemical to alter your consciousness or avoid dealing with life, it is indeed a problem. If your drug of choice interferes with your work, it is a problem.

One of addiction's sad ironies is that the afflicted person is usually the last one to know they have a problem. Therefore, regardless of what I write in this book, it will not mean much to you until you are ready to kick your own ass and accept responsibility or, as Steve would say, "quit whining and man up."

> MAN UP.

How We Respond to Stress, Anxiety, and Conflict

We've seen what manifestations occur when we negatively respond to life's stressors; so let's look at the process of *how* our responses contribute to our success or failure. Please see Figure 6.5 for an illustration of this. A larger version is also available on our web site.

Programming and Environment

Focus first on the circle surrounding steps one through three, which represents your external environment and internal programming. Your external

How We Respond to Stress, Anxiety, and Conflict

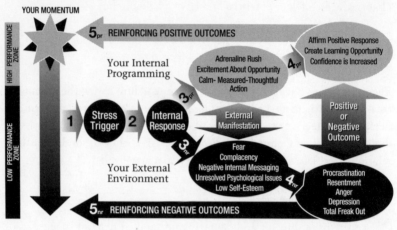

Figure 6.5   How We Respond to Stress, Anxiety, and Conflict

environment is the world in which you live. Is it positive and nurturing, filled with love and support? Your internal programming is the messaging that moves across your mental landscape through internal images, sounds, and thoughts. Are they positive thoughts, focused on helping others? Or are they similar to the negative internal messages we discussed earlier? Those two factors have a huge impact on how you respond to stress. Improving your environment can help you begin to change your performance significantly for the better.

KYOA Focus Questions

6.1. Is my external environment generally positive or negative?

_____

_____

_____

6.2. Explain why you gave the answer above.

_____

_____

_____

We're clearly affected by the stress trigger in the first block; something in our programming causes us to respond to a stressor. While these can be real-life situations, they're just as likely to be our responses to internal messages. Remember, the way we respond to stress is heavily influenced by our state of mind and environment at the moment it occurs. It literally takes a millisecond for us to decide if we're going to respond negatively or positively to a stressor. We typically react according to the groove in our brain, formed by years of internal programming. For example, an internal message may be a response we believe we *could* get, which might be negative. This anticipation could produce a negative response to an imagined stress trigger. Hey, *weirder things have happened today*.

KYOA Focus Questions

6.3. How do you typically respond to a stress trigger?

_____

_____

_____

6.4. When you respond positively what are the internal and external environmental conditions?

_____

_____

_____

In most cases, we manifest a positive or negative response that could be external, but can also be internalized thought responses to an internally generated stress trigger. Let's face it: we're weird. Most often, we react based on how we feel in our environment (according to Dr. Rotter). A negative response will elicit the previously discussed issues: fear, complacency, negative messaging, low self-esteem, or a psychological issue that impacts salespeople the most. Positive reactions manifest as excitement, adrenaline, or thoughtful action.

Our manifestation will dictate a behavior or realize an outcome; our reactions can differ wildly. Positive conduct includes affirming a positive response, increased confidence, and learning. Negatives might include procrastination, anger, depression, resentment, and the total freak-out.

POSITIVE RESPONSES TO STRESS FOSTER MORE POSITIVE
RESPONSES.

The final step in the process is the continuous feedback loop. Repeated and grooved positive responses to stress, anxiety, and conflict act as a magnet pulling our momentum up into the high performance zone. Repeated and grooved negative responses will kill our will and drive us down into the low performance zone.

Choose Your Path

If you connected with any of the issues discussed in this chapter, and you have awareness they are preventing you from changing the arc of your potential, and you are ready to make a change, there is hope for you. In the next chapter, we'll work on a behavior modification process designed to improve how you respond to stress, anxiety and conflict, and in the process, change the arc of your potential.

If you didn't connect with any of the issues in this chapter, it's likely you are in serious denial.

YOU CHOOSE YOUR PATH.

Chapter 6 Recap: The Will Killers

- *Reasons behind poor performance*. Most people face some core issue at the root of nonperformance. These problems are triggered by events that manifest themselves outwardly. The manifestation then elicits a certain kind of reaction, which we refer to as a "resulting behavior." We can reprogram our brains by rebuilding new neural pathways between the core issue and the *manifestation*, with the intent of changing the way we respond to stress, anxiety, and conflict.

- Two camps of mental health professionals take different approaches to changing our actions or behavior: *Behaviorists*—or *"time tellers"*—tend to ignore the core issue, and prefer to work exclusively on changing the synaptic firing mechanism between the manifestation and the resulting behavior, while psychoanalyists —or *"clock builders"*—offer therapy that works by peeling the psychological onion back to childhood, where psychologists feel that most of the damage that manifests itself later in life is done.

- Our brains make the connection between core issue, manifestation, and resulting behavior. It can therefore unmake them as well and change the way we process stress, anxiety, and conflict by reprogramming our minds. However, when we don't *know* the actual problem we're trying to solve, the applied behavior isn't very effective.

- Many experts believe our collective inability to execute is *a lack of will power and discipline*, and that we should buckle down and put our noses to the grindstone. Others maintain that it's our *profound inability to manage our time* that keeps us from reaching our potential. We need only to become better planners, and then we'll do and achieve more.

- While fear is essential to human life, an overabundance of it can often prevent us from reaching our goals. A *self-fulfilling prophecy* involving fear usually causes us to be so anxious that something is going to happen that we actually act in ways that *cause* it to happen.

- *Procrastination*—defined as the delta between our intention and our action—is a common manifestation of fear in salespeople. It's often linked to the concern that we don't possess enough knowledge of the topic we're covering, and has been partially linked to the anticipation of an undesirable outcome.

- We can learn to *control our fears* by simply *doing* what scares us the most. Most fear is simply anxiety over the future, and should be confronted head-on.

- *Complacency*—being self-satisfied and unconcerned—is another issue that salespeople face. It is usually a response to repeated setbacks and missed goals, wherein individuals begin to doubt their ability to do more with their careers and lives. People who possess strong or weak influences over the expected outcomes usually end up receiving exactly what they expect.

- *Negative internal messaging* is the destructive comments we make to ourselves that elicit the very behavior we fear. They are also triggered by anxiety about future events, and can be debilitating to your career and relationships.

- *Low self-esteem and self-image* hinder sales success greatly by forcing people to become so entrenched in the negative expectation cycle that they eventually anticipate that *everything* will turn out badly. A common trap for people dealing with low self-esteem is an ongoing inability to forgive others. Often, this punishes the person who refuses to forgive much more harshly than the person who has offended them.

- There are other issues—such as *chronic lying, OCD, other psychological disorders, and chemical dependency*—that can severely impede a salesperson's ability to alter his or her potential and outcomes. These issues can be resolved if the afflicted person is willing to acknowledge and manage his or her condition.

- Awareness of our *external environment* and *internal programming* can clearly show us how we respond to stress; and improving both can truly help us to change our performance for the better.

Fire Yourself Up
Five Simple Steps to Engage Your Will

Running in the Wrong Groove

Have you ever noticed the "crown" of a road, the dome shape that is higher in the middle than on the sides? Most suburban neighborhood streets are designed with a considerable crown to divert water into the gutters, making it safer for the drivers. And while heavily crowned roads with a greater slope are okay for automobiles, they're not so great for runners and walkers.

During my recovery from my aforementioned shoulder surgery, I walked for exercise, since the jostling motion of running too soon afterward could have undone the procedure. For nearly six weeks, I was a power walker. Upon my return to running, I immediately began to experience pain in my left heel, ankle, and knee. It was plantar fasciitis: a seriously painful, nondebilitating ailment common among runners. I didn't see that coming; I thought my six-week forced layoff from running would have actually been reparative for my joints and muscles. Silly me.

I asked about this new condition during a physical therapy session on my shoulder, and the physical therapist determined a possible contributing factor of the left-side problem was walking and running in the wrong part of the road. I had been walking for six weeks on the left side of the crown—which meant that my legs were walking at uneven levels. This caused an imbalance that put stress on my entire left side, manifesting as tendon and joint problems in various areas, including the plantar fasciitis. Essentially, I was running in the wrong groove.

As we discuss in Chapter 6, many of the will-related issues that derail or delay changing the arc of our potential occur when our neural signals transmit in the wrong groove. Our internal programming and external environment determines our response to anxiety, stress and conflict. If we chronically react negatively with the wrong groove programming, then it will be difficult—if not impossible—for us to find true, sustainable success.

Metal Memory

That being said, it's no easy feat to reprogram our brains. Consider sheet metal, the material used to make ventilation air-ducts in commercial and industrial buildings. Sheet metal fabricators know that once a piece of metal is bent in a certain way, it can be straightened to look nearly new, but it will always tend to rebend in the original spot, a term referred to as *metal memory*. Our brains have a similar characteristic: We tend to remember wrong-groove programming and will have a propensity to return to it. Reprogramming our brains to respond differently to stressors—and keeping us on the positive path to the High Achievement Zone—requires constant work and awareness, as well as a five-step plan. The five-step Potential Process is presented in this chapter for you to read, contemplate, and complete.

The Importance of a Mentor

Engaging in the Potential Process for the first time is not something I recommend you do alone. In fact, you will need someone you trust to go on this journey with you. Choose your mentor carefully, though, since he or she will help you work through the five steps of the Potential Process by listening without judging, offering assistance without worrying that you'll reject it, and clearly seeing the limitless potential in you, even though you may not see it yourself. This needs to be someone with whom you can openly share your honest feelings, experiences, and dreams. Most important, he or she needs to be able to confront you when they feel you're not being totally honest with yourself. Some of the work could be incredibly boring, while some of it might closely resemble a horror show; the Potential Process is therefore not for the faint of heart.

The Potential Process®—A Big Change from a Small Shift in Decision Making

You don't have to alter your behavior significantly to change the arc of your potential. You will, however, have to adopt a small shift in your thinking, and commit to a small shift in how you respond to stress, adversity, and conflict. The small shift is often actually *not* to respond, at least not too quickly. Over time, those seemingly minor alterations in your responses, will hugely impact your ability to reject the role your environment plays in your decision making. In short, you will begin running in the right groove. So let's get started in understanding how to implement the five steps. They are as follows:

The Steps of the Potential Process

Step 1. Accept where you are

Step 2. Create a new vision of yourself

The Steps of the Potential Process

Figure 7.1   Potential Process

Step 3. Set achievable goals

Step 4. Knock out adversity

Step 5. Achieve and become your new reality

Step 1: Accept Where You Are

Step 1 is meant to enable you to accept the reality of your situation. In order to do so, you will create a personal inventory, a snapshot of you at this exact moment in time. You'll share it with your mentor once it's complete. Clearly, this is a doozy. Don't get discouraged.

Change begins with a *moment of clarity*, wherein you *honestly acknowledge* and take ownership of where you are and of how you are going to change it. That means no more excuses, no blaming others, and understanding the chain of events—beginning with your core issue—that are connected to the manifestations that prompt your behavior. Don't overanalyze it; simply put it together and write it down. Once you have gathered the courage and energy to take a candid look at your situation, writing it down is the first step. This will allow you to let go of whatever is preventing you from reaching your incredible potential.

Your negative internal voice will resist this approach, and attempt to manipulate both you and the list. Don't listen! This is your brain attempting to control your behavior. Remember, *you are not your brain*; your brain is subservient to you. So kick your brain's ass. It doesn't matter how the list comes out—it could be a litany of core issues, manifestations, or your bizarre resulting behavior. It just matters that you acknowledge what your real problems are so you can figure out how to solve them.

Try to distinguish the links between the concerns you've listed in order to establish a working hypothesis of how the "why" is connected to the "what." At least you'll know the reasons behind your actions, and if you don't think you know, then guess. Don't be afraid to write down something "awful." I can promise you that people have dealt with worse.

Step 1a: Connect the Dots of Nonperformance
Answer the questions in the spaces provided.

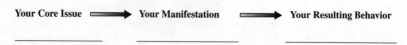

Your Core Issue ➡ **Your Manifestation** ➡ **Your Resulting Behavior**

_____ _____ _____

Figure 7.2 Connect the Dots

KYOA Focus Questions

7.1. My core issues are:

_____

_____

_____

7.2. My manifestations show up as:

_____

_____

_____

7.3. My resulting behaviors are:

_____

_____

_____

7.4. My negative internal messages are:

_____

_____

_____

Step 1b: Take an Inventory

You should now take a snapshot of your life, a look at where you are in each of the following areas at this very moment. Not where you'd like to be, and not where you want others to *think* you are; but where you *actually* are.

KYOA Focus Questions

7.5. My sales performance is:

_____

_____

_____

7.6. My net worth is:

_____

_____

_____

KYOA Focus Questions

7.7. My annual income is:

_____

_____

_____

7.8. My level of personal happiness is:

_____

_____

_____

7.9. My key relationship is:

_____

_____

_____

7.10. My physical health is:

_____

_____

_____

7.11. My mental health is:

_____

_____

_____

7.12. My sense of mission and purpose is:

_____

_____

_____

7.13. My spiritual journey is:

_____

_____

_____

Step 1c: Make a List of Your Resentments
Make a list of your resentments, grudges, sources of guilt, anxieties, angers, and regrets. This is a tough one, as it's hard to dredge up stuff from the

past. Yet unresolved issues have an ugly way of affecting your present and future. So, now is the time to let them go. And the first step to doing so is getting them all on paper.

KYOA Focus Questions

7.14. I have resentments about the following:

_____

_____

_____

7.15. I need to forgive the following people for:

_____

_____

_____

7.16. I need to forgive *myself* for the following:

_____

_____

_____

7.17. I have anxiety about:

_____

_____

_____

7.18. I have unjustifiable anger about:

_____

_____

_____

7.19. I regret:

_____

_____

_____

Step 1d: Summarize

Next, write a four- to five-sentence summary that depicts your situation. This is an opportunity for you to distill your thoughts regarding what is hindering you from changing the arc of your potential.

Say to yourself, "Today, I accept responsibility for my success and failure. I am not reaching my true potential for the following reasons." The following spaces are provided for your answers.

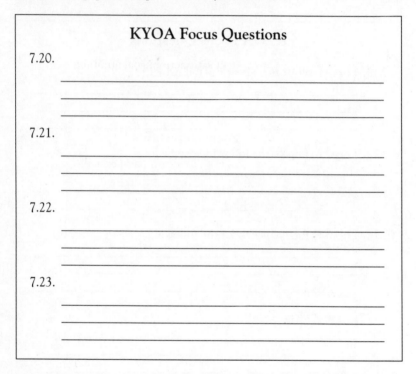

KYOA Focus Questions

7.20.

_____
_____
_____

7.21.

_____
_____
_____

7.22.

_____
_____
_____

7.23.

_____
_____
_____

Step 1e: Calculate the Cost of Not Solving Your Past Problems

What is the effect of doing nothing to change your current reality? We know that if a sales client perceives the cost of doing nothing to be less risky and expensive than investing in your solution, you will lose to "no decision" every time. The prospect is evaluating the investment against the potential return (either in satisfaction or dollars generated) on investment, and making a good decision not to risk it. And the same is true in changing the arc of your potential.

If you never connect the cost of doing nothing with doing nothing, you will always opt for doing nothing.

What is the lifetime financial impact for doing nothing, for staying on your current trajectory? Promotions you will not get, sales you won't make, jobs you won't be offered. Just take a wild guess at this. One simple way would be to think about the number of sales you won't make in a year due to not engaging in your potential process. Then, multiply that number by the number of years you intend to continue working. In Section III, we work on the skill of developing a value proposition. To help your customers, you'll have to help them understand their cost of *not* solving their dilemmas. I encourage you to consider the serious cost of doing nothing to change the arc of your potential over your career.

Beyond hard costs, there are also *soft costs* for doing nothing in terms of your relationships, happiness, career satisfaction, goal attainment, income potential, and so on that are generated by not changing the arc of your potential.

KYOA Focus Questions

7.24. What are the hard costs of not solving my past problems?

_____

_____

_____

7.25. What are the soft costs of not solving my past problems?

_____

_____

_____

Step 1f: Bask in Your Honesty

Once you've completed your list, it's important that you *bask in the honest assessment* of your situation. We might simply tell you to *consider* it, but the idea is really to bask. This will doubtlessly be a first for many, so be satisfied with the knowledge that these small decisions will encourage big changes in the right direction. Basking in honesty is very cathartic and affirming; let the list breathe like a good red wine. As you begin the process of sincerely accepting your position, celebrate the fact that you have done something great simply by being honest with yourself.

If you can't complete the list in a single sitting, fear not: It is unlikely that you will. This could take some time, and there's no particular rush to accept where you are, it's just helpful to know how you got there. Chances are that other people are dealing with the same issues that you are—or worse. People are imperfect creatures; we all have challenges.

Step 1g: Share the List with Your Mentor

Once you feel as though you have a grasp on where you are and how you got there, it is time to engage your mentor. The act of sharing the list is a simple yet effective way to let go of the issues. While sharing your list can be difficult, it can prompt you to release the barriers that are keeping you from growing. Remember, your true potential is waiting on you to get your act together.

Step 1h: Forgive Yourself and Others

When it's possible, seek out the people you've harmed—and for whom you carry unresolved guilt—and ask for their genuine forgiveness (only take this step, however, if you're sure it won't cause further harm). As we discussed in the last chapter, this is a power step that can transform you—and most likely the other person as well.

If you need to forgive yourself, get on with it already. You are one of billions of people who have made mistakes; so don't waste another moment worrying about the past.

If you owe forgiveness to someone else, you no doubt realize by now that hanging on to the anger and resentment is actually hurting you. Realize that forgiving others for the harm they have caused you in no way condones their behavior. It simply allows you to move forward and release the negative energy which permeates your being. This too is a power step. You will be transformed. I promise.

Step 1i: Burn the List

Now that you've forgiven yourself and others, you can consider burning the list—a step that moves your focus from the past to the future. Consider a driver's windshield and rearview mirrors: while both are helpful, the windshield is about 100 times larger. It's time to spend all your available energy focusing on where you want to go, and almost no energy thinking about where you've been. Regardless of what or how, it is behind you.

It's time to move on with your life.

> FORGET THE BAD AND REMEMBER THE GOOD—*EVEN IF THE BAD WAS MEMORABLE.*

Step 2: Create a New Vision of You

The purpose of Step 2 is to develop a working vision of you in a future state, a glimpse into the arc of your potential. If you have been conscious for the past decade or so, you've no doubt heard about the *law of attraction*. The premise is quite simple: We attract that about which we think. How this is possible—how our thoughts can turn into realities—can be initially hard to comprehend. But it is true, and it has given way to my very own Law of Direction:

Our lives move in the direction of our most dominant thoughts.

You must create a new vision of yourself to transform the way in which you see yourself as you move toward the future. To achieve this, you will develop a vision of your fully enabled self and share it with your mentor. Finally, you will develop your creed: a daily affirmation of your future self.

Step 2a: The Process of Becoming

To create true sustainable success, you have to see yourself as the person you want to become, and visualize in detail what it will be like once you get there. Imagine that you're looking over the hill and around the corner, and allow yourself to write what you see. Author Malcolm Gladwell argues in his book *Blink* that we often instinctively make the right choice extremely fast, only to have our brains—which we know can fail to work in our best interests—talk us out of the decision by playing on our fears. *Tell your brain to stop it,* and instead pretend that anything is possible. Which, by the way, it is.

Next, take another snapshot of how you'd like to see yourself in five years.

KYOA Focus Questions

7.26. My sales performance will be:

_____

_____

_____

7.27. My prosperity will be defined as:

_____

_____

_____

7.28. My annual income will be:

_____

_____

_____

KYOA Focus Questions

7.29. My level of personal happiness will be:

_____

_____

_____

7.30. My key relationship will be:

_____

_____

_____

7.31. My physical health will be:

_____

_____

_____

7.32. My mental health will be:

_____

_____

_____

7.33. My sense of purpose will be:

_____

_____

_____

7.34. My spiritual journey will be:

_____

_____

_____

Step 2b: Write Your Elevator Pitch for Your Future Self
You must next summarize the vision for your future state as you did in Step 1 for your present state. This is an opportunity for you to pull together an executive overview—similar to an "elevator pitch"—of the stuff that's most important to your new, actualized, running-up-the-arc-of-your-potential self. Imagine at least five aspects of the new you and write them in the following spaces.

KYOA Focus Questions

7.35.

_____

_____

_____

7.36.

_____

_____

_____

7.37.

_____

_____

_____

7.38.

_____

_____

_____

7.39.

_____

_____

_____

Step 2c: Write Your Creed

Once you have you've completed your "future self" inventory and elevator pitch, you can use this material to create your creed or declaration. This is a personal statement of belief that you will use to affirm your goals and intentions. A big part of reprogramming your brain is to replace any pessimistic internal messaging with new, positive messaging. Your creed then becomes your daily affirmation. For example, my creed is as follows.

Rob's Creed

This is a new day. It does not matter what has happened in the past, and I won't worry about the future. I am going to live in the Now. I forgive those who have harmed me, and I am going to let go of my anger and resentment. I forgive myself for the mistakes I've made, and

I let go of my own self-doubt. I am destined for greatness. Today is my new day.

Your creed is a daily companion that helps you learn to react positively to tough situations. When your internal messaging takes a negative turn, your creed serves as the tool that redirects your thinking. It goes a long way toward changing what you expect, which in turn has a profound effect on your future reality.

When you're developing your creed, keep the following guidelines in mind.

- Make it just long enough to say what you want to say.
- Memorize it.
- Place copies of it strategically in areas you encounter every day: mirrors, automobiles, refrigerator, desk, notebook computer, bedside table.
- Give copies to your loved ones and explain its purpose (they'll remind you when you should be reciting it).
- Make it your mantra.
- Change it when necessary.

KYOA Focus Questions

7.40. Write your creed.

_____

_____

_____

Step 2d: Share Your Future Self with Your Mentor
Just as it was essential to share your core issues, manifestations, and resulting behaviors with your mentor, it is absolutely necessary that you share your vision for your future self. Assuming you haven't scared off your mentor yet, schedule some time to review the elements of your future inventory, executive review, and creed with them.

Step 3: Set Achievable Goals

Your Step 2 work has provided you with a new vision of yourself, complete with future vision elevator pitch (something to use at parties to amaze your friends and coworkers). Step 3 requires that you put your vision into action, a core success activity for you. Along with developing your creed, proving to yourself that you can succeed is a significant step in reprogramming your brain's new neural pathways. To do so, you'll create a track record of making—and keeping—a thousand commitments. Sound like a lot? It is, but it will help you develop constructive habits and thinking patterns. You'll make these promises over and over, until you have reset your expectations and are moving toward your most dominant thought. Let's begin.

Step 3a: Choose a Goal

Pick a goal you would like to accomplish. We *don't* want some half-baked New Year's resolution goal that you have little to no chance of achieving; remember, we're trying to undo that behavior. We need to set attainable goals that meet the requirements of the "three Ms": they must be *manageable, measurable, and meaningful.* If you have habit or "groove" of making and breaking commitments, let's start with a slam-dunk, no-brainer goal, such as *saying one nice thing each day for 21 days to your closest personal relationship.* If that seems like it could be a *stretch* goal, then consider *breathing each day for 21 days.* It may sound crazy, but our intention here is to reconstruct the neural pathways with successful goal attainment. Since the actual *goal* itself isn't that important at this point, it's essential that you set a goal that you will keep. And saying one nice thing, or breathing every day, certainly meets the following criteria.

1. *Manageable:* It must be achievable in a reasonable amount of time. For our purposes, we'll use 21 days.
2. *Measurable:* You must be able to articulate the goal in specific and measurable terms, such as, "I will breathe every day"; or, "I will say at least one nice thing to _____ each day for 21 days."
3. *Meaningful:* The goal must support your vision. We don't want goals that move us away from our most dominant thought. Our aim is to begin moving our thinking away from the negative and toward the positive.

Step 3b: Develop an Activities Plan

Goals are the result of key activities executed on a timetable. Remember the list of activities that Steve and I created for the Ascent in Chapter 1?

Articulate Your Goal

7.41. My goal is:

_____

_____

_____

7.42. I will measure it by:

_____

_____

_____

7.43. It supports my vision by:

_____

_____

_____

- Lose 35 pounds in 7 months.
- Complete treadmill workouts at 11 percent grade.
- Do long runs of three to four hours.
- Do two-hour bridge repeat workouts on Saturdays.

Our next step was to create a daily, weekly, and monthly plan for executing the goal of running up Pikes Peak. The only reason I knew I was in serious trouble in April was *because* we had created an activities plan that had weekly specific and measurable milestones (meaning I was actually

---

Articulate Your Goal

7.44. My goal activities are:

_____

_____

_____

7.45. My daily and weekly milestones are:

_____

_____

_____

---

going to have to do this crazy thing!). Your plan should include a list of key activities, as well as daily and weekly milestones.

Step 3c: Make a Small Decision to Measure—Every Day
I call this *"getting on the scale."* Hey, how hard can it be? Simply make a record of your progress each day. Well, the answer is *"pretty hard."* However, the small decision to faithfully track your results daily— regardless of your actual progress toward the goal—can generate impressive results, and often make the difference between success and failure. Why does measuring work so well? The answer may be rooted in the results of the "Hawthorne Effect," a theory based on a Harvard Business School experiment conducted at a Western Electric plant between 1924 and 1933. The experiment essentially asked factory workers to track their work without requiring them to change their output. Workers who tracked their output increased their performance over 15 percent—just by getting on the scale.

You significantly risk failing to meet your goals if you don't mea- sure your progress each day. To make your objectives a reality, create a chart (I tend to use Excel for these) in which you'll make daily notes about your accomplishments. For instance—returning to our "breathe every day" example—your chart might look like this:

My Goal: Breathe Every Day		
Day	**Activity**	**Result**
Day 1	Breathe	Y
Day 2	Breathe	Y

Step 3d: Spread the Word about Your Goals
During the years I spent smoking, hating it, and wishing I could quit, I made and broke promises to stop literally every day—to myself. However, it wasn't until I made a commitment, sought medical help, and told every- one I knew I was going to stop on a certain date that it actually *worked*.

Goals don't seem to become "real" until you share them with others. So tell your mentor and others with whom you're close about your goals. Post them on the refrigerator. Create little reminder cards. Do whatever it takes to make the goal public. You are much more likely to succeed if others know that you're trying to.

Step 4: Knock Out Adversity

Into every plan, a little rain must fall. It's the order of the world. The sun and moon, happiness and sadness, success and failure are all linked.

Your brain is about to begin the full plan of attack on your attempts to regroove your neural pathways; it's actively fighting to keep the status quo. Be prepared: Adversity happens, and it's like an objection in the sales process. What would you do if you had no answer *whatsoever* every time a prospect told you they wanted to think about it, requested a discount, or claimed they had to discuss it with their manager? You would lose a lot of sales (and by the way, if you don't have an answer for those objections, keep reading). You're going to encounter serious setbacks; it's part of the program. You merely have to be prepared for them. As every runner knows, injury is unavoidable. We do our best to prevent it, but the best we can do is strive to reduce the risk, and manage through the injury and rehabilitation.

Adversity—like the locus of control we learned about in the previous chapter—comes in two primary forms: internal, which we create from within, and external, which we encounter from our environment and others. Internal adversity is often self-inflicted and reflects the ongoing battle of the human condition—that we repeatedly do what we wish to avoid. External adversity occurs when peripheral conditions change, at times rendering the original goal invalid. Even if we do everything right, external forces beyond our control can cause chaos in our execution. Whether internal or external, real or imagined, adversity stops your momentum toward your goal, and regardless of origin or nature, the following framework for managing through adversity can help.

1. *Acknowledge* the adversity. Whether real or imagined, once you feel or sense it, say it.
2. *Notify* your mentor. He or she will help you work through the issue.
3. *Create and execute* an adversity recovery plan as necessary. Whatever it takes, it takes. Do not be afraid of repeated failure.

Step 5: Achieve and Become Your New Reality

The goal of the *potential process* isn't just to spend 21 days tracking your breathing, but rather, to create a framework of repeated success, which leads to even greater accomplishment. Setting and achieving goals should result in an increased trust in your own abilities, which in turn creates the confidence to make commitments in other areas of your life. Goal attainment creates a new reality, and these new realities generate a new definition of a realistic goal. A smoker becomes a nonsmoker; a nonsmoker becomes a walker; a walker becomes a jogger; a jogger becomes a runner; and a runner becomes a racer. A racer runs a 5k, then a 10k, then a $\frac{1}{2}$ marathon, then a marathon, then goes wherever she or he wishes: from triathlons to ultraracing to coaching others. The possibilities are endless.

Reality is accepted. Vision is created. Goals are set and met. Adversity is overcome. New reality is created and accepted. New vision is created. New goals are set and met. Adversity is overcome. New reality is created. . . .

Come Out Swinging

We're just about ready to wrap up our work on engaging your will to succeed. This book's central message is that most salespeople fail to reach their true potential not for a lack of skill, but rather a lack of *will*. While I can't promise that you will become one of the 20 percenters, I *can* show you how to improve your performance in and satisfaction from a sales career, earn a great living, and have a lot of fun while you're doing it.

This section's primary lesson is to teach you to disengage from the behavior that's prevented you from reaching your true potential, and adopt new behavior by developing a process to alter how you respond to stress, anxiety, and conflict through the Potential Process. You can then begin the wonderful journey of changing the arc of your potential, leaving the rut of self-doubt and negative internal messaging behind, and embracing the new vision you have created. As we prepare to move into the skill and drill of changing the arc of our potential, you need to come out swinging—and keep swinging. Life is a series of moments, and it's in these moments that we choose our path. Keep going through the moments. If you do, the days, weeks, months, and years will take care of themselves.

However—even enlightened souls who know their personality and core issues and have executed a process to engage the arc of their potential can get off track. We can blame a unique quality of being human: *we do what we don't wish to do, and we don't do what we wished we would.* Often without warning, we realize we've drifted off course and are once again running in the wrong groove. It might come in the form of a return to negative internal messaging, self-doubt and fear, complacency, or an unresolved psychological issue. Realizing that perfection is an unlikely goal, the question becomes—*How do we structure our lives to stay out of the ruts and in the right groove?* There is no single answer to this question. In fact, there are eight.

1. *Begin and end your day with your creed.* Your creed is essential to changing the arc of your potential. Beginning and ending your day with it will serve as a constant reminder of your commitment to yourself, and keep your positive affirmations firmly planted in your brain—which is the best way to crowd out the negative. Your creed is kind of like fertilizer for your lawn, in that you grow grass to help kill weeds. In short, more of the "good stuff" helps diminish the "bad stuff." Print your creed on small cards that can be easily stashed in your bedroom dresser, office desk, briefcase, purse, on your bathroom mirror, and keep copies everywhere. I often recite mine multiple times a day.

2. *Develop a five-second point-of-impact breathing meditation.* As we discuss in Chapter 6, the way you respond to negative internal messaging, stress, anxiety and conflict – whether real or imagined, internal or external—is a single, seemingly small decision that can greatly influence your outlook on life. Before responding negatively, take five seconds to breathe slowly in and out, and concentrate on your breathing only. This idea came from a friend of mine and is a great way to change your outcomes. You move the focus of your energy from the trigger to your breathing, and interrupt the well-worn negative pattern of response.

3. *Consciously remain in the present.* The decision and process of forgiving ourselves—and others—is life changing. Contemplating the present removes some anxiety about the future and diminished regrets from the past. However, this typically isn't a *"once and done"* process: it's a decision that requires constant attention. Simple awareness of a slip is helpful, because from there, you can decide where to expend your energy. Use the five-second meditation or your creed to assist. It can also be helpful to just laugh at your brain's tendencies. One of my more annoying habits is that I often break into laughter for no apparent reason, which can irritate those around me. Normally when this happens, it's just me laughing at my own screwy brain.

4. *Stay focused on your new vision.* In Step 2 of the Potential Process, we began to alter the way you see yourself and your true potential. Your new vision is you on top of your own Pike's Peak. Most of you have your new vision locked inside your head right now. If your vision is to double your income and change your lifestyle, then pick out the new home you want to purchase, take a picture of it, and keep it with you at all times. If your new vision is an improved relationship with someone, focus your thinking around how that relationship will look and feel. Connect visual snapshots of the relationship in the new form. Perhaps your vision is how you can create more, give more, help more, do more—the definition of true prosperity. At the start of writing this book, I created a mock-up front cover from a picture my wife took of me running up the stairs at Red Rock near Denver Colorado. I printed out the cover and kept it with me at all times. It helped me see the book becoming a reality.

5. *Stay connected to your mentor.* You need guidance, nurturing—and to have your ass kicked on a regular basis. Your mentor is on this journey with you; he or she is the person guiding you through this rough terrain. Frequent, candid contact to discuss any hurdles is essential. An early sign of trouble for many is a move away from a mentor relationship. Once isolated, they begin what Zig Ziglar calls "stinking thinking," and a downward spiral often follows. If you sense or feel yourself drifting away, say so, even if you're afraid.

6. *Set and achieve goals.* Spinning up the Potential Process creates a pattern of achieving goals, which strengthens your self-trust. This in turn creates greater confidence, which leads to setting more achievable goals and overcoming bigger obstacles. The result of your increased confidence is a faster potential process. The faster you spin the wheel, the more momentum you create. Remember, big change comes from small decisions. Do this.

7. *Connect to the power of expectation.* According to Rotter's theory of expectancy (discussed earlier), certain behaviors create expected outcomes. The power of expectation, which his book connected to the laws of attraction, is the following.

> If we believe we will fail, we will fail. By failing, our belief in our propensity to fail is confirmed.
> If we believe we will succeed, we will succeed. By succeeding, our belief in our ability to succeed is confirmed.

Essentially, the power of expectation is Rotter's theory of expectancy in action. How we think affects how we act. How we act affects our outcomes.

8. *Commit to continuous learning.* In Chapter 4 we explore the importance of knowledge on your career. Seeking knowledge continuously brings with it the added benefit of keeping your brain focused on onboarding new concepts, skills and ideas. Flooding the brain with new information frankly leaves less time for the negative internal messaging to take over, and replaces it with your curious desire to try new things. Books of all genres are great sources of knowledge and inspiration. My personal annual goal is to read 30 to 40 books each year.

> READ A LOT OF BOOKS!

The brain is a reprogrammable device. Doing so is relatively simple, but not easy. As we learn in this chapter, big changes come from making very small decisions differently from before. We can choose to interrupt our patterns of behavior and dramatically change our outcome. As we prepare to move to focus on the key skills every salesperson needs, take a moment to review this section, and if necessary, reread it. It is essential you connect your will by letting go of your old paradigms and engaging in a new process of managing stress, anxiety, and conflict. When you do, you will be well on your way to changing the arc of your potential, and your life.

Chapter 7 Recap: Fire Yourself Up: Five Simple Steps to Engage Your Will

- Our brains remember wrong-groove programming and return to it, especially when we're not consciously choosing *not* to. Reprogramming our brains to respond differently to stressors—and keeping us on the positive path to the High Achievement Zone — requires constant work and awareness, as well as a five-step plan, the *Potential Process*.

- You need to choose a mentor for your journey who will listen without judging, offer assistance without worrying that you'll reject it, and see your limitless potential (although you may not see it yourself.) It must be someone with whom you can be completely open and honest.

- You don't have to alter your behavior significantly to change the arc of your potential. Simply committing to making very small decisions in how you respond to stress, adversity, and conflict can go a long way toward altering your reactions.

- The five steps of the Potential Process are: (1) accept where you are, (2) create a new vision of yourself, (3) set achievable goals, (4) knock out adversity, (5) achieve and become your new reality.

- Step 1 requires that you honestly acknowledge and take ownership of where you are and of how you are going to change it. Candidly assess your situation and make a list of your core issues, manifestations, and resulting behavior. Summarize your situation, and bask in the truth that you've forced yourself to admit. Share the list with your mentor, forgive yourself and others of any transgressions, and, finally, burn the list to symbolize moving on with your life.

- Rob's Law of Direction states that our lives move in the direction of our most dominant thoughts; therefore, Step 2 is to create a new vision of yourself to transform the way in which you see yourself as you move toward the future. Tell your brain to stop second-guessing yourself, and pretend that anything is possible. Write your own "elevator pitch" to give about your future self. Use these to craft your own creed, or a personal statement of belief that you will use to affirm your goals and intentions.

- Step 3 is to set achievable goals that are manageable, measurable, and meaningful. Develop an activities plan toward meeting these goals, and commit to measuring some aspect of them every single day. Next, spread the word about your goals. Our goals often don't become "real" to us until we tell other people about them, so share them with your mentor and other important people in your life. You are much more likely to succeed if others know that you're trying to.

- Step 4 is to knock out any internal (self-created) and external (based on environment) adversity that you might face in your path to achieving your aims. You can do this by: (1) acknowledging the adversity, (2) notifying your mentor so that they can help you work through the issue, and (3) creating and executing an adversity recovery plan.

- Step 5 is to achieve and become your new reality. Setting and achieving goals should result in an increased trust in your own abilities, which in turn creates confidence in other areas of your life to make commitments. Goal attainment creates a new reality; and these new realities generate a new definition of a realistic goal.

- Even those of us who develop the most stringent of objectives and aims can occasionally wander off course. The following guidelines help structure our lives to stay out of the ruts and in the right groove: (1) begin and end your day with your creed, (2) develop a five-second *point-of-impact* breathing meditation; (3) consciously remain in the present; (4) stay focused on your new vision; (5) stay connected to your mentor; (6) set achievable goals; (7) connect to the power of expectation, and (8) commit to continuous learning.

Now that you've confronted the issues that may have prevented you from reaching your true potential, and developed a program for creating sustainable success, it's time to move to Section III to begin the journey of examining the essential skills every salesperson, regardless of product or industry, needs. Read on, my friend.

Essential Skills

The Logic and Emotion
of Selling

Selling Is a Skill

Martial artists know that it takes roughly 1,000 times practicing a particular skill or technique before they achieve anything close to competence. The development of skills requires preparing the body to accept the required movement, and then breaking the desired skill into a series of components. After each component is mastered, they begin to assemble them into a fluid movement. Speed, accuracy, intensity, and velocity come after competence in the learning curve. The acquisition and development of selling skills is the same. The skills discussed in this book are the basic building blocks needed to achieve competence in sales. They are: developing a sales process; creating new opportunities; developing trust and intent; listening; creating a value proposition; presenting a solution; engineering a decision; and responding to questions, concerns, and objections. These are abilities that you can learn and master with practice.

Selling Is Simple

Selling is a simple process based in logic and reason. Perhaps *Bull Durham's* baseball manager Joe "Skip" Riggins—played by the late Trey

Wilson—said it best when he gathered his team in the showers for a quick meeting to explain the basics of the game: "Baseball is a simple game. You hit the ball. You throw the ball. You catch the ball. Got it?"

Selling *is* an equally simple concept. *"We find the prospect. We qualify the prospect. We present to the prospect and we close the prospect. Sometimes we win. Sometimes we lose. Sometimes the economy crashes. Got it?"* Of course you do. But just because something is simple doesn't mean that it's easy.

The Old Definition of Selling

The old definition of selling was "getting people to buy." Sadly, that is how most salespeople have traditionally defined an exchange of goods or services for an agreed-upon sum of money. In this paradigm, selling is a pursuit of persuasion and transference of feeling that essentially boils down to *"I feel like selling you this, and I want you to feel like buying it."* This corruption—created and sustained by unscrupulous salespeople—is a primary reason that prospects have been conditioned to become defensive as a salesperson approaches them. In turn, this dysfunctional relationship, unsurprisingly, creates major barriers to the sales process.

The H&R Shuffle

This old type of selling methodology is primarily based on a persuasion technique known as *Hurt and Rescue*, based on the idea that *a drowning person will grab at anything, so push them in the water and then throw them a lifeline.* However, you best be a fast runner, or make the push look like an accident—as you *will* get your ass kicked once they get out.

The "Hurt" of the H&R Shuffle is designed to uncover common fears and create tension by upsetting the prospects' homeostatic balance. The longer a prospect remains in this agitated, upset state, the more likely it is she or he will actively seek to resolve it. The resolution is known as the "Rescue."

Salespeople attempt to reveal the hurt and generate stress by asking questions about a customer's "pains." "What keeps you up at night?" "What scares you the most about not having a working alarm system, especially with those children?" "Tell me, what would happen to your family if you should die suddenly?" "You do realize that your firm is vulnerable to malicious attacks without security—don't you? How bad would it make you look if the entire company's accounting system and customer list were lost—due to *your* oversight?" And herein lies the challenge: If the prospect doesn't trust your intentions, it is next to impossible to get them to open up about their true issues.

It would be ridiculous to go to the doctor's office only to refuse to answer questions about the nature of your complaint. We are open with our physicians because we have a basic trust in their intent to help. But this is not the case with salespeople who utilize Hurt and Rescue. Salespeople and sales organizations who employ this method must realize that their products or services aren't all that helpful, and feel forced to rely on scare tactics, guilt, fear, shame, or any number of well-worn tactics to close a deal. Sadly, the result is often a customer who deeply regrets their decision.

You Are Terrible Parents!

My first sales position entailed selling vacuum cleaners. I lasted exactly one week. At the end of my tenure, I decided that construction would be a better career path for me; at least this provided an essential service wherein I would see the result of my labor. I am not attempting to cast dispersions on the great companies who create and the professional salespeople who help families evaluate, select, and purchase vacuum cleaners. I just didn't happen to work for one of *them*.

I received the job by responding to an ad in the paper that said, "Closers Needed! Big Pay! No Cold Calling!" At least twenty of us must have answered the advertisement. We underwent a day of training on how to conduct a sale and work the product, and were then set loose to work a neighborhood. The sales process followed roughly 14 steps.

1. Teams of two would walk through blue-collar neighborhoods, placing cards in mailboxes. The cards offered a free set of steak knives (no kidding—they were nice, too) in exchange for a 30-minute preview of the latest technology in home cleaning. Those who received the cards simply had to call to arrange an appointment.

2. We'd then sit in the office and wait for the phone to ring. Which it did, incredibly, off the hook.

3. Next we would answer the phone and qualify the prospect based on the following list:

- Must be married with children (several little ones would be even better).
- Must have a job.
- Must have a credit card or car payment.
- Both husband and wife must be present.
- Ask the client to not vacuum the floor. (We'll do that for you—how's that for value!)
- Set the day and time for the appointment—generally that or the following day.

4. Show up at the prospect's house, always with two salespeople—a junior/senior, good cop/bad cop strategy.

5. Build rapport. Get to know the kids. Find out what kind of work the head of household does. Determine if they are "players—likely buyers." If deemed not to be players, hand them the knives, and bolt. Go to back-up appointment. *Always* have a back-up appointment.

6. Ask to see the vacuum they currently own. Vacuum their floor, sofa, and mattresses with their existing equipment.

7. Launch into a discussion about the dangers of the deadly "mite." Show pictures of the awful-looking critter, as well as the damage they can do to human skin. Provide the medical evidence report of how improperly cleaned homes are an ideal breeding ground for mites, which actually hurt children and cause all sorts of diseases.

8. Get out the new equipment. Revacuum all previously cleaned areas with white cloth filter—showing the filth that the old equipment has left behind. Remind them about the medical evidence, and comment on how it was a shame that such a sweet couple was hurting their family, just by being ignorant of the problem.

9. Go on to proclaim that, thankfully, *we* have a solution. Move from the living room to the kitchen table. Offer to sell them this demonstrator model, thereby saving thousands off the retail suggested list price, getting a great deal, and being the best parents on the block.

10. Get out the paperwork. Explain the investment—including lifetime guarantee—return on investment, and so on. Ask for commitment and a check for $2,500 dollars (without laughing—a small but important point.)

11. When they object, absorb the objection, pivot back to the hurt they'll endure from failing to purchase the machine. Offer two-year

financing and a discount to $2,300. Slide the pen across the kitchen table.

12. When they object again, absorb the objection, and bring out the big gun: "I can't believe you would let your child live in this filth, knowing that you could fix it for only $95 dollars per month. *You must be terrible parents!*," and then to the fellow salesperson, "Junior, pack up the machine. These people hate their kids. We're leaving."

13. Step #12 normally did it. The mom would usually start crying and claim that, of course, she loved her kids, and could she just talk to her husband in the bedroom for a quick minute?

14. Back to the kitchen table, where the couple signs a three-year note to invest in a better life for their family. The senior has me teach the mom how to use the equipment, while he finishes the paperwork with the dad. He reinforces how smart they are to have bought this, thus sealing the deal. We leave; everyone's happy.

It was incredible. And I felt like puking after we did it. My senior—who by the way, was the top rep and someone that the boss *adored* and the rest of the team admired—was laughing his ass off. Everyone told me how "super lucky" I was to be working with him. I believe the thrill of almost getting into a fistfight with the husband—but then still managing to close the deal—was what really turned this guy on.

Three of these interactions did the trick. After that, I concluded that sales was simply not for me.

We do not trust salespeople. Even *salespeople* don't trust salespeople. In fact, we're often repelled by them. Though my brief experience in the vacuum cleaner business is an extreme example, too many sales organizations still build Hurt and Rescue–based sales processes and just give them different names. And they are needlessly screwing it up for the rest of us. The entire industry suffers. Just visit an automobile dealership or a retail center, and observe your own immediate reaction as the salesperson approaches. We either run away, or, if confronted, respond to the inevitable question of "May I help you?"—or worse, "Hey, you looking for a car?"—with "Nope. Just looking." Now that is just silly. Of *course* we need help. Of *course* we're looking for a car; why else would we be on a *car lot*? We just don't want *their* help. It takes a ton of work by businesses and salespeople in the sales process just to get a basic level of trust.

It would be easy to blame Hurt and Rescue for our collective troubles; but the reality is that prospects must realize the cost of not solving in order to move forward, and connect with the impact of doing nothing, which could easily be defined as a form of "hurt." The trouble comes in how we handle the Rescue. If we twist facts to heighten the hurt—and remove all other potential options for how the client could solve their problem—we paint them into an emotional corner. We have made *our* solution the only solution, thereby taking away *choice*—something that's essential for a client to make an informed decision. In many cases, the choice of doing nothing is the best move.

Abandon Hurt and Rescue

Another concept, discussed and explored by sales guru and renowned author Mahan Khalsa, is called *Awareness and Choice*. You help your prospect gain awareness of their issues, and the impact of doing nothing, by creating a trust-based environment of exploration. Then, you help them develop choices on how best to solve them, including the option of doing nothing. Ironically, by creating an environment where all options remain on the table, you actually make doing something *different* a legitimate option worthy of consideration. If your solution truly meets a client's needs and improves their quality of life, you are obligated to help them. The best way to approach this is by giving them awareness and choice. Therefore, *the new definition of selling* entails enlightened salespeople who *help prospects and clients make good decisions.*

Art and Science, Emotion and Logic

Many experts have discussed the concept of the "art and science"—or emotional and logical components—of selling. To execute the process of selling, salespeople must master both components of logic and emotion. Once achieved, a bond with the prospect is created. This bond often manifests in the form of likeability and trust; without it, clients will rarely buy. I have made sales in amounts anywhere from tens of dollars to millions of dollars, and sales ranging from a single buyer to multiple teams of buyers, and the rule remains the same at all levels: the "best" product rarely wins. Prospects are more than willing to sacrifice functionality to build a trust-based partnership. In those cases, they make a logical decision to buy an inferior product with a superior trust-based emotional connection.

PROSPECTS WANT A TRUST-BASED RELATIONSHIP.

Selling Is Logical

As stated at this chapter's beginning, the selling process is rooted in logic, a method of human thought that involves a linear, step-by- step approach to solving a problem. In fact, most elements of the selling process are based on common sense. Finding and creating new opportunities, for example, is a logical process that requires consistent research to find them. Assisting the prospect in assessing their current situation and calculating the impact of doing nothing are both logical steps, as well. Developing a summary of findings that includes their key issues, impacts, and potential investments can be super logical. The entire process is logical: It's based on facts, clear rational thought, and sensible reasoning.

What's more is that prospects use logic to justify a purchase decision. Often we've helped them understand the overwhelming reason for going ahead with a purchase. *"Honey, the Corvette just was so much more aerodynamic than the Corolla, that it was just logical that it would get better mileage when going 186 miles per hour. I had to get it to save on the gasoline."* Or, *"Well, the department store was having a half-off sale, so I decided to stock up on shoes, just to show you what a logical and frugal shopper I am."*

Selling Is Emotional

Selling is also an emotional process; however, it is one that requires intuition and insight into buyers' attitudes. Like two tracks on a video editing timeline, the emotional track must sit just above the logical track. Without being able to sense your buyer's outlook and developing the ability to know *when* to say *what*, all logic will fail. The first car I learned to drive was my mom's VW with a standard four-speed manual transmission. I found that the trick to driving a manual shift automobile is the management of the clutch in relationship to the gas and brake pedals. Apply too much gas too soon, and the car lurches forward, and then stalls. Likewise, too little gas and too much clutch brings on stall city. The act of initiating movement from a dead stop requires a little skill known as *feathering the clutch*. Ironically, it's based on a blend of feeling the pedals, hearing the sound of the engine, and sensing the movement of the vehicle. No amount of logical explanation can prepare a driver for the "feel" that's needed to operate the vehicle. Once true competence is achieved, the driver will no longer avoid stopping on inclines. Moving forward without rolling backward into the car behind you becomes second nature.

The Logic versus Emotion Continuum

A good portion of the sales process—the skill and feel of managing the relationship between logic and emotion—is akin to feathering the clutch. The entire affair is complicated by the fact that most buyers have different personalities (as we discuss in Chapter 5), and therefore respond to the emotional versus logical argument differently. Further confusing this is the fact that *you* have a personality, as well, complete with your own preferences between logic and emotion.

A prospect can also develop a strong "feeling" about a given product or salesperson. *"Yes, I'm well aware it doesn't actually have any of the features we listed on our 'features we must have' list; but the salesperson seemed very trustworthy, so I felt we could work around it."* Or, *"Yes, I realize we were buying a dump truck, and this is a convertible. But the salesperson and I thought of that, and the dealership offered to install a trailer hitch for free. Pretty smart, huh."* Indeed.

Selling Is Pure Emological

Emological is a newly coined word, invented by me to describe how selling is both a logical and an emotional enterprise, both left- and right-brained. You can execute a flawlessly logical sales process and lose the sale if you don't have the right mix of these elements. Selling is about helping your clients explore their situations in a safe, trust-based environment, and helping them make the best possible decision. To do that, you have to be prepared to manage both the "art" and "science" of selling. You need to operate the gas, brake, and clutch in concert with one another, smoothly and simultaneously.

Sales Disaster: Logic and Emotion Gone Berserk While Attempting to Build Rapport

Let's explore the concept of "building rapport" to emphasize the importance of both logic and emotion in the sales process. In the "sales training intervention" discussed in Chapter 2, we learn about this invaluable skill. My initial tactic upon learning about this concept was to try to build rapport with everyone whom I cold-called. However, I learned that most people don't actually want to "make an instant emotional connection" with perfect strangers, especially strangers trying to sell them something over the phone. Therefore, people hung up on me a lot. I occasionally managed to get in touch with an extreme extrovert; however, those people often had a lot of time on their hands. So while they were happy to talk about nothing all day, they were hardly ever in a position to make a decision. It took a while for me to figure out when to build rapport and how to *read* voices on the phone. Now, I can usually discern someone's dominant personality type—as well as his or her current mood—after about three seconds of dialogue. For example, there is a distinct difference in a high Ds voice if they are happy, sad, or mad; listen for it.

I learned a lot of great techniques for building rapport during the sales training intervention, such as "look for common interests to discuss," "find something nice to say," or "compliment them on something." However, the trainer failed to mention the fact that most people instantly recognize rapport-building as a "sales technique"—and hate it. She also neglected to instruct us in the use of common sense, which—in hindsight—would have been useful.

The Worst Recorded Moment in Sales History

Not too long after the training, I went on a sales call in the rolling-hill horse country of Ocala, Florida, where I was calling on a small "mom and pop" homebuilding operation. I parked my vehicle in front of a model home that doubled as their office, and went inside. The "pop" was on the phone, so I was standing in the front office waiting for my appointment with the "mom." I realized this would be an excellent time to whip out one of my shiny new sales techniques for building rapport. I first looked around for a picture of her doing something athletic upon which I could comment and, finding no conceivable common interest, I started down the path of commenting on how nice their model home looked, and that I bet they were selling a ton of them. "Actually, we aren't," she replied, which I should have known. This was during the great depression of 1986, when homebuilders were barely hanging on. I vowed to win her over no matter what it took, and decided right then I was really going to build some good rapport. She was going to like me, because I distinctly remembered the sales trainer saying—*with feeling*— "People buy from people they like!"

I continued looking for a possible connection; and it occurred to me that it appeared she was going to have a baby. Fantastic! I had recently become the father of my second daughter; this would give us tons to talk about.

What happened next is something I recall in slurred-slow-motion, perhaps as the worst moment ever in sales.

I looked at her and asked, "Sooooooo, whennn arrre youuu duuue?"

She replied, "Who me? Oh, I'm not pregnant."

"Ohhhhhhhhh, Fuuuuuuuuuuuuudge."

I didn't see that coming, and I bet she didn't either. All I can say is that she sure *looked* pregnant. In the ensuing gulf of silence after the worst recorded moment in sales history, to say that I struggled to find the appropriate words would be an understatement. My brain executed the process of flipping through the thousands of options for "how to recover from an inappropriately asked question" as if it were rifling through my friend Jerry's index-card system. The sales trainer didn't mention *this*. Among several options that I considered were:

1. "Oh really? You sure look pregnant."

2. "I'm sure sorry I assumed you were pregnant, when you were really just a little heavy in the middle—maybe you're just retaining about ten gallons of water . . . "

3. "I am so sorry I said such an ugly thing, I have a strange, yet-to-be diagnosed strain of Tourette's syndrome, which causes me to say the exact thing that is crossing my diminished mental landscape, without pause. I'm pretty certain that it's a disease, anyway. I hope to begin treatment immediately. Please forgive me."

4. "Gosh, I am sorry to have thought you were pregnant. Perhaps your tent dress caught a gust of wind, causing it to puff out . . . Oh, it's not a tent dress? Wow. It sure looks like a tent."

As hard as I tried, *nothing was coming to mind*. It was a little like when my boss informed me that my raise would "become effective" when I did, but a billion times worse. Eventually—and this "eventually" seemed like a *cosmic light year*—I managed an apology, which she immediately accepted and told me not to worry about it. I also managed to get through the meeting with her husband, yet somehow I never got an opportunity to help them improve their competitiveness through computerization. Imagine that.

(By way of footnote, I have had several decades to ponder this moment, and I have concluded that the only possible way out of a situation as disastrous as this would have been to immediately hit the ground and feign passing out due to some form of "cataclysmic brain event." The pandemonium of calling for medical assistance might have distracted her into forgetting that a sales rep had just called her fat. Granted, it has a low probability for success; but after twenty-some years, it is still the best solution I've come up with.)

It was a valuable lesson, and one that made me vow—as a matter of form—never to ask anyone, ever, about *anything* related to or concerning pregnancy. *Ever.* While it's true that "people buy from people they like," the following is even more true: No one will *ever* buy from an idiot *whom they hate.*

Clearly, my "feathering the clutch" skills weren't fully operational at that moment in time. Selling *is* a logical pursuit, which requires an emotional awareness not to screw it up. So now we're going to work on putting all that logic and emotion into action.

Chapter 8 Recap: The Logic and Emotion of Selling

- Just because the *concept* of selling is simple does not mean that the *process* is easy. The old definition of selling—"getting people to buy"—is a primary reason that prospects usually become defensive when a salesperson approaches them. In the "Hurt and Rescue" approach, salespeople attempt to reveal common fears and generate stress by asking questions about a customer's "pains" and then "Rescue" them by providing a solution.

- While prospects must realize the *cost of not solving* in order to move forward, and connect with the impact of doing nothing—which could easily be defined as a form of "hurt"—the trouble comes in how we handle the Rescue. We must make sure to provide *choice*—something that's essential for a client to make an informed decision.

- A much more client-friendly approach is *Awareness and Choice*, wherein the salesperson creates awareness by helping clients understand their issues, and then creates choice by giving them options on how best to solve them. Therefore, the *new definition of selling* entails enlightened salespeople who *help prospects and clients make good decisions.*

- Salespeople must master both the *emotion and logic* of selling to execute the skills and process of selling, and create a strong emotional connection to the prospect. Selling is both a logical and emotional process—and salespeople must appeal to both. Without being able to sense a buyer's outlook and knowing when to say what, all logic will fail.

- Since most buyers have different personalities, and therefore respond to the emotional versus logical argument differently, the objective of selling is to help clients explore their situations in a safe, trust-based environment, and enable them to make the best possible decision.

- Although there is a lot of material on "building rapport," many clients quickly recognize these techniques and tend to shy away from them. It's therefore usually best to use common sense.

Create Your Own Unique Super Successful Sales Process

Cooking Is a Little Like Selling

Creating a meal and selling are somewhat alike, since they are both process-driven activities. You can't, for instance, start baking a cake before you mix the ingredients; it will end up an inedible mess. In the same way, you can't request an order from a prospect before understanding his needs or wants, as he will look at you as if you are a Martian. Yet one of the most common challenges for salespeople is their tendency to do just that—to present a solution before the proper time, often with a poor outcome. That is why it is so helpful to have a sales process map to follow, as if you were following a recipe.

Cooking Strategies of Different Personality Types

Staying with the cooking theme, let's harken back to Chapter 5, where we discussed the four basic personality types: extroversion, dominance, patience, and conformity. Now I'd like you to consider how each of these styles would approach the process of preparing dinner (see Figure 9.1).

High D	Runs 12×1200 repeats after work at the local YMCA track in preparation for Death Valley race. Leaves the track and inhales a sandwich while driving and talking to office. Once home, throws anything not obviously spoiled in fridge, *Rocky style,* into blender and drinks dinner while responding to late-in-the-day e-mail.
High E	Sends blast e-mail from smart phone to entire neighborhood—about fifty people—without getting the OK from the spouse for an impromptu weeknight cookout. Cops arrive after a "noise" complaint, are invited to join, and end up in the swimming pool for underwater karaoke contest. Family therapist simply shakes head.
High P	Crock pot is on at 8:30 AM for pot roast. Works all day in kitchen to make homemade biscuits, vegetables, salad, and the very popular "marshmallow delight" brownies. Delivered to homeless shelter at 6 PM. Choosing not to eat any, orders drive-thru on way home, and is very nearly hit by crazy driver eating sandwich and talking on cell phone at same time. Smiles and waves while proclaiming, "My gosh."
High C	Research Venetian recipes from an eighteenth-century Italian cookbook, choosing to focus on local fall northern Italian seafood recipe. Orders live fish via airfreight. Premeasures out all ingredients three days prior.

Figure 9.1   How Different Personality Types Prepare Dinner

Process . . . What Process?

The examples in Figure 9.2 are somewhat exaggerated, needless to say. The type of person you are also plays a substantial role in how readily you accept structured sales processes as well. While creating stereotypes isn't healthy, it *is* fun, and there are *general* behaviors associated with particular traits that can impact how we accept assigned tasks.

For example, it is possible that the dominant personality types would respond to a formal sales process in the following ways (see Figure 9.2).

What *Is* a Sales Process?

We've determined that selling is a logical process infused with an emotional connection that utilizes a systematic approach to selling a product or service. The first skill to acquire is to create a *formal, mapped-out sales process.* This will serve as your guide for aiding your clients in

High D	Prefer to jump to the closing and objection-handling step, and fly past the qualifying and presenting portions entirely—which they do often.
High E	Would likely lose the sales book entirely, forget there is a process, and just "wing it." When pressed on the issue, they would respond, **"Process—what Process? I thought you were kidding!"**
High C	Would embrace the process wholeheartedly, and volunteer to spearhead a *Sales Process Improvement Committee*.
High P	Would enjoy being on the high Cs sales improvement committee; would strictly adhere to the rules, and strive to be the best report filler-outer.

Figure 9.2   How Different Personality Types Approach the Sales Process

making good decisions. It should include activities and milestones that have to occur for a client to understand their issues, the impact of not solving, and choices for moving forward. Regardless of your personality, developing a systematic approach to selling is essential to changing the arc of your potential. Remember Julie in Chapter 3? She had significant problems closing sales, largely because she didn't have a process. Her challenge wasn't an *inability* to close sales—a common misdiagnosis— rather, her issues entailed an inadequate pipeline and rushing the sales process to the presentation, as well as denying the prospect the opportunity to understand fully the cost of *not* solving the problem. In reality, if you are currently selling, you have a process. You may not consistently *adhere* to it, or it may be flawed in some way. After all, few of us take a different route to work each day; we stick with what we know because we want to make sure we're taking the right route.

Why Have a Sales Process?

Many organizations rely on a sales presentation book as a means of managing their sales process. When a salesperson meets with a prospect, they likely use a binder or PowerPoint to walk the prospect through the phases of their sales process. Sales training usually instructs sellers to go through the entire procedure in a linear manner. The reason for this is because their firm has considered the logical and emotional aspects of buying, and created a process that first takes the prospect through a "hurt," thus upsetting their emotional homeostasis. They then develop a form of "rescue" that typically includes their offering. For example, the vacuum company at which I began my sales career used a very well-designed sales process. I took issue with their intent of selling at any cost, and of not helping the customer make a good decision. A big part of their training was simply designed to train nineteen-year-old former roofers who could read to follow the steps of the sales process. If they did, they would inevitably sell vacuum cleaners to many people.

It's a good idea to construct a formal sales process, because it:

1. Improves *predictable* outcomes. Having a process greatly increases the probability of a successful outcome. In other words, *you will sell more.*

2. Creates *measurable* metrics and increases your ability to gauge performance and diagnose problems in the process, which makes it much easier to correct and improve skills and thereby reduce overall anxiety.

3. Creates a *repeatable* pattern. The nature of a systematic method makes it easier to bring scale and efficiency to a process and to an organization.

4. Makes the job *manageable*. One of a sales manager's primary tasks in many organizations is to forecast revenue. A defined sales process with clearly defined milestones greatly enhances their ability to forecast accurately. A salesperson's primary job is to execute a sales process, and having a predefined road map makes everyone's job go much more smoothly.

The Four Elements of Selling

Regardless of what you sell, your chosen sales methodology, or the price point for your product or service, nearly all sales processes are comprised of four basic elements: *prospecting, qualifying, presenting, and enabling a decision.*

- *Prospecting* is the practice of creating and developing opportunities.
- *Qualifying* is a broad category of steps to determine the fit of the prospect for your particular product or service, as well as helping them

understand the nature of their issues or opportunities, the impact of not solving them, and the benefit to solving them.

- *Presenting* is the phase where you take information from the qualifying phase and present your *best thinking* on how you could help your prospects solve their problems or capitalize on their opportunity.

- *Engineering a decision* entails helping your client make a decision that is right for them. *Remember, our role is to help our prospects make good decisions.*

The two most important elements of the four—by a long shot—are the first two: prospecting and qualifying. The best *prospectors*—not the "best closers"—are the ones who win all the top sales awards and make the most money.

PROSPECTORS WIN SALES AWARDS.

Create Your Super Successful Sales Process Map

A sound sales process will help you achieve consistent, superior results, and is comprised of the following four sections:

1. Customer Process
2. Sales Process
3. Sales Actions and Milestones
4. Sales Tools

We will walk through each section in order to help you build your sales process. (See Figure 9.5.)

Special Note: *The steps are the same, regardless of the size and scale of your particular product or service. They do not denote actual meetings or events. For example, my first software sales position was executed entirely over the phone; our typical sale included an initial call, a need analysis call, and a call to review the contract and close. However, there were times when all those happened at once—or, over several years. Even so, the steps of the customer and sales processes were the same: the steps were simply compressed or expanded.*

Section 1: The Customer Process

Begin building your own sales development map with the customer. It makes sense to build a procedure that will mesh with how the prospect actually *considers* the logic and emotion of a decision to buy. It is unlikely that prospects will abandon their buying behavior en masse to conform to your particular method. However—and this is a big however—this doesn't mean that we advocate letting the prospect control the process. It does mean that you need to understand buyer behavior for your particular product, and then build your process to match. Let's carefully consider each step; and remember, this is simply an example to stimulate your creative thinking to help generate your own wildly successful sales process map. (See Figure 9.3.)

I have intentionally omitted a myriad of steps here, since the idea is to illustrate a *general* idea of what a customer process might look like. Your challenge is to think of your own customers' buying process; and one way to figure this out might be to ask them. You can find helpful tools to assist in developing your own sales system at www.willskilldrill.com.

KYOA Customer Process

Step #	Step Title	Description
1b	Unrecognized Need	The prospect fits your target qualification profile, but are unaware of either a problem, an opportunity, you, or your product. Your outreach programs target these opportunities.
2b	Recognized Need	The move from steps one to two is considerable, since the prospect has recognized a want, problem or an opportunity—either by your efforts, or due to some other factor.
3b	Gather Information	Now typically done on the internet, a buyer's first step is to look for possible solutions, compare offers, and so on. This can make some salespeople uncertain since it's is the first encounter they have with the prospect; and it's easy to mistake gathering information for a commitment to buy. Again, without an understanding of the cost of not solving, a perception of value, and the commitment of time and money, decisions ordinarily aren't made in this way.

Step #	Step Title	Description
4b	Decision to Solve	Based on their initial findings, prospects decide to go forward to the next step in which they begin to consider buying something. This vital step moves prospects from casual spectator to an engaged potential customer. But most prospects don't do this; they simply fall back to step two.
5b	Pick Potential Partners	Once step four is completed, customers choose potential partners with whom to work based on filters such as previous experience, referral, advertising, and brand/name recognition.
6b	Perform Due Diligence	This step determines the outcome of the process, wherein either the buyer or the salesperson creates the value proposition here. If left to the buyer, the transaction often does not occur, as they typically do not consider the cost of not solving. There is no single method for due diligence; high Es approach it dramatically differently than high Cs might. Committee decisions often reflect the leader's personality. However, there are generally two elements of due diligence: technical and strategic.
7b	Select Partner	Once the buyer has made it through this process, he or she will select a partner; or, in some environments, a group of finalists.
8b	Negotiate Price & Contract	Once the buyer chooses a finalist or small group, he or she will negotiate the price and contract terms. Warning: If you don't have a strong value proposition, expect to be hammered on price.
9b	Review Value Proposition	Once buyers have reduced risk and investment impact as best they can, they will review the entire opportunity and weigh the benefits of going forward against the risk and anticipated return on investment.
10b	Buy or Not Buy	Once they've completed the value proposition review, buyers will decide whether to purchase or not.

Figure 9.3 The Customer Decision to Buy

Section 2: The Sales Process (Create Your Sales Book)

Once you have a grasp on the logical and emotional process your potential customers use to buy, you can build your specific sales process that will assist and enhance their experience. For our example, we are using a seven-step sales process. (See Figure 9.4.) When creating your sales

	KYOA Sales Process	
Step #	Step Title	Description
1s	Create Opportunities	The toughest part of the job for many salespeople, creating opportunities requires developing a target market and creating outreach campaigns to initiate contact with potential customers that fit this profile.
2s	Initial Meeting	This step is often the first contact with the prospect. The goal for the IM is to confirm profile and to explore potential reasons to connect for further dialogue.
3s	Needs Analysis	This is the fulcrum of the sales process, wherein a salesperson learns of the prospect's issues, opportunities, wants, the impact of not solving the problem, and benefits created when they do.
4s	Summary of Findings	A recap of the needs analysis phase, the SoF is both the process and the document that outlines your findings and—if appropriate—suggestions for moving ahead. This gives both the salesperson and prospect a chance to walk away from the process.
5s	Present "Best Thinking"	This is an opportunity for you to tell a prospect how you propose to solve their problem. We prefer "best thinking" as opposed to words like Demo or Solution.
6s	Engineer a Decision	Once the prospect understands how a salesperson can help, we then begin the process. This step encompasses completing the order process; handling questions and stalls; etc.
7s	Deliver Results	Once the relationship moves from potential customer to actual customer, your focus moves to delivering great results.

Figure 9.4   KYOA Sales Process

process, create your sales presentation book. This will assist in developing a process road map. As you do, consider each of the following carefully, as you will add them to your process map under the tools section:

- What information must the customer have to make a well-considered, informed decision?
- What is the purpose and goal of each step?
- What information must be gathered and milestones achieved to move to the next step?
- What selling/product tools are required?
  - Plan letters, Summary of Findings, Needs Analysis checklists, Pricing options, Product Presentation information
- What would disqualify a prospect at each step?
- If you sell in a complex environment—to multiple departments and decision makers, for example—how do you manage multiple sales processes simultaneously?
- What is your communication road map for the entire sales process?
  - Meeting prerequisites and reminders
  - Meeting follow-up and next step confirmation
  - Formal findings, pricing, proposal, contractual
- Where are the natural predictive points in the process?

Your sales process may have from 1 to 10 steps. The actual sales process for many products, services, and price points rarely follows the same process; buyer types are different, their particular situations and the competitive landscapes may differ, and so on. Still, it is important to have considered and developed a best practice for how best to work with a prospect that will create the most consistent, positive outcome.

Sections 3 and 4: Sales Actions and Tools

Once you have mapped out the customer and sales process, it's relatively easy to develop the benchmarks, actions, and tools needed for each phase. The example shows key milestones for each stage that make it simpler to manage the opportunity. In the Initial meeting, you know what key information you need in order to move the opportunity to the Needs Analysis phase. Do you have the list of key issues? If not, it's probably not worth moving forward. Do you have an agreement to have access to the decision maker? If not, again, it's probably not worth moving forward. Some items to create and embed in your sales process are the following.

- Prephase communications
- Required information from the prospect
- Checklists, guides, forms
- Post-phase communication
- Presentation materials
- Red-light signals
- Likely objections
- Percentage complete, closing probabilities

Putting It All Together—A Sales Process Case Study

Judy owns a small business that helps nonprofit firms improve their fund-raising and grant management. She is a certified public accountant and runs a very traditional practice; she's never thought of herself as much of a salesperson. In fact, like many, she didn't much like the idea of being a salesperson. Once Judy began to work with her first nonprofit client, she knew she has found her passion and her niche. As she claims, "I just felt good working with firms who were trying to help others."

However, Judy began to realize two things as she moved her business away from traditional public accounting to a firm that focused on nonprof-its. First, she was indeed a salesperson by default, and second, she had no idea how to sell. She did know that her strategy of setting appointments, presenting her solution, and sending the prospect a proposal wasn't work-ing—at all. As much as Judy wanted to help these companies handle their fundraising grants more efficiently, she struggled to convince her potential clients that this would be helpful and, as a result, her business struggled as well. She had yet to learn the lesson that clients don't want a solution; they want a solution to their problems. Her sales process completely skipped the essential element. Oops.

Judy had terrific product knowledge, was an expert in the nonprofit industry, and knew the competitive landscape extremely well. In other words, she already had three of the four knowledge elements required to succeed in the bag; all she lacked were the skills and process for helping her clients evaluate their issues, understand the cost of not solving, and make a good decision. In desperation, Judy signed up for a Sales Academy program. It was her first exposure to any form of formal sales skill development, and a last resort for her.

The training program focused on teaching her the fundamentals of the selling, developing a formal, structured sales process, and mastering a few basic skills. The result: she really connected with everything she learned, and her sales have literally skyrocketed.

Judy loves processes, and the super successful, yet super simple sales process we helped her develop gave her a road map to follow with each prospect, which she did.

Develop Your Super Successful Sales Process

In all likelihood you have a sales process. A very good exercise to test the effectiveness of your process is to map the four elements of customer, sales, actions, and tools. Just as Judy transformed her business, you have the opportunity to do this as well. Whether starting from scratch or tuning up your current process, this process is time well spent.

Take time right now to consider the four primary sales process elements, the need for awareness and choice, and the emotional and logical components necessary for the prospect to buy. Then begin to develop your own super successful sales process.

1. *Customer process.* Considering the logical and emotional aspects of your particular product, what is the process your ideal customer uses to become aware of an issue (problem or opportunity), gather information, make a decision to pursue, evaluate the offer, and make a decision? Diagram this process in the form of a *step-by step process* (see Figure 9.5).

2. *Sales process.* Now that you have considered the buying process, imagine what each page of your "sales book" will look like.

3. *Sales actions and milestones.* For each step or page of your sales process, there are specific actions that must be taken and milestones achieved in order to advance to the next step. What are they?

4. *Sales tools.* What specific tools in the form of data gathering or presentation will you need for each step?

KYOA SALES PROCESS MAP

	Unrecognized need	Recognize need	Gather information	Decision to solve	Pick partners	Perform due diligence	Present "Best Thinking"	Select partner	Negotiate price & contract	Review Value Proposition	Buy or not buy
Customer Process	Unrecognized need	Recognize need	Gather information	Decision to solve	Pick partners	Perform due diligence	Present "Best Thinking"	Select partner	Negotiate price & contract	Review Value Proposition	Buy or not buy
Sales Process	Create Opportunities		Initial Meeting	Needs Analysis		Summary of findings	Present "Best Thinking"	Engineer a Decision			Deliver Results
	1		2	3		4	5	6			7
Sales Actions	PROSPECTING			QUALIFYING			PRESENTING	ENABLING DECISIONS			
	Create Matrix Develop plans Execute 5% Plan	Initial call Pre-Conditioning letter—move up to a 4 or back to a 2	Develop quick list, agree to next step, schedule mtg with Financial Sponsor	Perform Needs analysis, establish decision process & resources, constraints, Cost of not solving, Benefit to solve		Present findings to Financial Sponsor, gain agreement on next steps, id decision process and resources	Present Proposed Solution & review options for working together	Closing checklist	Negotiating guide lines	Objection handling guidelines	Closing assistance provide feedback
Tools	Marketing plan, prospecting guides	Initial call Pre-Conditioning letter	Buying process, ground rules pre-needs analysis letter	Needs analysis worksheet, ROI tools		Summary of findings	Presentation tools	Closing checklist	Negotiating guide lines	Objection handling guidelines	Closing assistance provide feedback
Pareto	Inquiry 80%							Advocacy 20%			

Figure 9.5   Blank Sales Process Form

You can improve your sales performance by implementing or improving your sales process. If you are looking for a "big spike in performance," consider changing the process you use when working with prospects. Next, we'll work on a few simple methods of filling your sales pipeline and building an ocean of opportunities. Come on.

Chapter 9 Recap: Create Your Own Unique Super Successful Selling Process

- One of the most common challenges for salespeople is their tendency to present a solution before the proper time. That is why it is so helpful to have a sales process map to follow. Dominant personality traits play an important role in how different people accept and respond to a structured sales process.

- A sales process road map should include activities and milestones that have to occur for a client to understand their issues; the impact of not solving; and choices for moving forward. Regardless of your personality, developing a systematic approach to selling is essential to changing the arc of your potential because it improves predictable outcomes, creates measurable metrics, establishes a repeatable pattern, and makes the job manageable.

- Nearly all sales processes are comprised of four basic elements: prospecting, qualifying, presenting, and enabling a decision. The two most important elements are the first two. The best prospectors—not the "best closers"—are the ones who win all the top sales awards and make the most money.

- A sound sales process will help you achieve consistent, superior results, and is comprised of the following four sections: (1) Customer Process, (2) Sales Process, (3) Sales Actions and Milestones, and (4) Sales Tools.

- A general Customer Process pattern includes bringing an unrecognized need to the customer's attention; gathering information; making the decision to solve; picking potential partners; performing due diligence; selecting a partner; negotiating price and contract; reviewing the value proposition; and choosing to buy or not.

- A general Sales Process includes initiating opportunities, holding an initial meeting, conducting a needs analysis, reviewing the summary of findings, presenting "best thinking," engineering a decision, and delivering results. No matter what your industry, 80 percent of your sales process should be focused on inquiry—assisting your client to understand their particular issues—and 20 percent focused on advocating a solution, if one is warranted.

Once you have mapped out the customer and sales process, it's relatively easy to develop the benchmarks, actions, and tools needed for each phase. These might include prephase communications; required information from the prospect; checklists, guides, forms; post-phase communication; presentation materials; red-light signals; likely objections; and percentage complete/closing probabilities.

Build Your Own Ocean of Opportunities

C *reating new opportunities* could arguably be the most important step in the sales process. If we look at selling strictly from a "numbers" perspective, we see that the more opportunities that go into the top of the funnel, the more sales pop out the other end. It's the law of probability, large numbers, and gravity all rolled into one. Yet something so obvious is often incredibly difficult for many to grasp; therefore, this chapter is dedicated to generating and perfecting strategies to create more opportunities.

Several years ago, a gentleman attended one of our Sales Academy training programs. He did very well in the role-play competition, and connected strongly with our trust-based approach to the sales process. In the field, he utilized many of the skills taught in the class, except for one: He simply refused to do any form of prospecting outreach. To him, the notion of developing relationships and creating opportunities was so distasteful that he simply refused. As you could imagine, his boss was quite distressed—a salesperson who won't pick up the phone, or attend a networking event? What universe are we in? But he was adamant about his position. Despite his manager's readiness to work with him on alternatives, this particular salesperson clearly faced a significant obstacle in reaching his true potential. Early in his career, leads were provided to him through advertising and demand for his product, thus concealing the true impact of the issue.

What's Up with This?

What are some of the potential reasons that a salesperson might simply refuse to do any form of outreach? Considering what we cover in Chapter 6, it would appear there is a significant "core issue" that is manifesting as either fear, poor self-image, or an inflated ego. The resulting behavior is call avoidance, fear of rejection, or a refusing to engage in a process this salesperson believes to be "beneath" him. This is a classic "Your Raise Becomes Effective When You Do" situation. It took a little over a year before his boss cut him loose. To be fair, there are numerous methods for doing outreach, but in this case, our friend wouldn't do anything. His entire strategy was to *wait* for a lead to appear. His issue isn't a lack of skill, but a lack of will—whether an ego issue or a fear issue, he has a *core issue that is manifesting itself* as a refusal. Regardless of his excuse, it isn't unreasonable to expect salespeople to reach out to potential customers; in fact, it's unreasonable for this *not* to be a major part of nearly *any* sales position. At this point, this man's career as a salesperson responsible for generating new relationships is likely over, which would be a total waste.

Fear of failure and rejection and a reluctance to try new things is normal, but allowing these fears to completely destroy your career is abnormal. If I can ride a roller coaster, anyone in the world can make a phone call. You are responsible for your success. Therefore, you are responsible for building your ocean of opportunities. If this is an area of struggle, confront and solve the problem using the process in Chapter 7. For most salespeople, doing outreach and developing a sales pipeline is half to three-quarters of the job.

Create Your Own Ocean of Opportunities

You can create endless waves of prospects without spending a fortune. This is a great skill to develop, as self-sufficient salespeople never miss quota, earn a very good living, can literally find work in any city and economy, and are highly sought after. The best prospectors are the 20 percenters, and they win the big awards. Achieving this status will require that you adopt a systematic approach to building your ocean. Remember, your goal in creating opportunities is to schedule a preliminary meeting with a prospect. The following five-step process will help you to open up your sales career to boundless opportunities.

Step 1: Define Your Perfect Prospect

As we discuss in Chapter 4, the paradox of prospecting is that a bigger pool of suspects is not necessarily better. How many target prospects you have will largely be dependent on the size of your transactions and the number of sales you wish to make in a year. In Chapter 16 we work on your annual success plan, which will help clarify these questions. However, you will recall from an earlier discussion that the orthopedic surgeon's specialization in surgery of the shoulder made him an absolute expert. The lesson here is that the more narrowly you can define your market, the more of an expert you will become—which will make you more valuable in the eyes of your prospects. And the more valuable you are, the more they will choose to work with you.

Therefore, the first step is to identify the characteristics of your "perfect prospect," and to do that we consider the three primary elements of *demographic, psychographic*, and *geographic*. If you have existing customers, identify who your "perfect customer" is as a place to begin to develop your perfect prospect profile. Part of this process will include a fact-finding mission to help answer the questions and identify the exact criteria that makes them such a good fit as a customer. The big idea, of course, is to get a bunch more of them.

Typically, the first area to consider is *demographics*, which takes into account the size and type of a potential oppurtunity. In my first software sales job, the demographic was small- to medium-sized homebuilders. In business-to-business transactions, an easy way to identify and research the demographic data is through the use of a database, such as one provided by Dun & Bradstreet (D&B). The more specific the information you can get, the better able you'll be to home in on your target audience. There are numerous factors that can help you discern the exact right demographic to assist in defining your perfect prospect. For example, revenue, employees, type of work, years in business, current solution, type of ownership, transactions per year, professional relationships, associations, and educational institutions—are all potential features to use, and there are hundreds more.

Once you have identified the demographics, delve deeper into those targets with a look at their *psychographic* qualities. For example, look at their attitudes toward change and innovation. It's likely that you'll have two fairly identical companies that do the same business and are a similar location and size, but that have dramatically different views on technology. That *matters*. Identifying psychographic qualities can be harder, but it's not impossible; in fact, your perfect customer can help with this. Dominant personality traits, education level, current systems, associations, type of work, subscriptions, and purchasing behaviors in other industries are all characteristics that can indicate a prospect's level of comfort with technology.

Once you've assessed the demographic and psychographic qualities, you'll likely want to operate within a certain *geographical* area. Whether it's a city, state, region, country, or hemisphere, you will have a preferred operational territory. Typically, you want it to be as small as possible, but big enough to provide the right number of potential opportunities. Smaller is usually better from a territorial perspective, and your territory's size will depend upon the other two factors we've discussed.

These three components are what comprise your perfect *Prospect* profile—the unique blend of elements that make your perfect prospect perfect for you.

Step 2: Create Your Prospect Universe

Once you have developed your perfect prospect profile, you'll want to create your prospect universe—a list of as many people as possible who fit your unique criteria. You will want to store this list in your contact management system with a label such as "Act!" Gathering information and building your prospect universe is an ongoing, never-finished task, so the list is dynamic and ever-changing as well. Your prospect universe is one of your greatest assets; you should treat it as such.

To keep your prospect universe organized, consider using a nomenclature system that clearly identifies where each prospect is in the buying lifecycle at any particular moment. (See Figure 10.1, for instance.) If you are

Prospect Matrix Grid		
A	Perfect Prospect	Buying
B	Perfect Prospect	Looking
C	Perfect Prospect	Responding
D	Perfect Prospect	No Current Interest
E	Profile Not Complete	
F	Not in Matrix	
G	Dead/Do Not Call	

Figure 10.1   Prospect Matrix Grid

a stockbroker, your current active clients would likely be As, and those on your target list would be Bs and Cs. Later, as you build strategies and plans to reach out to your prospect universe, it will be helpful to have this in place.

In Chapter 4, we discussed Larry's selling metrics, which you might recall aren't as good as they could be. It is important for you to know your own as well; specifically, how many sales or transactions you want to make in a year, how many A prospects you need to complete a transaction, and how many touches it takes for you to produce an A prospect. My advice is to be conservative in your thinking. Again, we'll delve into these issues in greater detail in Chapter 16. It's important, however, to consider the number of prospects you'll need to generate to reach your annual sales goal, as this will have an impact on your outreach strategy.

Step 3: Create Your Outreach Strategy

There is no single way to develop opportunities. There is only *your* way. I've worked with thousands of salespeople, and something that the best performers have in common is that they have developed a system for conducting outreach. A valuable plan for creating an ocean of opportunities doesn't have to be complex; usually, it is quite the opposite. Simple is better and more effective. Let's look at how a few do it.

The Referral Builder

First up is Andy, whose method of generating opportunities is to build referrals through networking. Andy opts to build a self-propelled momentum generator of leads by personally knowing every client, every potential referral source, every association, and nearly everyone else in his demographical and geographical territory. More importantly, they know *him*. He's active in associations and on committees. He is in constant touch with his clients and referring partners. He's not a fan of cold calling, so he does very little of it. In most cases, prospects call *him* after having spoken to one of his referring sources. Andy puts a lot of effort into staying in touch with his flock, and it works for him. When he does initiate a call, his first order of business is to connect the dots among the people whom the prospect knows that likely know him. This typically takes about 10 seconds, and after he connects the dots, he schedules an appointment. Andy works in a very tight, vertically oriented industry. He manages to make an exceptional living by focusing on his one thing: building referrals through *networking*.

In all types of selling, networking is essential. The reason: networking creates referrals. And, an introduction to a new opportunity through a referral is about five times more likely to result in a sale than any other type of lead. A few sources of referrals in a business-to-business environment are existing customers, association members, accounting firms, insurance companies, banks and credit unions, industry partners, friends, civic clubs, religious organizations. Furthermore, web sites like LinkedIn, Facebook, and blogs are essential elements of every outreach plan.

A good example of building referrals through networking is a colleague of mine who provides accounting services to micro businesses. His number one source of new customers is his banker. Every time a startup company sets up a commercial checking account with this particular bank, they get his card and a strong recommendation to call him. The reasons are simple; first, my friend helps small businesses set up their accounting systems, which greatly increases the likelihood they will succeed, and enables them to qualify for a loan. Second, he has a reputation for doing great work. Third, he asked his banker if he would spread the word. Great outreach programs don't have to be fancy to be effective.

The thought leader and expert at building referral-based outreach programs that work is John Jantsch, President of Duct Tape Marketing, and author of the book, *Duct Tape Marketing: The World's Most Practical Small Business Marketing Guide*. If you want to rev up your referral-based marketing, I encourage you to read his book, and visit his web site, www.duct tapemarketing.com.

The Phone Jockey

Another selling hero of mine is Eric, who, as opposed to Andy, *hates* networking. His approach is to wear out the *telephone*. He's a caller: cold, warm, hot, and everything in between. Here's how he does it. Every Friday, his assistant prints out about 150 perfect prospect records from his Act![1] Database and puts them into a manila folder. He keeps the folder stuffed under his arm for the entire week, wherever he goes. His goal: Reach everyone and move the needle "somewhere" on each one. The outcome might be an appointment, a removal from the list, a call-back in the future, or a presentation.

---

[1] Act! is one of the leading personal contact management tools in the world. Perfect for salespeople, Act! makes it possible to manage your career and improve the arc of your potential. For more information, visit www.act.com.

Eric is relentless, and his prospects know it. He'll see a company sign on a building with contact information, and call them while driving by. This approach pays off more often than you might think. Rather than making special "prospecting" appointments and scheduling a follow-up, he simply prospects *constantly*. At the end of the week, his assistant trades him a new folder of 150 more names for the existing one and updates his Act! Database. Eric is consistently a top producer in his industry. Nothing fancy with this approach. Just consistent.

The Expert Speaker

Our next example is Thomas. As the owner and chief salesperson of a small business, Thomas loves to *speak publicly*. He's also a blogger and published writer on topics concerning his industry, as well as an active participant in his professional associations. Thomas's strategy is to become as knowledgeable as possible in his chosen field, and to get as much press in his particular industry as often as he can. This strategy has enabled him to become the de facto expert in his industry. As a result, he and his company are quite well known. While his firm does little in the way of traditional marketing, they are constantly a top performer. Becoming the expert allows Thomas to choose with whom he works and charge a premium for his services. His clients are actually buying the "Thomas brand" as much as the services he provides.

The following are some tips on ways to develop your public speaking skills.

- Join a Toastmasters[2] group.
- Develop a speech that you can deliver to a variety of audiences. Some suggestions for subjects:
  - Five Power Selling Secrets I Learned from a Gecko
  - Four Fantastic Secrets to Outselling a Fifth Grader
  - Three Reasons Why Selling Is a Lot like Baseball

    It's simple enough to swap out the word "selling" and replace it with almost anything in any one of these titles; managing, teaching, running, thinking, learning, weightlifting, catfish noodling, and so forth. Virtually any other "-ing" word will work, making the subject suitable for nearly every conceivable audience.

---

[2] Toastmasters is a nonprofit organization dedicated to helping its members improve their public speaking skills. There are roughly 250,000 members in 12,500 clubs in over 100 countries. Learn more and join at www.toastmasters.org.

- Practice the speech on your kid's kindergarten class. A tip: bring lollipops and helium balloons. They will love you, and won't really care what you say.

- Write up a one-page overview of yourself and your speech and send it to every local chapter of nonprofits, trade groups, associations, and so on. Volunteer to speak for free. Again—lollipops and helium balloons will win you some surefire fans here.

The Canvasser

Next up is Sean, who has created a mash-up of Andy and Eric's approach of developing prospects and referral relationships by *prospecting face to face*, and enjoys tremendous success with canvassing. He literally walks into businesses and initiates opportunities by simply asking to speak to the decision maker by following the process described here.

First, Sean maps his customers using a computer-based mapping product. He then adds his perfect prospects and potential referring sources to the map, and continues by calling and setting appointments to meet with his clients. When he's there, he brings out the list of potential clients and referrers in the immediate surrounding area, reviews it with the client, asks if she or he knows any of them, and requests permission to use them as a reference. His clients inevitably know some of them, and happily agree to be a reference. Customers will occasionally even call or write e-mail introductions on Sean's behalf. Next, Sean walks into the potential referring partner or prospect's office, introduces himself to the receptionist, and asks to speak to the decision maker. About 25 percent of the time, he actually does. The rest of the time, he leaves a company brochure with a letter of introduction.

Once he returns to his office, Sean sends the target a follow-up e-mail in which he references the client, who is often in the same industrial park. He gets through about 50 percent of the time when he follows up by phone, and then he schedules an initial meeting. This form of face-to-face prospecting works well for Sean because he has tied it to referral marketing—the most effective form of marketing.

Each personality type lends itself to a particular style of doing outreach. There isn't a single right way to fill your pipeline; there is *your* way. In most industries, creating opportunities—filling the sales pipeline with prospects—is the single biggest part of a salesperson's job, as I bet it is in yours as well.

Finding your own style is essential to changing the arc of your career. Our friend at the beginning of the chapter who refused to cold call stunted his potential by refusing to face his fear. Therefore, he can't creatively find his particular method for doing outreach; yet he's literally *one small decision* away from having a much better career, full of enjoyment and satisfaction.

Finding your style is probably easier than you think. Begin by talking with your mentor about their ideas. Then, talk with your perfect clients about how they prefer to be approached with new ideas. Be open. Don't be afraid to fail repeatedly. You'll find your own approach, eventually, and once you do, you'll love doing it.

> PREPARE TO FAIL REPEATEDLY—AND LOVE IT.

KYOA Focus Questions

10.1. Does one of the four types—the Referral Builder, the Phone Jockey, the Expert Speaker, or the Canvasser—make the most sense or appeal the most to you?

_____

_____

_____

10.2. Consider and describe your current strategy and activity level.

_____

_____

_____

10.3. What changes would make it more effective?

_____

_____

_____

Step 4: Create Your Outreach Plan

Once you know how you're going to create your ocean of opportunity, you need to develop a plan for doing so. Considering the matrix grid (see Figure 10.1) of prospects from A to E, the goal for your plan should be two-fold: first, move as many as possible either out of the E category and into an "in-matrix" slot, or into either the F or the G buckets. Optimally, your number of E prospects will be quite low. Second, develop specific strategies and programs to move prospects up the ladder from D to A status. For example, D prospects are in the matrix but have no interest; they would be great prospects if and when they recognized a need. To become a C prospect, they need to become curious or connect with an issue or opportunity. In our industry, peer-led educational workshops work well in this area, since they provide an opportunity to learn in a low-pressure environment. A great way for a C prospect—a declared looker—to move up to a B is to schedule a one-on-one meeting to explore their situation, or perhaps social interaction such as going out to lunch or, my favorite, a golf game might be an easier way to move them up the ladder.

Step 5: Do One Thing Today

Building an ocean of opportunities is an essential part of your success. Remaining constrained because of fear of failure, misplaced ego concerns, or

---

KYOA Focus Questions

10.4. My perfect prospect has the following characteristics:
Demographic:

_____

_____

_____

Geographic:

_____

_____

_____

Psychographic:

_____

_____

_____

10.5. My Super Simple Prospecting Plan is:

_____

_____

_____

confusion over methodology is delaying your inevitable accomplishment. *You* are responsible for your success, and you *can* do it. You simply need to find your way. Be prepared for repeated failure and rejection. It's the only way to reach competency. Embrace it.

Chapter 10 Recap: Build Your Own Ocean of Opportunities

- Skill number two in the sales process is to "create *opportunities*"— arguably, the most important step, as the more opportunities that go into the top of the funnel, the more sales pop out the other end.

- Sales reps will occasionally exhibit behavior manifesting from some core issue that impedes their ability to successfully complete this part of the sales process. A fear of failure and rejection and a reluctance to try new things is *normal*, but allowing these fears to completely destroy your career is *abnormal*. If this is an area of struggle for you, review Chapter 7 and develop a plan to overcome it.

- You must adopt a systematic approach to building your ocean of opportunities by taking the following steps.

  - Define your perfect prospect by taking the three primary elements of *demographic* (the size and type of an entity or person), *psychographic* (attitudes, opinions and viewpoints such as dominant personality traits, education level, current systems, associations, and type of work), and *geographic* (a prospect's location) aspects into account.

  - You want information that is as specific as possible for a demographic and psychographic profile, and you want a geographic territory that is small enough to handle but big enough to provide the right number of potential opportunities.

  - These three components make up your *Prospect Matrix*: the unique blend of elements that make your perfect prospect perfect for you.

- The next step is to develop your *prospect universe*, a list of as many targets as possible who fit your unique criteria. This is an ongoing, never-finished task, so the list is dynamic as well.

- It's also important to *know your own metrics*—such as the amount of sales or transactions you want to make in a year, how many A prospects you need to complete a transaction, and how many in-matrix touches it takes for you to produce an A prospect.

- Next, create your outreach strategy. There is no particular "best" way to create opportunities. Whatever works best for you—that which you will execute regularly—is your ideal approach. Some people excel at making personal connections and *networking*; some work best by consistently *calling* and following up with others, whether they know them or not; some elicit clients by *speaking publicly* and joining associations; and some are best at *prospecting face to face*.

- To find out which style works best for you, ask your mentor about their ideas and talk with your *perfect clients* about how they prefer to hear about new ideas.

- The next step is to *create your outreach program* using your matrix in the following way. First, move as many as possible either out of the E category and into an "in-matrix" slot, or into either the F or the G buckets. Second, develop specific strategies and programs to move prospects up the ladder from D to A status.

- Finally, committing to *do one thing every day* to build your ocean of opportunities is an essential part of your success.

Develop Your Trust and Positive Intent

O n a recent Friday night, my family discovered that our washing machine had stopped draining water. This was a big problem. At our house the washing machine is considered a "mission critical" appliance. We typically run multiple loads each day, so any operational hiccup can cause significant problems to the running of the household— such as a certain T-shirt or pair of jeans not being available at the exact moment it is needed. (If you have never reared teenagers, that remark makes no sense; if you have, you understand implicitly.) The machine, getting on in years, was on the brink of being not worth repairing. So we accepted our reality and developed a plan: call a repair shop in the morning for a Saturday visit. If that didn't work, we would head to the big-box retailer with the pickup truck and pull the trigger on a new model. By sundown on Saturday, we were going to have this situation resolved.

Luckily, we connected with a repair shop in good time and made an appointment for early Saturday afternoon: so far, so good. Michael, the appliance repair person, arrived on time, and quickly diagnosed the problem as a broken motor. He didn't have a replacement on his truck but "might have one at the shop." It just so happened he was going to be working at the shop on Sunday, would confirm whether they had one, and planned to return Sunday afternoon to install it. We were set . . . or so we thought.

My wife Anita got Michael's mobile number, and he let us know that he would call and confirm whether they had a new or used motor and when he'd be coming back. By Sunday at noon, we hadn't heard anything. Anita placed a call to Michael's number and left a message. By 2:00 PM, we had left a message, sent a text message, and had called the company's main number. Nada. Ix-nay on the return call-ay. By 4:00 PM, we had moved to plan B and were on our way to purchase a new machine.

At around 5:00 PM, we received a call from another person at the repair company who informed us that they didn't have the motor in question in stock, and asked if we would like to buy a used washing machine instead. When we inquired about Michael's whereabouts, she casually mentioned that he had "gotten tied up." We never received a call back from him. Obviously, we didn't take their offer, nor will we ever take any other offer they put forth. Why, we wondered, did Michael promise to do something and then not deliver?

UNDERPROMISE AND OVERDELIVER—IT'S BETTER THAN THE ALTERNATIVE.

As Anita and I loaded the new washing machine in our pickup truck, we decided that without a change of trajectory, Michael would be destined for an unhappy career, complete with low earning power and poor job satisfaction. All of this is unnecessary, as he seemed to be a cheerful, competent person. However, he scored a zero in the trust department, as a big part of our relationship depended on him making and keeping his commitments. If Michael had simply kept the promise he made to call us Sunday, the outcome would have been completely different. We would have happily waited to have him come back Monday to install the new motor. We would be satisfied clients wanting to refer their business to others.

This is an example of how a very small shift in thinking can have a *huge* impact on a given career's trajectory. You can make a series of seemingly insignificant choices to not keep a commitment, and soon, you are labeled as "untrustworthy" and someone with whom very few people want to work. While Michael may well have wanted to help us, his ability to keep his word was nonexistent—rendering his intent completely invalid.

The good news for Michael—and for all of us—is that trust is a skill, and skills can be strengthened and improved. It's somewhat like a bicep; repeated use under stress—even very light stress—causes it to grow.

Author Stephen M. R. Covey claims in his book *The Speed of Trust* that: "*Clients must trust your Character plus your Competence*; where your character equals your integrity plus intent, and your competence equals your capabilities plus results."

In other words, your clients must believe that you intend to be helpful, and are competent enough to actually make it happen. And, as we saw with Michael, a big part of competence is doing the little things—like returning phone calls.

The benefits of having a high degree of trust in business are immeasurable. It's especially important to consider the impact that trust has on the *speed* of a sales transactions. High-trust transactions lack a sense of fear—of both competence and honest intent.

For example, I have a highly trust-based relationship—in both of these areas—with my mechanic, Wade. I know that Wade knows how to repair the vehicles, since I've enjoyed quality results from him for twenty years. I also know this because in those instances when Wade wasn't comfortable, he said so. When I take a vehicle to Wade, either for preventative maintenance or because I suspect a problem, I drop it off, notify him of the issue, request that he "look the whole thing over" and let me know the damage. We don't really have a sales process where he does an estimate. We operate in the absence of fear, and the result is *increased velocity*.

Some time ago, I suspected the clutch was going bad, so I dropped the car off with Wade, fearing the worst. Clutches aren't easy to reach in that vehicle and can be quite pricey to replace. Later that day, I answered a call from Wade with the trepidation of facing a bank-draining report, but he simply told me to "Come pick it up." How was this possible—and so fast? He replied, "Your clutch cable just needed adjusting. It took five seconds. Oh, and we changed the oil." "Was it low?" I inquired. "No; it had been over a year and just needed to be changed, that's all." "How much?" I asked. "Twenty-five bucks," said Wade.

Wade could have done an unnecessary procedure, and I would have been none the wiser. But he didn't, and wouldn't. *That* is why I trust him.

> OFTEN, IT'S THE SALE YOU DON'T MAKE THAT CREATES THE GREATEST ROI.

Another significant benefit of creating and maintaining trust-based relationships is *increased profit* in your transactions. Buyers typically negotiate price to *reduce* the impact and *risk* of not getting what they expect when they expect it. Conversely, when customers trust salespeople, they are typically willing to pay a premium for the relationship. For example, manufacturers who buy parts to assemble and resell rely on their suppliers to provide materials for their products in a timely manner. Vendors who fail to deliver the right product at the right time not only risk missing sales and losing clients, they put their customer's business at risk as well. There is real value in making and keeping your commitments.

The Haggler Gene

Now, I know there are a few of you who have a genetic mutation which forces you to negotiate price on *every little thing*. It's like a sport to see how much you can get. My advice: Leave that for your trips to the Tijuana or the street merchants in Venice. They expect it there; it's part of the atmosphere and experience.

SOMETIMES "CHEAP" COSTS THE MOST.

Cheap Plastic Surgery?

However, when you insist on whittling down your vendors' and partners' prices, you usually receive less than the best—which could end up costing *you*. Let's get real—who really wants the "cheapest" plastic surgeon? If you go the low-priced route, you may need to have a do-over, something that never works out very well.

When we build trust in our relationships, we attract customers who value reliability, intent, and competence—characteristics we also admire. These very customers are quite willing to pay a premium to receive it. For example, Wade's garage charges at least double what the chain-store mechanic charges for a standard brake job. But Wade uses only factory parts, and they rebuild the entire brake, change the fluid, and bleed the lines. So the job he does is worth it to me. I mean, who really wants the cheapest brake job? I feel safe, and Wade makes a profit, which is even bigger due to our speed-of-light sales process.

Trust also positively impacts sales in *increased referrals* from your clients. Clients typically refer a friend or a colleague to a business because they're satisfied and happy with the relationship and wish to share their good fortune with others. The reverse is also true: When friends won't make a referral, they're usually concerned that the business won't take good care of their friend. In other words, they have a low degree of trust. Using Covey's definition of trust as "Competence plus Intent," to receive a referral, a client must trust both your competence to do the task and your intent behind doing it; and they must feel good about the relationship. If they do, watch out: You are about to sell a whole lot of stuff to a bunch of people.

Referred Trust

When someone makes a sales referral, they are, in effect, referring trust. In "farmer"[1] selling, you build trust over a period of years by demonstrating both your competence and intent to help. In new account "hunter"-type selling, the salesperson has to establish trust very early in the sales process. Trust is essential to creating meaningful dialogue and understanding the prospect's true issues. The most efficient way to do that is through a referral. When someone says *"Give Chris a call, she has been super to work with,"* not only is Chris getting a lead, she is inherently receiving trust from the prospect based on the faith her client has in her.

Business author and strategist Fred Reichheld's recent book, *The Ultimate Question*, takes a very hard look at the impact that referrals have on a business's growth and profit. Reichheld's research concludes—not surprisingly—that companies that "delight" their customers receive more referrals than those that don't. The result of all those referrals is increased sales, fueling greater growth and profitability.

But How Does This Work?

The foundation for increasing sales velocity and outcomes; generating higher profit margins; receiving more referrals from customers and strategic partners, and creating faster growth is *establishing trust*. A client must have faith in your ability to do what you say you are going to do, as well as confidence that you know how to do it.

---

[1] A sales methodology term where a "farmer" refers to salespeople engaged in relationship-based selling to existing accounts, as opposed to "hunter" selling, where the idea is to actually "kill and devour" your prospect. *Just kidding*. Hunter selling is where you hunt down and close the prospect, and then move on to the next one, leaving the nurturing function to the farmers.

DEVELOPING TRUST REQUIRES KNOWLEDGE, INTENT, AND MAKING AND KEEPING COMMITMENTS.

How Do I Develop My Trust Skill?

As we explore in Chapter 4, the more you know about your product, industry, and competition, the more valuable you are in your clients' eyes. Combining that with your intent to help them find the best solution without regard to your commission check—along with expert selling skills—creates a safe environment for them to explore options. It's an atmosphere that promotes awareness and choice, and that allows you to engage in the kind of meaningful dialogue that's only possible in the absence of fear. Meaningful interactions are the key; therefore, the first step to developing your trust skill is to shore up your knowledge in the four areas of product, industry, competition, and selling skills.

The second component of creating trust in your relationships is your *intent*—the purpose behind your actions. Intent is fairly easy to read. Many researchers believe our faces are the windows to our brains and consistently betray our thoughts. Consider your most significant relationship. Can't you usually determine how the other party feels immediately, without him or her ever having to say a word? Emotion is usually evident in someone's eyes and their face. Malcolm Gladwell discusses the science behind how this works in his bestselling book *Blink*. Our brains are very adept at reading faces, which is one of the mechanisms we use to form initial opinions of people. Intent works the same way: Your intentions are written all over your face. For example:

- Your prospect reads your face and decides what your intent is (good or bad)—whether you want them to or not.
- Their impression acts as a spigot of meaningful dialogue. If they believe your intentions are focused on their best interest, they will open up the flow of dialogue. However, if they think that you're focused solely on your commission check, they will likely withhold information.
- The flow of dialogue has a huge impact on the transaction's outcome.
- You therefore have the ability to influence your propect's perception of your intent (without saying what it is).

YOU CAN'T FAKE INTENT.

One thing to remember: *you can't fake your intent.* In fact, if you try, your prospect will instantly know it and write you off as someone to be avoided. Intent begets a cycle of profitability in the following way: if you focus your effort on your clients' success instead of your own, they will be instantly attracted to work with you—which will result in greater performance. So give it a try. Consider the question below and create your intent statement. Then, share it with your mentor.

KYOA Focus Questions

Develop your Professional Intent Statement by answering the following questions.

11.1. What is your intent for your prospects and customers?

_____

_____

_____

11.2. What is your intent for your most significant personal relationship?

_____

_____

_____

Make and Keep Commitments

The third aspect of developing trust in the sales process is *making and keeping commitments*. It would be a shame to do an awesome job of being an expert and truly help your client succeed, only to fail to fulfill your commitments on time. As discussed previously, it can be difficult for high Es to master this discipline, but necessary for building lasting trust-based relationships. You must do what you commit to do, and be strong enough to avoid making promises that you are unwilling or unable to keep.

YOU ARE YOUR WORD.

The Dog Ate My Commitment

For many, not keeping commitments is a matter of simple forgetfulness or lack of self-organization. For others, it is a resulting behavior of fear or another manifestation of a core issue. In either case, it is tiresome to invent excuses for why commitments were missed, including the classic "The dog ate it." As if that is going to work. Often, the client sees right through the flimsy excuse, which begins the rapid descent of your relationship into irrelevance due to a lack of trust. Whatever the case may be, one way to improve your skill of self-trust is to reprogram your neural pathways, as we discuss in Chapter 7 with the Potential Process. Doing this will help your brain believe that you *can* indeed make and keep a commitment. In keeping with the concept that we retrain our brains on a 21-day cycle, try this four-step refresher.

1. Set a "no-brainer" goal for each day.

   Option 1: *Say one nice thing each day* to your most significant partner.

   Option 2: If Option 1 seems too hard, try *"breathe every day"* as your daily goal.

2. Before going to bed each night, update your goal log.

3. On day 21, celebrate your victory.

4. Rinse. Repeat.

This may sound ridiculous, and it might well be. But if you tend not to do a very good job of making and keeping commitments, beginning with these "no-brainers" will help you retrain the pathways correctly. You can and will change the arc of your potential by improving in this area.

GET YOUR ACT TOGETHER!

Another way to improve your ability to keep commitments is to become organized. This concept is a struggle for certain members of the personality spectrum (you know who you are), but necessary and essential to ensure that you keep your commitments, which will greatly improve the arc of your potential. We dig deeper into this concept in Chapter 17.

Chapter 11 Recap: Develop Your Trust and Positive Intent

- Trust is a *skill* that sales professional must develop and hone; your clients must believe that you intend to be helpful, and are competent enough to actually make your promises happen.

- It's especially important to consider the impact that trust has on the speed of a sales transactions. High-trust transactions lack a sense of fear, which is essentially mistrust of both competence and honest intent.

- Another significant benefit of creating and maintaining trust-based relationships is *increased profit,* since buyers typically negotiate price to *reduce risk.* Customers are willing to pay a premium for the relationship when they can trust salespeople.

- Trust also positively impacts sales by resulting in *increased referrals* from clients who share their good experiences with friends or colleagues. The reverse is also true: People won't refer businesses that they worry won't take good care of their associates. When someone makes a sales referral, they are, in effect, referring trust.

- Developing trust requires *knowledge, intent,* and *making and keeping commitments.* The more you *know* about your product, industry, and competition, the more valuable you are in your clients' eyes. Customers must also believe that your *intent* is to serve their best interest. Finally, you must do what you *commit* to do for clients, and be strong enough to avoid making promises that you are unwilling or unable to keep.

Learn the Subtleties of Power Listening

The single biggest problem in communication is the illusion it has taken place.
—George Bernard Shaw

Fun with Miscommunication

Great humor is often based on the concept of miscommunication. For example, Abbott and Costello's "Who's on First"—a comedic skit first performed in the late 1930s—portrays a dialogue between two gentlemen who are discussing the names of a baseball team's players, which happen to be *Who* and *What*. It is perhaps one of the funniest sketches of all time. It is rooted in the Vaudeville era, and is the foundation as well for many television situational comedies that followed. The next time you're watching a sitcom, keep an eye out for the comic possibilities of miscommunication.

However, miscommunication is markedly *less* funny in a sales environment. As a sales manager, I often traveled with salespeople in the field to observe their selling skills. I took a trip with a rep named Ken. As we sat in the prospect's conference room, the prospect asked Ken about a particular feature of the product. Ken went on to describe literally everything about the product—*except* the very aspect that the potential client had asked about. It soon became obvious to both the prospect and me that Ken either hadn't heard the question correctly or had absolutely no idea what he was talking about. After what seemed like five minutes of Ken confidently providing useless information, I couldn't take it any longer; I interrupted Ken and suggested a clarification. Not only was he moving in the wrong direction, he was doing so at a high rate of speed, making it difficult to interrupt him.

Ken is by no means unique; this same scenario has taken place numerous times. Miscommunication is nearly an epidemic in the sales profession. The primary culprit is that somewhere along the line, the phrase "selling is telling" was socialized and adopted en masse by every living salesperson. For the record, "selling is *not* telling." When we consider the nuance of language, nonverbal communication, political posturing within organizations, and distractions on the part of the speaker and listener—it's surprising that the buyer and seller *ever* manage to have a meaningful dialogue on issues and solutions.

> *What we got here . . . is a failure to communicate.*
> —Strother Martin ("Captain" in Cool Hand Luke, 1967)

Miscommunication can get downright *unfunny* when it invades personal relationships, sometimes with disastrous effects. Consider this purely hypothetical example:

- Party A makes a statement about not feeling well to Party B.

- Party B—not listening closely—assumes incorrectly that Party A said that Party B was looking fat and out of shape (stranger misreads have happened).

- Party B responds to this with a misplaced attempt at humor (which goes awry) about how Party A could stand to "drop a few kilos and hit the gym every once in a while." (Party B might be feeling a tad guilty for never getting on the $5,000 treadmill that now sits in front of his TV, and is taking it out on Party A for bringing it up by using sarcasm as a way of getting even.)

- Party A is shocked and horrified that Party B could be so ugly, insensitive, callous, and mean-spirited.

- By the time Party B realizes the mistake, he is camping out on the spare bedroom futon.

- It takes the better part of the next day—through a series of conciliatory e-mails, flowers, and dinner reservations—to regain admittance into the master bedroom and to begin to repair the damage, however innocently it was caused.

Components of Communication

Verbal communication can be described as *inquiry and advocacy*, *listening and speaking*, or remaining *receptive and going active*, depending on which books you've read. I tend toward *receptive listening*, a term that many authors and professionals use, but which I define as "creating an environment of trust to allow my dialogue partner the freedom to explore their thoughts, feelings, and emotions without interruption, judgment, or redirection." Regardless of labels, all communication has a purpose: to engage in interaction with others to fulfill a need. Expressing our desires, thoughts, and feelings is part of the process. Understanding others' desires, thoughts, and feelings is essential as well, as *effective* communication requires both listening and speaking. Otherwise, we are just ranting in the wilderness. How fun is that?

> "SELLING IS LISTENING"—SAY IT WITH ME—"SELLING IS LISTENING"—WITH *FEELING*.

Remember Pareto?

The general rule of thumb in the sales process is to listen about 80 percent of the time and speak about 20 percent of the time—which is almost diametrically opposite to what actually *happens* in most selling situations. We've somehow equated talking with selling, when the reality is that listening is selling. Perhaps we didn't get the memo. To make a bold statement that effective communication is essential in selling would still be a dramatic *understatement*, because selling *is* communicating. The degree to which we are able to converse with prospects in order to understand their issues (inquiry, listening, remaining receptive) and then convey a proposed solution (advocacy, speaking, going active) will measure our success. As Ziglar says on his *Secrets of Closing the Sale* tapes, "We have two ears and one mouth, we should listen twice as much as we talk." He's right.

Listening Is Harder

Not to pay any disrespect to speaking, but between listening and speaking, effective listening is the tougher skill to master. In fact, most people don't even consider it to *be* a skill; they simply ignore it, which becomes evident in virtually every aspect of the sales process. For example, we'll tackle creating a value proposition in the next chapter—something that's virtually impossible without honing your ability to listen receptively and communicate in a trust-based environment.

One of the challenges of listening well is that the ability to communicate varies from one person to the next. Use of language can create barriers that are hard to overcome, and disparate needs of and purposes for the exchange can increase a misunderstanding's likelihood. Furthermore, there are levels of communication, which can create difficulties when both parties are not corresponding on the same level.

Levels of Communication

Four basic levels of communication—which often can determine the outcome of a dialogue—are:

1. Clichés
2. Facts
3. Beliefs
4. Emotions

Considering the list from a sales process perspective, we know it is essential to include logic and emotion in a dialogue with a prospect. We have to get *emological* to truly help clients achieve their goals. From a communication perspective, we have to get to level four with our prospect to understand what is truly behind their issues. This is understandably difficult—*especially if we aren't listening!*

CONNECT ON AN EMOLOGICAL LEVEL.

The Four Levels of Communication and Your Sales Process Map

Consider the relationship between the sales process map and this list of communication levels. When we begin dialogue at the *create opportunities*

LISTENING STYLES OF DIFFERENT PERSONALITIES	
High D	Easily distracted; finds it difficult to listen to high Es and high Ps as they wander from the point. Can become impatient and will pivot conversation to a topic they prefer, or interrupt speaker to finish sentences. Tips: don't bring anything to meetings that could be distracting; watch, phones, paper, etc. Try to practice meditating to find your happy place.
High E	Can be good listeners if they are interested in the person; if not, look out. They will take over to talk about something of interest, typically themselves.
High C	Don't care much for small talk, so conversations in general are not a strong suit. As a result, listening can be a struggle, especially if the topic isn't serious or productive. They love to engage in dialogue on topics that are technical in nature, or that are intellectually stimulating.
High P	These are the best listeners on the planet. Pick a topic, and they are yours all day long. Plan to have someone call you as an escape hatch—or it could go on all night.

Figure 12.1   Listening Styles of Different Personality Types

step, we often use a cliché, as it potentially builds rapport without risking much. The next step of the *initial meeting* requires that we dig for and disclose facts. The *needs analysis* phase entails relating the facts to the impact of doing nothing—what we term the *cost of not solving*. To do that, we must connect with our prospect's beliefs. Finally, as we begin to *engineer a decision*, we move beyond beliefs and into our prospect's emotions and fears to help them solve their problems. None of this is possible without creating a trust-based environment (a skill) and becoming an expert listener (a skill).

Receptive listeners have the power to move the dialogue to different levels and, usually, our partners will go where we lead them. Forging an emotional connection takes bravery on your part and requires you to share your emotional side. Let's consider how the different kinds of personality traits that we discussed in Chapter 5 might approach listening. (See Figure 12.1.)

Why Do We Struggle to Listen?

First, and foremost, we are preoccupied. If you're like most people, you have a plethora of internal and external stimuli competing for your attention at all times. For example, it is impossible for me to have a mean-ingful dialogue with anyone if I am near my computer, Smartphone, or television. Since I travel a great deal, the major opportunities I get to catch up with family and friends often take place in a hotel room over the phone. A few years ago, while on a call with Anita, I was simultaneously surfing the Internet. She was attempting to have a level four conversation, and I was checking out something important like "vintage Honda motor-cycles" on the Internet. Then I heard this: *"Are you on the Internet?"* "I was. But not anymore," I lamely answered.

However, external stimuli are only a small part of the problem. As con-versationalists, we have numerous other issues to contend with as well, such as:

- *Waiting for an opening:* We're often not very interested in what the other party has to say, so instead of listening to them, we're simply waiting for a break in order to share our own ideas/opinions/stories.

- *Interrupting the speaker:* In many cases, we don't even bother to wait for an opening: We create one. We're so anxious to make our point that we simply interrupt the speaker midthought. Just as bad, we will use body language (head nodding, glancing at watch, and so on) to convey to the speaker that we've grown weary of their dialogue, and want to take over ourselves.

- *Formulating a response:* Frequently while the other party is speaking, we're busy formulating our response. It may have been a single word they said that triggered it; from that moment forward, we are think-ing solely of our own point of view.

- *Judging the speaker:* We lose the thread of the dialogue by focusing our attention on the actual speaker, instead of focusing on what they are saying.

- *Winging it:* Rather than admit we lost focus, didn't understand, or didn't hear what our dialogue partner said, we wing it by attempting to carry on the dialogue even though we have no earthly idea what was said. Instead, we should ask a clarifying question such as: *"I to-tally didn't listen to that because I was focused on how much I hate your outfit and how hungry I am for an egg sandwich. Would you please repeat it if I promise to actually listen?"* Or, another option could be, "I'm sorry, I didn't quite get that, do you mind repeating?"

- *Conversation stealing:* We change the direction of the dialogue from being a listener to being a speaker by taking a statement made by the speaker and using it to pivot the exchange to an issue of our choosing.

The struggle to listen isn't only our own issue; many struggle with speaking as well. A few of the challenges that people face as active dialogue partners are:

- *Lost threads*: Some lose the thread of the dialogue in the middle of the statement and never actually get to the point. In fact, I have personally witnessed a speaker begin on a topic, lose the thread, realize that it happened, try to regain it by morphing the dialogue in a new direction—only then to remember what they had temporarily forgotten, and complete the statement.
- *Inappropriate anecdotes*: In a clumsy attempt to build rapport or be funny, speakers will tell an inappropriate story, perhaps one that is either off-topic, too long, or on a subject unsuitable for the audience.
- *Overspeak*: Some people just go on and on. (Clearly, they've never heard of Pareto.)
- *Volume control*: Another challenge for speakers is inappropriate volume and intensity. We began to learn the concepts of "inside" and "outside" voices" in kindergarten, but not all of us have quite mastered this. Alternately, some actually speak so softly that their dialogue partner cannot hear them.
- *Mumbling*: Using impossible to understand speech patterns makes it difficult for prospects and customers to communicate with them.
- *Body language*: Some speakers convey strange facial expressions, eye contact, or seating positions.
- *Fear of public speaking*: To paraphrase Jerry Seinfeld, "If having to choose between being in the casket or giving the eulogy, many would choose the casket."

Developing Your Conversational Construct

We've discussed how communication is comprised of listening and speaking. Therefore, we must establish a framework to begin creating a more meaningful dialogue. Ours will include three primary areas:

- *Receptive listening:* Fostering an environment of trust to allow your dialogue partner the freedom to explore his or her thoughts, feelings, and emotions without interruption, judgment, or redirection.
- *Active participation:* Providing feedback, personal views, and experiences; contributing facts, emotions, and feelings to the dialogue in an open, sharing environment.
- *Observation:* Observing and understanding the external environment and the physical behaviors of your dialogue partner. Consider what is being said—along with what isn't—and why.

Conversations are like a dance, a choreographed movement between a leader and a follower, and subject to ebb and flow before reaching a natural conclusion. Like dance, conversations have a cadence or rhythm that you can enhance by allowing your partner to finish their thought completely before you respond. Let silence permeate the air before replying; it allows you to wait to formulate a response until your partner has concluded, and it makes your dialogue partner feel as though you are really listening—which is the point.

Ironically, this law of dialogue is often counter to the law of dialogue shared among salespeople: *The listener is in complete control of the dialogue.*

The listener directs the dialogue by asking questions; whoever is active is simply following the listener's commands. Unfortunately, this is an area that takes a lot of practice to correct when coaching salespeople.

LISTENING IS POWER.

Be Like William

An associate of mine named William is the best receptive listener I have ever encountered: He can have a 30-minute conversation with anyone without *ever* going into "active" mode. He will take any topic his dialogue partner introduces and move it to areas he finds interesting without ever *stealing* the dialogue; in the process, he almost never talks about himself. He will, of course, answer a question if the active partner asks, but he'll then end his answer with an open-ended question and put himself back into receptive mode. He remains completely focused on the other party while he or she is speaking; no glance at a watch or phone; no looking around the room. He makes them feel as though they are the most important person in the world, and this is the most important conversation in the world—regardless of who they are or what they are discussing. The result is that William's dialogue partners walk away from conversations with him feeling absolutely great about themselves—and William.

To improve your process for engaging in meaningful dialogue with prospects and customers, consider the following nine dialogue guidelines:

1. Create a trust-based environment that enables you and your partner to get to level three and level four conversations.
2. Commit to receptive listening.
3. Engage the 80/20 rule.
4. Develop techniques for ignoring the inner dialogues ("noise") that preoccupy your brain.
5. Ask clarification questions.
6. Recognize your own personality style and that of your dialogue partner, and modify your behavior to meet them.
7. Avoid conversation stealing.
8. Let the speaker finish his or her thought.
9. Change the conversational cadence by introducing silence between dialogue exchanges.

Selling is an act of *communication*, a balance between receptive listening and active participation. How you converse is as important as—often more than—what you say. How you speak and listen is a window into your personality. You can build trust and credibility quickly by how you interact. Communicating, listening, and speaking are skills, all of which you have the ability to improve.

Chapter 12 Recap: Learn the Subtleties of Power Listening

- Though miscommunication is a great foundation for comedy, it is a serious barrier to an effective sales process.
- Regardless of labels, all communication has a purpose: to engage in interaction with others to fulfill a need. Expressing our own and understanding others' desires, thoughts, and feelings is part of the process, as *effective* communication requires both listening and speaking.

- Applying Pareto's rule to conversations, the sales process works best if we listen about 80 percent of the time and speak about 20 percent of the time. Unfortunately, many sales professionals do the complete opposite.

- The degree to which we are able to converse with prospects to understand their issues (inquiry, listening, remaining receptive) and then convey a proposed solution (advocacy, speaking, going active) will measure our success.

- Between listening and speaking, effective listening is the tougher skill to master and the one most often ignored.

- The four basic levels of communication are clichés, facts, beliefs, and emotions, all of which play an important part in the course of the sales process.

- Each of the different personality types approach listening in various ways; some are markedly better at it than others.

- We struggle to listen because we're distracted by stimuli such as television and e-mail, as well as by our own self-imposed goals, such as waiting for an opening, interrupting or judging the speaker, formulating a response, winging it, or conversation stealing.

- Speakers encounter difficulties as well, such as losing the thread of the discussion, telling inappropriate anecdotes, overspeaking, not controlling the volume, mumbling, using the wrong body language, and having a fear of public speaking.

- A framework in which to establish a meaningful conversation will include receptive listening, active participation, and observation. Always remember that the listener is in *complete control* of the dialogue.

- The way you speak and listen to others provides a window into your personality and allows you to build trust and credibility. Communicating, listening, and speaking are all skills that you *can* improve.

Gather the Facts and Develop a Value Proposition

What Is a Value Proposition?

The tipping point in any sales process is the establishment of a value proposition—which, simply put, is the logical argument for *what makes your product or service worth buying*. Will it create more value than it consumes? Will it provide enjoyment or safety, or any other possible definitions of value? If you are able to specify a strong value proposition that supports your solution during the needs analysis phase, the prospect will typically move forward with your offer. If, however, your claim is weak, your prospect will either elect to do nothing (causing you to lose to "no decision"—your biggest competitor), or buy from a competitor who they believe has a better offer. *Without a value proposition, "no decision" will beat you like a drum named Silly.* So will all of your competitors, for that matter.

The tangible result of creating a value proposition is often referred to as ROI, or Return on Investment—which you can calculate by following this basic formula: $R - I = ROI$.

For instance, if your product sells for $100,000, and the value received in terms of fun created, problems solved, and opportunities created is $500,000, then the client's return on investment from your product is $400,000: pretty nice!

$$\$500,000 \ (R) - \$100,000 \ (I) = \$400,000 \ (ROI)$$

Most salespeople are fairly good at calculating the required-investment portion, but not quite as good at figuring the value-received portion. In fact, as we discuss in Chapters 11 and 12, without a trust-based relationship and the ability to listen, it is unlikely you'll get access to the belief and feeling level of dialogue necessary to determine the value-received portion. As you might imagine, this becomes problematic, as the prospects aren't good at calculating the value received, either. And when the boss sees the $100,000 investment and nothing else, "no decision" begins to look like the *smart* decision.

However, before we begin the process of building a value proposition, we should first focus on the concepts of value, which are coincidentally known to me as *Rob's Laws of Value*. (Small world!)

Rob's First Law of Value

Value isn't what your product does; it's what your product does for the customer.

For example, let's consider the value of a heart transplant, the value proposition for which is pretty compelling. It provides the recipient the opportunity to walk the planet and pursue life, liberty, and happiness for longer than would be otherwise possible. The ROI here is incalculable. But, as miraculous as they are, heart transplants have no inherent value *in and of themselves*. I know that sounds crazy, but consider this premise: As I write this book, I have a healthy heart. I exercise regularly, generally eat well, have low cholesterol, and am not plagued with any genetic heart problems. In other words, I am thankfully not currently a candidate for a heart transplant. Therefore, if a heart transplant salesperson called on me with an offer to do a heart transplant for me, it is extremely unlikely I would consider their offer at any price with any special incentives; even with a free set of Ginsu knives, a free three-day cruise, a drastically reduced

price on installation, an extended maintenance plan, or any other induce-
ment they might fling at me. It's a no-go on the heart transplant for
me, because no amount of money could induce me to take the offer to
have dangerous invasive surgery with high potential for complications if
I have absolutely no need for it. Call me crazy.

Consider this the next time a prospect flat-out rejects your offer: They
might be under the impression that you are trying to sell them the equiv-
alent of an unnecessary heart transplant. They are likely thinking "No
amount of money could induce us to buy X with its potential for complications, along with a significant investment, if we have absolutely no need
for it." And you wouldn't either! Remember, the stuff you sell has no
intrinsic or inherent value. The worth of your solution is derived from
what it allows the purchaser to do as a result of buying it.

Rob's Second Law of Value

Value isn't a cheap price. Value is a big return on investment.

Another important element of value is its relationship to price.
We have corrupted the meaning of value in advertising by equating the
term with something cheap. Calling something "value"-priced indicates
that it's somehow cheaper, or even worse: the *cheapest*. The fast-food
industry, of which I am a fan, is partially to blame by introducing the
concept of a *value* meal. These brilliant marketers simply bundled components together and knocked a dime off the total price, compelling most of
us to suck them down like giant shop-vacs. But value creation has nothing
to do with price. In fact, while most consumers want a good deal, they
don't want the *cheapest* product or price. After all, as we have previously
asked, who really wants the *cheapest* plastic surgery? Or fire-suppression
system? Does anyone want the cheapest tires, computer software, day-care
center, or dinner out? What about the cheapest engagement diamond or
automobile? I don't think so. What we want is a good deal on a *quality*
product. We want a return on our investment that we can measure in
terms of how much enjoyment we derive, the problem it solves, or the
opportunities it creates. What we want is a great product that creates
value for us at a fair price, working with a competent salesperson focused
on our success . . . and so do your clients. A value proposition is an essential ingredient in the sales process. Next, we'll examine the principles of
building one.

When to Create the Value Proposition:
The Needs Analysis and Summary Findings Phase

Where or when you create the value proposition in your sales process will differ from one situation to the next, but in the KYOA sales process, we generate it during the needs analysis and summary of findings. The amount of time and effort you spend developing one will be determined by the size and complexity of the opportunity. For example, I've worked with many organizations that sell lower-priced items over the phone. Their entire sales process occurs over the course of one call; their initial meeting, needs analysis, summary of findings, presentation of best thinking, and enabling a decision all take place in one ten- to fifteen-minute time frame. Regardless of size, scale, or scope, all phases of the sales process are executed, including the development of a value proposition. And, the requirement for an emotional and logical connection of their issue to a solution is the same across virtually any sales process. A common sales mistake is to move to the "present your best thinking" step and attempt to enable a decision without developing a compelling value proposition. The result is likely a loss to "no decision." Keep in mind that value isn't what your product is or does, it's what your product can do for your prospect. Value is created from the use of the product. The value proposition is derived by understanding the expected benefits received from its use, less the required investment.

For a refresher on the KYOA Sales Process, refer again to Figure 9.4.

The Four Levels of Dialogue

Perhaps you recall our discussion in the previous chapter of the four basic levels of dialogue: cliché, facts, beliefs, and emotions. As our level of trust increases, the deeper and more connected our dialogue becomes. (See Figure 13.1.) It is therefore vital that we are able to create the environment of honest exploration with our prospects and become aware of their most compelling beliefs and emotions—because *that* is where true value is understood. It is there the prospect will feel safe to discuss the "why" behind the "what."

Communicate with Purpose: Map Your Dialogue

It's essential to understand the levels and progression of dialogue in order to create a value proposition. It's also helpful to have a road map, a framework

Value Proposition Dialogue Progression		
Cliché/Initial Meeting	"We're looking for a _____."	Low Trust
Facts/Needs Analysis	"We are experiencing _____."	
Beliefs/Needs Analysis	"Need to invest in modern technology to stay competitive."	High Trust
Emotions/Summary of Findings	"Our employees are afraid of change, and we need help on this journey."	

Figure 13.1   Value Proposition Dialogue Progression

within which you can explore topics with the prospect. By creating a trust-based environment focused solely on raising awareness—*without* the expectation of selling something—you give the prospect the freedom to explore possibilities. This kind of sincere examination is what will elicit a level-four discussion. An easy-to-implement four-step communication format is shown below.

KYOA Dialogue Road Map

1. Make a list of the *topics* they would like to discuss.

2. Clarify your *understanding* of each topic.

3. Choose an order of importance.

4. *Explore* the topics in the following areas:

    a. What are the *facts* of the topic?

    b. How does the topic impact them in these two areas:

        i. If they do *nothing* (cost of *not solving*)?

        ii. If they *do* (benefit to *solve*)?

    c. What is the *financial impact* of the topic?

        i. If they do nothing—downside.

        ii. If they go ahead with your solution—upside.

    d. What are their *personal beliefs and emotions* regarding this topic?

This simple four-step process makes it easier to understand your potential client's issues. By creating a list before you go into detail, you're able to minimize the risk of missing the most important issue. When you explore each issue individually in step four, you help them see the potential effects of either solving the problem or living with it. Keep in mind that our focus is to create a trust-based environment to help your prospect explore without fear of being sold; and that our intent is to help them make a good decision.[1]

Asking versus Telling

Your unique dialogue road map will likely differ from what I've presented here. However, all sales process models should conform to the aforementioned 80/20 rule: 80 percent focused on inquiry (asking)—assisting your client to understand their particular issues—and 20 percent focused on advocating or proposing a solution, if one is warranted. I cannot overstate the importance of this. The reason is that, in order to make a change, customers must fully understand the impact of *not* changing. And it is our collective nature to respond to and accept new ideas using our own cognitive abilities, and not those of others. Therefore, when anyone says to us, "Rob, let me tell you what your problem is . . ." we tend to discount it, and potentially become defensive. Conversely, if we discover the issue and impact on our own, we believe and own it. It is our job to help the prospect understand their issues and their impact through receptive dialogue. A needs analysis, or discovery, is a process to allow the prospect the opportunity to understand and feel the impact. It is a process we do for them, not to them.

> THE NEEDS ANALYSIS IS FOR THE PROSPECT.

A common challenge for salespeople is to listen patiently while a prospect goes through their personal discovery without interrupting. For most salespeople, once you gain competency in knowledge, you will know what the prospect needs well before they do. Yet, it is essential they get to go through a complete process of discovery. We do this by listening, not telling. It is very difficult for a prospect to share their issues if you are shaking your head in anticipation of your answer—as a device to hurry them along—"*OK, I got it. You can stop talking now.*" Even if you have heard the same stories one billion times before, just remember it is their first time sharing it, and it is very meaningful to them. Which is why you are there.

---

[1] To learn more about creating meaningful dialogue, read Mahan Khalsa's book, *Let's Get Real, or Let's Not Play*. In my opinion, it is perhaps the finest guide to creating a value proposition through meaningful dialogue ever written.

Moving too rapidly to the solution stage denies the prospect the chance of feeling the impact and conveys to them that you don't care much about their issues.

> YOU CANNOT TELL A PROSPECT WHAT THEIR PROBLEM IS; YOU MUST ASK.

Communicate with Purpose—Speak in Their Language

When we read sales books or attend training, we're often taught to *find the pain. "Tell me where it hurts, so I can sell you something."* While incredibly efficient, this strategy rarely works—unless the prospect begins the relationship by declaring that "We're in huge pain and we need someone to sell us something to make it go away!" If we attempt to start with the "show me your pain" tactic—or something like it—in almost every other imaginable scenario the prospect's *personal danger alarm* goes off, and the likelihood of having a meaningful dialogue goes down dramatically.

However, we *do* have to have a meaningful conversation with the prospect; otherwise, we can't be of much help to them. So, rather than focus on the pain, it's easier to let them tell us what vernacular in which they are the most comfortable speaking. For example, I often begin conversations with prospects by saying something very generic, such as "Would you mind starting by sharing your situation?" They will typically focus their answer in one of three areas: a desired product or solution, an opportunity for gain, or a problem they wish to solve. If they begin with either the opportunity or problem, we launch right into the Step 1, "make a list" option outlined above.

However, if they choose to begin with the desired solution, then we want to let them begin there. Think of a desired product or solution as a "what" and the issue behind the "what" as the "why." The why shows us how to develop a value proposition. My response to a desired solution is generally, "Great; tell me what you are looking for, or looking to accomplish." I know I'll get to the why eventually, but if we attempt to move there too quickly, we usually get poor results. "Sure, we have the fetzer valve; but tell me, what pains do you have about not having the valve installed?" They will stare like you are a Martian, and then leave. And who could blame them?

> TO GET TO THE "WHY," YOU MUST FIRST EXPLORE THE "WHAT."

If the prospect wishes to begin the dialogue around the solution, then go for it. Remember to stay receptive and genuine; and then when the time is right, you will have earned the right to move the discussion to the "why." After all, this is the reason they're looking in the first place. We call the skill of moving them back to the issue a *pivot*.

The Pivot

A pivot is a common communication redirection technique and the basis for many skills required in selling. Pivots can be used when the prospect asks a question that we can't answer without more information (like a feature of the solution), or when we prefer not to answer until we have developed the value proposition (such as one about price). We also use pivots to regain receptive control of a conversation that has gone too far off topic. It is an essential skill in developing a value proposition, and one that you can practice and improve regularly. A few examples are:

- "Bill, now that you've gotten a brief look at the fetzer valve, would you mind if I ask you what need you have that requires this product?"
- "Bill, I'm happy to show you the fetzer valve; but there are many different models. I would be able to show you the exact kind you need if I could ask you a few questions; would that be okay?"
- "Bill, let's agree that fetzer valve pricing is an important topic. However, before I can provide even a ballpark number, it would be helpful if I could ask you a few more questions. Would that be okay?"

Starting the dialogue where the prospect feels comfortable is smart; it creates an environment of trust and allows you to begin developing deeper level three and level four discussions. You can use a pivot to move them into our communication format where we get to the core issues.

The Value Proposition of a Backhoe

Let's pretend that we work for a company that sells backhoes for approximately $80,000 each, including training, installation, mobilization, and maintenance for the first year. We're currently calling on a ditch-digging company with just two employees: the owner (CEO) and his son, the hand-shovel operator (ditch digger.) The CEO has recently learned of a potential opportunity for new work digging a ditch for a customer who wishes to install an underground drainage system. However, he determines while assessing the project plan and scope of work that his current resource allocation (his son) would take him approximately 400 years to complete the job, thus removing his company from serious consideration. The job pays about $100,000 and has to be finished in eight weeks—399 years and 10 months faster than he could currently complete it. Also, the current opportunity represents the first phase of a potential of 9 total phases in the project.

Communicate with Purpose: Backhoe Company Dialogue

Remember: We must move through the four levels of communication as we construct the dialogue with the backhoe company. Clearly, these folks have needed a backhoe for some time, but something has kept them from taking action. Though this logical point will help you move ahead, you will need to understand the emotional side as well, and understand what has prevented them from purchasing this equipment. The dialogue progression in the form of their responses to your questions is shown in Figure 13.2.

Once you've uncovered the underlying fear as to why they've avoided moving ahead in the past, you are ready to move to the next step: Creating the summary of findings.

Summary of Findings

The *summary of findings* is the tangible result of performing a needs analysis. It forms the foundation that helps the prospect make a reasoned,

Backhoe Company Dialogue Progression		
Cliché/Initial Meeting	"We're looking for a good-looking, cheap backhoe."	Low Trust
Facts/Needs Analysis	"We have an opportunity to bid on a big job."	Low Trust
Beliefs/Needs Analysis	"Need to invest in modern technology to stay competitive."	High Trust
Emotions/Summary of Findings	"We're very afraid of change, and we're glad you are here to help us on this journey."	High Trust

Figure 13.2 Backhoe Company Dialogue Progression

thoughtful decision. The format in Figure 13.2 is a sample structural framework of how this might look. I've seen them as short as a single page, and as long as a small phone book. I personally prefer the executive overview size of a single page, because it forces you to put your thoughts together in a concise manner. The intent of the summary of findings is to convey your comprehension of both the logical and emotional elements of the prospect's situation. Let's face it—the ditch digger needs a backhoe. You're not merely "selling them equipment," you are helping them transform their business and their quality of life. How you present and format your summary of findings will be unique to your situation.

- Key prospect issue: Seeks opportunity to grow business.
- Current situation: One owner (dad) and one shovel technician (son). Very constricted revenue potential due to operational limitations.
- Backhoe investment: $80,000
- Associated revenue: $100,000
- Return on investment: $20,000
- Cost not to solve: If they elect not to go forward, they would lose the opportunity to earn $20,000, and get an $80,000 asset that could become a huge revenue generator and potentially transform their business.
- Benefit to solve: If they go ahead with the order, they earn the $20,000 as well as the prospective to bid on additional work that the sewer client has—and nine more phases of the project. The $80,000 investment could yield a potential $920,000 in increased revenue to the business from the contract.
- Critical sales issue: Fear of financing. Lack of experience securing phase one contract. Operator training.

Value Propositions Don't Have to Be Written

However, value propositions aren't only for large construction equipment; and they don't have to be delivered in a Summary of Findings. For example, if you sell clothing, electronics, or musical instruments, you create value propositions when you help the client understand how darn good they will look in the swanky suit, how much they will truly enjoy watching their favorite movie or sporting event on the new television, or how satisfied they'll feel once they finally master the ukulele. You create value propositions by helping the client comprehend the value they will receive by owning your product or service.

The Value of a Value Proposition

The value proposition is the fulcrum of the sales process. The more prospects you help understand both the cost of not solving as well as the benefits of solving their particular issues, the more prospects will become your customers. However, in some cases, the *real* value is created when they *don't* become your customer.

The Perfect Needs Analysis

Several years ago, I inquired about having corrective laser eye surgery. My vision isn't terribly bad; I only wear corrective lenses for driving (especially at night), or when I'm in a movie theatre. And while I don't yet need reading glasses, it is getting harder to read with my eyeglasses on, so I constantly take them off or push them up on top of my head when I need to read. Therefore, I spend a great deal of time either looking for my glasses, or walking around with them on top of my head, while looking for my glasses. It's somewhat pathetic.

So laser eye surgery seemed like an option. I found an eye surgeon through a referral and called his office for an appointment. After checking in, the staff had me fill out an extensive medical history, and then a brief description of my current situation, what I was trying to fix, and so on. Additionally, they wanted to know what I did for a living, sports, and hobbies. It was a detailed questionnaire.

Once complete, I began the process of having every eye examination conceivable. There must have been over 20 separate tests, which took a total of about 90 minutes. Then, a technician put drops in my eyes to dilate them, and put me in a darkened room to watch a video on the "dangers of eye surgery" while my eyes became fully dilated. The video was factual and a little scary—although the success rate of this particular procedure is extremely high, I appreciated knowing what the risks were.

The technician ran several more tests, after which I returned to the darkened room to wait to speak to the ophthalmologist. Eventually, I was escorted into his office. After the introductions, he began a dialogue with me that closely resembled the four levels of communication. He began by reviewing the results of the eye exams. Then he went into great detail about my work, hobbies, and attitudes about life. At one point, I forgot the purpose of the dialogue was about eye surgery. Finally, he said, "Rob, I could do the surgery for you, and you would never have to wear glasses to drive or at the movies. However, you would immediately have to wear glasses to read. In other words, you would be trading one pair of glasses on top of your head for another." He then continued, "If I were to recommend this for you, I'd have to recommend it for myself—we have almost identical eyesight—and I would never have this surgery."

I was stunned. He could have sold me the eye surgery and I would have done it—and would be wearing reading glasses today. However, he put my needs above his. He completed a very thorough needs analysis and developed a value proposition that favored doing nothing.

Performing a needs analysis and developing a value proposition is a chance for you to develop a relationship, gain a deeper understanding of what drives your prospect, and guide them through the catharsis of understanding the connection of their issues and the impact of not solving them. In some cases, the best course of action will be no course of action. How you conduct this process gives your prospect a glimpse of what working with you will be like.

If the cost of not solving looks like it costs nothing, doing nothing will always win.

Chapter 13 Recap: Gather the Facts and Develop a Value Proposition

- A *value proposition* is the logical argument for *what makes your product or service worth buying*. If you are able to specify a strong value proposition that supports your solution during the needs analysis phase, the prospect will typically move forward with your offer.

- The tangible result of creating a value proposition is often referred to as ROI, or return on investment, which you can calculate by subtracting the required investment from the value received.

- Value isn't what your product does; it's what your product does *for the customer*. The stuff you sell has no intrinsic or inherent value; its worth is derived from what it allows the purchaser to do as a result of buying it.

- Value is not synonymous with a low price, but rather with a big return on investment that we can measure in how much enjoyment we derive, the problem it solves, or the opportunities it creates.

- In the KYOA sales process, we generate the value proposition during the needs analysis and summary of findings phase. The amount of time and effort you spend developing this will be determined by the size and complexity of the opportunity.

- It is vital that we are able to create the environment of *honest exploration* with our prospects and become aware of their most compelling beliefs and emotions—because *that* is where true value is understood. That is where we help them discover the "why" behind the "what."

- It's helpful to develop a *framework* within which you can explore topics with the prospect by following these steps: (1) make a list of the topics they would like to discuss, (2) clarify your understanding of each topic, (3) choose an order of importance, and (4) explore the topics in detail.

- It's best to let customers tell us—in the vernacular in which they are the most comfortable speaking—what about their situation they're trying to change, or what particular problem they want to solve.

- A *pivot* is a common communication redirection technique that we can use when the prospect asks a question that we can't answer without more information, when we prefer not to answer until we have developed the value proposition (such as a feature or the price), or to regain receptive control of a conversation that has gone too far off topic.

- The *summary of findings* is the tangible result of performing a needs analysis and is where we articulate the value proposition. It forms the foundation that helps the prospect make a reasoned, thoughtful decision. The shorter and more concise this can be, the better.

- A value proposition is the *fulcrum* of the sales process. The more prospects you help in understanding both the cost of not solving as well as the benefits of solving their particular issues, the more prospects who will become your customers.

Engineer a Decision

Helping Your
Customers Buy

E ngineering a decision is the process wherein you help your prospect make a good decision. If you have assessed their situation properly and developed a compelling value proposition—one that supports an argument for moving ahead—then the good decision you are going to help them make will be to buy your product. Otherwise—as in the laser eye surgeon example at the end of Chapter 13—you would likely have halted the sales process at the end of the needs analysis phase when you reviewed the summary of findings with your prospect. This is where you begin to shift your focus from a mutual exploration of the prospects issues to advocating a course of action. To paraphrase renowned business author Stephen Covey, you move from seeking to understand to being understood.

The ability to successfully engineer a decision depends completely on the quality of the value proposition. If the prospect sees a high reward/low risk value proposition, they will likely buy. If they don't, you could lose to "no decision" or a competitor, or be forced to substantially discount your offer to tilt the value proposition in your favor.

Rob's Rule of Closing is: *A strong close doesn't overcome weak qualifying.*

If a strong closing did overcome weak qualifying, I could have written a book titled *Top 10 Power Closes to Slam Deals and Slay Your Competitors!: Power Closes for Power Closers*. And, it would have been the cure-all, magical, acai berry of closing manuals.

Engineer a Decision—Prospects Close Themselves

If you have developed a compelling value proposition for the prospect, engineering a decision will take about five seconds; it's merely a matter of handling logistics. After reviewing the summary of findings, the prospect might say, "*So, what's our next step?*" Your answer hopefully won't be "*Hey, you can't buy yet. I haven't shown you my Demo!*" A better response would be, "Let's review the paperwork and get you started."

The Logic and Emotion of Buying

It would be great if all sales happened by having the prospect close themselves, but they don't. In the continuum of the logic and emotion of buying, making a decision swings hard to the emotional side. It is difficult to choose—even when the logic is overwhelming, the cost of not solving is huge, and the benefits are many. People will put off making commitments that include risk and uncertainty simply to avoid them. That is why most sales opportunities end up in the file known as "stalled." Nevertheless, our job is to walk customers through this process and get them what they really want—a solved problem or an opportunity seized. You have to be well prepared to get them over this hump.

Good at Selling, Bad at Closing . . . Not

I get calls from sales managers and salespeople needing help with "closing skills." Their complaints are very consistent: "Rob, I'm really good at selling; I'm just not good at closing." My response is typically, "Look, you are horrible at selling and closing and there is nothing you can do to improve. So, quit whining, and go find another line of work—like ditch digging." I really don't say that; and of course, I don't think it. Heck, I just wrote that to get a cheap laugh! Struggling to close sales is more likely a result of not having enough prospects to work, working with unqualified prospects, not establishing a strategic competitive advantage, or rushing to present a solution without developing a value proposition—all of which can be improved through hard work and focus. Many opportunities—especially competitive ones—require intense work in the engineering decision phase to secure the sale.

The Concept of "Best Thinking"

A key component of engineering a decision is to frame your solution in the correct light. It shouldn't be a one-size-fits-all, *take it or leave it* proposition; rather, it should be something like "Based on our last discussion, our team huddled up and developed a scenario for solving your problem that we feel is ideal for you. However, despite our experience, we still occasionally miss getting it exactly right. Our purpose today is to simply present and discuss our *best thinking* on the subject. If, as we're going through this process, you see something that isn't cutting it, please say so. That way, we can continue to refine our best thinking in developing an exactly right solution for you. Fair enough?"

There is nothing to be gained by putting the prospect in the position of having to choose between "yes or no." Creating instead an environment of collaboration around best thinking, we make it okay for the prospect to object to components of the solution without rejecting the entire relationship. Introducing the concept of best thinking into your sales process will have a profound impact on how you approach selling—and how your prospects respond to you.

The Mechanics and Process of Engineering a Decision

It's impossible for me to accurately describe the exact approach you should use to help prospects engineer a decision without knowing your particular selling situation. I'll therefore discuss a general business-to-business approach, leaving you to interpret the rest. Since decisions typically require meetings—either face-to-face or over the phone—we'll work as if we will meet in person.

Presentation Prep

Let's begin by imagining what your prospect's premeeting checklist would look like. It is important to consider and prepare for the questions and objections you may likely encounter. Our industry's list would look something like the one below, which we crafted from interviewing chief executives about their primary concerns when contemplating a large capital investment. Review this list from the prospect's perspective and consider how you would answer these questions for them. Are there any other questions you don't see that should be added?

Prospect's Predecision Meeting Checklist

- What decision are we being asked to make?
- What problem does it solve or opportunity does it create?
- What is the impact of delay or denial?
- What are our other options for solving the problem?
- What criteria are we using to make a decision?
- What is the value proposition?
- How do we measure and define success?
- Who at our firm is responsible for the success of the project?
- Why is firm X the best choice as a partner?

Your Predecision Meeting Checklist

In addition to the prospects checklist, you have your own checklist. Before proceeding to a presentation meeting, it is essential that you are able to answer these questions as well:

- Are our desired outcomes in sync? Are we expecting a yes or no decision, or are they're still reviewing other options?
- What are the objections we are likely to encounter?
- Are the right people invited to the meeting? What is our exit strategy if not?
- Are we in a position to engineer a decision?
- What is our presentation road map?
- Do we have the right "best thinking" solution and pricing?

The Meeting

I prefer to meet with prospects in the morning. My experience with afternoon meetings is not as good, especially if there is a product presentation involved that might require sitting in a darkened room, staring at a Power-Point presentation while attempting to keep attendees from falling asleep. If I'm presenting to a group, I like to print out the key issues on a huge sheet of paper and tape it to the wall. I also like to include the actual cost of not solving along with each issue, to help participants understand why we are actually meeting. The wall becomes like a great big refrigerator door, with urgent information posted here and there. When it's taped to the wall, it makes it much harder to ignore.

I like to begin a presentation with introductions and confirm that the necessary players are present. If someone who should be there isn't—especially the financial authorizer for the project—I am likely to reschedule the meeting. My experience is that if they aren't there, they aren't interested in buying, and we're merely spinning our wheels. It's better to simply let the attendees know that your corporate policy requires you to present your best thinking to *all* key decision-makers, and that you are happy to reschedule. If they are interested, they'll reschedule. If they're not, they will ask that you leave the proposal behind—which you will not do.

Once the introductions are complete, I'll review the agenda and confirm the meeting timeframe. (I make sure to leave at least $\frac{1}{3}$ of the meeting's total time free for an open discussion on the issues at the end.) It is essential to have enough time to discuss the solution as a group—even more essential than giving your demo. Really.

After this, I'll begin by reviewing the issues. I'll ask if anything new has arisen, make sure that we're covering the right topics, and that the parties agree to the cost of not solving. This is important to establish, and if we're good there, then we can proceed to the presentation.

Presenting Your Solution

Presentations differ dramatically depending on what the product or service offered is and to whom it is being presented. For example, presentations to executives are very different than those to users. However, the underlying purpose doesn't change; its point is always to convey your plan for assisting the prospect in solving their problem, capitalizing on their opportunity, or increasing their enjoyment. The elements of a presentation should include only whatever it takes to demonstrate your ability to help. A good rule of thumb is to appeal to the interests of the highest-ranking person in the room. If it is the business owner, for instance, concentrate on the financial aspects of the offer—

including total cost of ownership, lease or financing information, and reliability data. And keep in mind that if this person is a high D personality type, you likely want to keep your discussion under 15 minutes.

Presentation Road Map

Regardless of whether what you sell is tangible or intangible, your presentation is the natural next step that follows from the summary of findings. As opposed to the popular "throw spaghetti at the wall" approach of showing every imaginable solution until your audience falls asleep, your information should be based on the list of key issues discussed during the needs analysis. For example, a presentation road map in the technology arena might be as follows.

- Explain their current situation.
- Discuss the problem or opportunity impact of the current situation, including the cost of not solving and the benefit to solving.
- Provide a quick demonstration of how much smoother and better the process will work once solved with your solution.
- Recap how this solves their problem (value proposition) and creates value for the company.
- Elicit feedback on solution.
- Repeat as needed.

Your presentation process might differ from this, depending on your product or service. However, having a road map based on exploring your best thinking and connecting the issues to the future "solved" state usually works quite well. You and your prospect need to agree that the proposed solution for each issue could work before you move on to the next step of review options.

> PRESENTATIONS SHOW THE FUTURE STATE: PROBLEM SOLVED, OPPORTUNITY REALIZED.

Reviewing Options for Proceeding

Once you have completed the presentation, you can then review options for proceeding—including legal matters, logistics, scope, and resource allocation, or any other number of elements. A quote, summary of findings, plan letter, proposal, or statement of work are all possibilities that can serve as the basis for reviewing options.

Eliciting and Receiving Feedback

It is useful to have a mechanism for eliciting and receiving feedback on your proposed solution. If the opportunity is closable on the spot, you will be looking for an up or down/yes or no response for each solution component. If the opportunity isn't immediately closable, you can measure feedback on a scale of one to ten. For example, *"It is essential to share your honest feedback to ensure we create a solution that will work for you. I'd like to suggest we work on a scale of one to ten—one being the worst idea ever, and ten being perfect in every way. As we go through our session, we'll poll you to see how confident you are that each component would work for you. Please don't be afraid to give it a low score if you feel it wouldn't work. That is the only way we can be sure to get to a workable solution."* This approach is particularly essential if you are presenting to a group or several groups. Your goal is to create an environment where each member of the team feels comfortable raising their concerns about your offer. This requires a trust-based environment, open to collaborative exploration. You and your prospect are working in a dynamic setting to collaboratively create a solution; you are not presenting a static solution for them to either accept or reject.

An especially powerful way to work through this phase is to put the list of key issues and decisions to be made up on the white board. That way, as you are working through them, you can have the prospect check them off the list.

Choice in Pricing

It is helpful as you review options with the prospect to give him or her options for participating when possible. Similar to the small, medium, and large options in the fast-food industry—and practically everywhere else—buyers like to have a choice in what they purchase.

Mom's New Heater

Several years ago, my mom's home heating system began to falter, and for good reason: It had been in service for nearly 50 years. To replace it, we planned to get quotes from three heating and air conditioning companies; since we had no experience with any HVAC companies, this was a way to reduce our potential risk. The first company we called scheduled a time to come do a needs analysis. The owner spent nearly two hours in the home both completing a technical assessment and discussing my mom's future plans for the house—a relevant topic as she is—as they say in the Midwest—no spring chicken.

After he finished the needs analysis, he called me (as the kid designated to help mom with this project) to review his findings. The heating system was long past its useful life expectancy and needed immediate replacement. We explored various topics: Did we want to upgrade and add air conditioning? Did we want variable zones? Did we have a particular brand loyalty? Would she want a best-of-the-best-available system, with a lifetime guarantee? Perhaps the 20-year guarantee would be okay. We had a very good conversation, and I got the sense he was trying to create a solution that would work for her needs. At the end of our call, he told us that he would come up with some options for us to consider, e-mail them to me, and then reconnect on the phone to review and discuss. What I received looked a little like what's shown in Figure 14.1.

- The pricing included multiple options based on different configurations.
- Each option had options for various grades of equipment.
- There were three levels of service plans.

This strategy of creating a complex value pricing metric was a brilliant way to change our dialogue from "Are you going to buy?" to "Let's explore what options seem to make the most sense for you." After receiving the quote from this particular company, I completely abandoned the notion of getting the other ones. My logic was this: the owner spent time to understand mom's issues, and she and I developed a feeling that he was both competent and had the intent to be helpful. Plus, his pricing strategy satisfied my need to shop price by creating options.

The idea of tiered pricing isn't new: Sears & Roebuck pioneered the idea of "Good, Better, and Best" in their paint and tire departments in the middle of the last century. Consumers are accustomed to variable pricing strategies: consider movie theater popcorn sizes. A typical three-tiered popcorn pricing set drives consumers to buy the gargantuan size. A well-known national hamburger chain created a monstrous triple burger,

Mom's AC Quote	Good	Better	Best
Option 1 (single zone, no a/c)			
Variable 1 10 year warranty	$ XXX		
Variable 2 20 year warranty		$ X,XXX	
Variable 3 lifetime warranty			$ XX,XXX
Option 2 (single zone, with a/c)			
Variable 1 10 year warranty	$ XXX		
Variable 2 20 year warranty		$ X,XXX	
Variable 3 lifetime warranty			$ XX,XXX
Option 3 (multiple zone, with a/c)			
Variable 1 10 year warranty	$ XXX		
Variable 2 20 year warranty		$ X,XXX	
Variable 3 lifetime warranty			$ XX,XXX
Service Plans			
Bronze Service	$ XXX		
Silver Service		$ X,XXX	
Elite Service			$ XX,XXX
Installation and Service Total			

Figure 14.1   Mom's AC Quote

simply to make the double burger the commonsense alternative . . . and they succeeded in creating that impression.

DO YOURSELF AND YOUR PROSPECTS A BIG FAVOR: CREATE CHOICE IN PRICING.

Another option for choice in pricing is a concept known as value pricing. The idea behind the concept is to base pricing on how much value is created, rather than on a percentage markup over costs. Ronald J. Baker[1] is a pioneering value pricing thought leader. He has written a number of books on this subject, including one entitled *Pricing on Purpose*, in which he explains the concept of how and why people buy. An area of focus is his work with professional knowledge firms to move away from their dependence on the billable hour, a classic cost-based model, to a value

[1] Learn more about Baker's methods at the VeraSage Institute by visiting www.verasage.com.

pricing model. The result is higher profitability for the firm, motivated employees, and happier customers. Ron and I have worked together on many workshops and presentations, since creating a value proposition is an essential foundational component to value pricing.

Closing—a process we call engineering a Decision, because we're attempting to help clients make informed decisions—carries baggage from sales practices that imply that the process is about doing something *to* someone instead of *for* someone. As both a student and a practitioner of this profession, I've heard—and admittedly, used—some pretty wild closing lines. A few of my favorites are listed below. The reality is that there is no magic line that will make someone buy. There is your way . . . your authentic way of helping your prospects through the process of making a decision.

The Top Ten Power Closes of All Time!

1. *Let's Make a Deal Today Close:* "*Floyd, what do we need to do to put you in this ERP Software today?!*"

2. *Create Urgency to Buy Close:*
   "*Tom, that model backhoe is not being manufactured anymore, and we only have this one left. The new model might be more expensive and have fewer features. I'm don't know this for sure, but I'd hate to see you hesitate to take action and lose out on a terrific opportunity to own this legend of backhoes. Let's at least get the paperwork taken care of today. Press hard, Tom. There are at least five copies attached to that contract.*"

3. *Find a Way to Win Close:*
   "*Floyd, in addition to the fact that you hate me and our company, our product doesn't fit any of your needs, and the price is more than double our nearest competitor—is there any reason why we can't ink a deal today? Don't answer that before I show you our contract. If you were going to buy today, all you would need to do is sign here. See? Right here. What? Yes. If you sign the contract, I will commit to leave and never come back, and you have my word on that Floyd, which is kinda like gold. Yes. Right here. Floyd, you won't regret this for long. Press hard on that contract, Floyd.*"

4. *Play on Their Fears Close:*
   "*Chris, I guess you know what happened to the Smiths, right? Do you really want to be the only house on the block without a working alarm system? Press hard, Chris.*"

5. *Reduced to the Ridiculous Close:*

"How many times do you think you'll actually wear that pair of blue jeans, Tom? Let's say at least one hundred times. That will be impressive, Tom. Now, I know that a $180 dollar investment for blue jeans might seem ridiculous, and even slightly stupid—until you spread the blue jean investment amount over their useful life of roughly one hundred instances of wearing them. That means you are only investing $1.80 per instance. Now, Tom—isn't it worth $1.80 to look like the lady killer you are? Dude, if I were a chick, I'd be checking you out. Sign here, Tom. Tom?"

6. *Keep Selling until They Scream Close:*

"Bill, those shoes look great; but they seem lonely. How about another pair to go with it? What about some socks? We have a special, 'buy ten pairs, get the next half-price' offer. Seriously Bill, what are your plans for taking care of your shoe investment? I assume you'll need shoe trees, right? Two words, Bill—shoe cream. You have got to have shoe cream. Bill, did I mention we now sell shoe insurance? Terrific! With the shoe trees, 11 pairs of socks, the cream, and the insurance, that'll be $1,100 dollars. Press hard, Bill. Are you sure you don't want that second pair?"

7. *My Kid Needs Surgery Close:*

"Bill, I realize this may not be the ideal time for you to take advantage of our offer. Hey, have you seen a picture of my son Johnny? Look at that poor guy. He needs very expensive head transplant surgery that we were hoping to get for him with the commission check from this sale. It's okay; he'll probably live without it, for a while. Oh? Gosh Bill, that would just be great if you could do it today. Press hard, Bill."

8. *I'm an Idiot Close:*

"Jerry, I have a confession to make. Last week, to celebrate Presidents' Day, we had very special pricing on the ERP software you are considering—and it would have made a significant reduction in your initial investment. But like an idiot, I forgot to notify you, which is completely my fault, and I got in really big trouble for not letting you know. But I've got great news! My manager approved a one-time, never-before-or-again, extension on the incentive, just for you, if you buy right now. Just sign here, Jerry. Here's my pen. Be sure to press hard, Jerry."

9. *Appeal to Their Ego Close:*

"We reserved these top-floor condos only for the select few who could afford such luxury. We reserved it for you, Tom. We know you can do it. Become the heavy hitter you were meant to be. When your friends and coworkers find out you live here, they will be stunned with envy. This is *your chance to shine. Just sign here to begin your new, enchanted life-style. Press hard, Tom."*

10. *Reverse Psychology Close:*

"Tom, perhaps you aren't ready to declare your spot as 'world's biggest heavy hitter' by claiming the most luxurious, intriguing condo address in town like yours. . . . Oh, really? You are? I knew you were. Tom, be the heavy hitter right now. Sign here. Press hard, Tom."

Rob's Secret to Closing

Be your authentic self.

You are what your customers are buying. They believe in your intent and your competency to deliver. Engineering a decision is the result of a lot of hard work. My personal favorite close is the assumptive close. By the time you are ready to make the prospect your customer—and begin to deliver the results they need—the act of "closing the sale" is merely a small step of authorizing the paperwork. *"We've reviewed the issues, and it seems as though we have a workable solution. We need to get started by taking care of the paper-work and scheduling the implementation. Next Thursday looks good for us; how about for you?"* More than likely, they will say Thursday looks great. If they hesitate, it is probably fear creeping in. In the next chapter, we'll look at a couple of simple strategies to help them work through it.

Chapter 14 Recap: Engineer a Decision: Helping Your Customers Buy

- *Engineering a decision* is the process whereby you help your prospect make a good decision. If you have assessed their situation properly and developed a compelling value proposition, then the good decision you are going to help them make will be to buy your product.

- *Rob's Rule of Closing* is that a strong closing doesn't overcome weak qualifying.

- *Emotion* often plays a more prominent role in decision making than *logic* does. It's difficult for potential clients to commit, even when the logic is overwhelming, the cost of not solving is huge, and the benefits are many. People prefer to avoid risk.

- Salespeople who claim to be good at selling but "bad at closing" likely do not have enough prospects to work, are working with unqualified prospects, are not developing their strategic competitive advantage, or are rushing to present a solution without developing a value proposition.

- Creating an environment of collaboration around best thinking makes it okay for the prospect to object to components of the solution without rejecting the entire offer.

- Salespeople must envision what the *prospect's premeeting checklist* might look like in order to consider and prepare for questions and objections they may encounter. Additionally, salespeople must prepare a list of their own questions that need to be answered.

- It is usually best to meet with prospects in person, and in the morning; introductions and confirmations that all key players are present should come first.

- No matter what your industry, presenting your solution should always *convey your plan for assisting the prospect in solving their problem, capitalizing on their opportunity, or increasing their enjoyment.*

- The next step is to *review the options* for moving forward and elicit feedback from the group. You want to give your prospects options for participating when possible, because buyers like to have a say in what they purchase.

- Tiered pricing is one popular method for offering customers choices along a continuum of options. A close cousin to this approach is *value pricing*, which bases pricing on how much value is created, rather on a percentage markup over costs.

- Despite the myriad of closing "tactics" that have been touted, the best approach is simply to be your true, authentic self. Your customers are buying *you*; they believe in your intent and your competency to deliver.

Don't Screw Up

Handling Questions, Concerns, and Objections

Human beings exhibit strange behavior at times; for example, when asked to make a commitment during the sales process. People get nervous when they have to commit to something; even when it's something that we want and need. An *objection* is often an underlying psychological desire on the part of the prospect to have the salesperson reassure them that the purchase is a good idea. However, instead of saying *"You know, I'm just a little nervous about the commitment, and would really appreciate it if you would review the issues, cost of not solving, your solution, and why partnering with you is the right move"*—it often comes out as *"We're going to need to think about this."*

Prospects like to use price as a smokescreen objection to mask the real issue that's preventing them from buying, as they feel it will be impossible for the salesperson to handle it without dropping their price. And if the salesperson *does* drop their price, known as the *drop your pants close*, the prospect has managed to lower the price, thereby reducing the risk to a more tolerable level.

Prospects will occasionally ask a *question*. This can be dangerous, of course, as there is a chance the salesperson isn't listening, and answering questions without listening often leads to answering the *wrong* question—accompanied by a 10-minute diatribe that wrecks the entire sale. Or perhaps the salesperson launches into an hour-long demonstration in an area of the product marked "Beta" with which they are not entirely familiar—which causes the product to crash and also wrecks the entire sale.

Occasionally, it isn't the prospect who is concerned; it's us. Perhaps the prospect isn't keeping his commitments, returning phone calls, or granting access to the right people. Instead of acting like an adult and raising the issue, salespeople often ignore the warning signs of a derailed sales process and march forward with an opportunity that has little to no chance of progressing. My experience as a sales manager is that many of these opportunities show up as "A" prospects on the salesperson's 90-Day Hot List, with a 90 percent chance of closing this quarter. Ha—right.

Three forms of communications malfunctions—questions, concerns and objections—don't only show up when trying to close a sale; they can emerge at any time throughout the entire sales process. Consider the following situations.

- *Creating an opportunity*: Let's face it; we're busy. And when a stranger calls, it's easy to blow them off, even if we are interested in what they are selling.
- *Value proposition*: Prospects feel uneasy about sharing sensitive data with people they don't know well. The reluctance manifests as either a concern on the part of the salesperson or a stall or an objection from the prospect.
- *Engineering a decision*: It's easy to opt for "no decision" when considering several alternatives and preparing to commit, since the perceived risk is lower.

Be prepared to respond to questions, concerns, or objections throughout the sales process. Our role is to help the prospect make a good decision, which we do by helping them overcome their natural response of doubt and anxiety when faced with new situations. There is no *"right way"* to handle these obstacles; there is simply *your way*. Your personality and that of your prospect are hugely important in discerning how to handle communication. The examples contained in this chapter are designed to stimulate your thinking on how to handle questions, concerns, and objections. You likely get the same questions and objections over and over, so remember: learning how to respond to them is a *skill*. There are strategies to modify the sales process to pre-emptively deal with them and ways to respond when they arise. Once you learn these, you will use them constantly, and you will sell more.

Ask yourself: How good would you be if you practiced handling a "need to think about it" objection 1,000 times? *You would be bulletproof.* Let's get started. We'll begin with the skills around handling questions.

Handling Questions

Questions from prospects can sound a lot like an objection. For example, "Why is it priced this way?" could be either a question or an objection. The price question could be a mask for "this price is too high"; conversely, it could simply be an honest question on how the pricing works. How we respond can impact the outcome of the sale. It's important to establish an easy-to-follow framework for handling questions.

1. *Align:* Provide reinforcement for asking the question.
2. *Clarify:* Clarify the question to ensure you understand it.
3. *Explain:* Provide an answer to the question.
4. *Confirm:* Confirm that the prospect is satisfied with the answer.

When asked *"Why is it priced this way?"* we could *align* with the asker in a number of effective ways.

- "Thanks for asking that question."
- "That is a great question."
- "That's a tough one, let's talk about it."

Aligning first allows you to reinforce your commitment to mutual trust-based exploration. If you were to react in an aggressive, trite, or defensive manner, the dialogue, for all practical purposes, would be over. Even if your initial internal response is negative, remember—your brain has a history of fallibility. This method of responding immediately in a positive way emphasizes to our prospects that we encourage dialogue about their honest feelings.

Attached to the end of your alignment statement is a *clarification* question. This is a good idea for every question, as we often don't hear, listen to, or understand the real intent behind the question that was actually asked. When someone is asked to reiterate their question, they are able to further clarify their own reasons for asking. This approach keeps you in a receptive position and allows you to really understand their question before answering.

- "Thanks for asking that question. Exactly what do you mean by [insert topic or phrase used by asker]?"
- "I really appreciate your interest. *That price* means many different things to different organizations; how exactly would you define it?"
- "That is a great question. I'm not sure I follow you; could you explain further what *priced that way* means to you?"

Once the prospect further clarifies their question, you are in a position to answer. Typically, there are three explanation options:

1. We do it.
2. We need more information before answering.
3. We don't do it.

The best strategy for option number one is to answer the question and ask if the prospect needs further information rather than just launching into a detailed explanation. For example, "Yes, the backhoe will dig a hole fifteen feet deep" is probably sufficient. If you can't answer a question yourself and need to call on outside resources, make a note and a commitment to follow up. As a rule, triple the length of time your brain is telling you as the time frame for responding. There is nothing worse than needlessly losing a prospect's trust because you make an unreasonable commitment that you can't keep. This extra built-in time will make you look like a hero when you respond quicker than promised.

This brings us to the toughest part: getting a question for which you do not have a solution. Here are three possible outcomes for the "*We don't do it*" answer.

1. It's no big deal.
2. There is a work-around.
3. It is a big deal.

Most questions asked in the sales process are prompted by curiosity and don't have a huge impact on the outcome. For example, *"Could we get the backhoe in pink?"* could be answered *"We don't do it"* or could lead to a work-around such as *"We could have it painted for you."* Until you clarify and truly understand the thinking behind the question, it's difficult to know or understand why a company would want a pink backhoe. Is it the owner's passing whimsy, or part of a color strategy to improve the brand's visibility? You won't know until you clarify the question. The rubber meets the road when it is a big deal to the prospect and you don't provide a solution. Cases wherein you can't do something and it's a "big deal"— which are rare—are best handled in the following two-step method.

1. *Explain your position.*

   "This isn't part of our business model, and we would not be able to provide a solution for you. We'd be happy to work with you in any way possible to assist you in this."

2. *Complete your thought with a question.*

   "Knowing that we won't have a solution for _____, is this a red flag, or is it okay to proceed?" If it is something that will hinder your ability to continue the sales process, it's better to know now. The client will decide what is in their best interest.

Interestingly, clients frequently choose options that are not as feature-rich in order to work with companies whom they trust. Your willingness to be open and honest about potential weaknesses in your product shows your true intent. The way that you handle these types of issues will go a long way to attract your prospects to you.

Once you have explained your answer, it's a good idea to *confirm* that they understand your response and that it will work for them. For example, *"Just to make sure we're on the same page, you'd like the backhoe to be painted pink as part of your branding strategy. We agree it's important to the success of the project, and we will add the painting to the scope of the project. Fair enough?"*

To recap, don't take handling questions for granted. Adopt this simple four-step process of align, clarify, explain, and confirm: ACEC.

Concerns

If you are going to hit the ditch in a sales process, doing so earlier is preferable than later. There are few things worse than rocking through a sales opportunity only to have it derail at the last minute. When we conduct post–lost sale reviews, we often see huge warning signs that were missed early in the process. Salespeople tend to ignore that sense that some-thing-is-wrong-with-the-sale, and instead move boldly forward. Perhaps they are hoping to use a power close to pull victory out of the jaws of de-feat. *Not likely.* This reluctance to confront reality is sometimes connected with fear of failure, a lack of opportunities to work, or a simple misunder-standing of how to handle a *concern*. Mastering this skill begins by recog-nizing that it is senseless to extend an opportunity if the prospect isn't qualified or willing to engage at the appropriate level. It's best to deal with it immediately and move on to other opportunities. Stopping a doomed sales process early in the process isn't failing, it's winning: win-ning more time to go work a real opportunity.

Common Warning Signs That Your Sales Opportunity Could Be in Trouble:
- Your prospect suddenly stops returning your calls and "goes dark."
- They won't give you access to the money person.
- They ask for more than they are willing to provide.
- They are not keeping all competitors at the same stage of the sales process.
- They attempt to refuse to follow your process.

The best way to handle a concern that *something doesn't feel quite right* is to say it. An example of what to say could be *"I get the feeling by the fact that you are refusing to give us access to your financial sponsor that we may have a problem. As you know, this is an essential step for us in the process of creating a solution for you, and without access, this simply won't be possible. What do you think we should do?"*

Ordinarily, this will bring the issue to the surface and make it easier to handle. Either the client will say *"Thanks for bringing this up; we need to put this on the back burner for a while"* or *"Thanks for bringing this up. I apologize for being so tardy. I've been procrastinating and feeling guilty. Let's set up the meeting right now."* Either way, you're a winner. You have a prospect more fully engaged in the process, or you have more time to prospect. Moreover, you have confronted your fear head-on, which means you are an Ass Kicker.

Objections

Salespeople typically get less than five objections, and they're most often about a delay, a price issue, or something technical in nature. Managing objections is a fairly easy skill to master, as there are so few to learn. Take a moment to consider the most common objections you hear; I bet you have a hard time coming up with five.

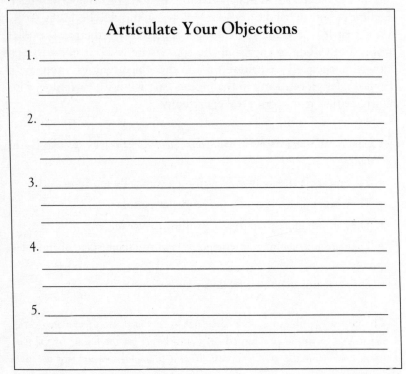

Articulate Your Objections

1. _____
   _____
   _____

2. _____
   _____
   _____

3. _____
   _____
   _____

4. _____
   _____
   _____

5. _____
   _____
   _____

The key to handling an objection is to know exactly what the objection is. Prospects are usually reluctant to share their concerns with salespeople, which means that you have to develop a process for helping them speak their minds and share their concerns. While there are an infinite number of techniques for this, most salespeople find one or two methods for handling their five most common objections. For our purposes, we'll focus on three.

The No-Brainer

The first of these techniques is designed to approach the issue in a non-threatening way if the prospect isn't bringing it up. It's very similar to how we might handle a concern.

"Jim, I hope you don't mind me saying this, but something seems out of whack and, truthfully, I can't understand why we are not further along in the process of working together. When I look at the value proposition we have created, it seems like this would be a no-brainer decision to make. Level with me; is there something I should know?"

The Real Deal

The second objection handling skill is designed to use price to get at the real objection.

"Jim, I'd like to explore the opportunity with you. Let's assume that price is not a factor in your decision. Taking price completely off the table, how do you feel this solution would really work for you on a scale of one to ten?"

If they answer with a ten, thank them and then ask them why. This will confirm the reasons why they will go ahead with you. If they answer anything other than a ten, thank them as well, and then ask them *"Jim, what would you have to see in our solution to make it a 10?"* This will help you home in on the real issue.

Successfully handling price objections in the "engineer a decision" phase requires that the prospect understand both the value proposition and your unique strategic advantage. This is especially important in competitive situations, since prospects—when forced to choose between two proposed solutions—will always choose the less expensive option unless there are compelling reasons to do otherwise. Without being able to differentiate your offering by creating unique strategic advantages (see Chapter 4) and a solid value proposition that ties their success to your firm (see Chapters 11 to 13), the client will typically opt to save a few bucks, because *in the absence of value, all you have is price.*

The Stallinator

The third technique can be used when the prospect brings their doubt to your attention, and is attempting to stall the sale. This skill is most commonly taught as a derivative of the *feel, felt, found* objection-handling procedure. *"This is awfully expensive; I don't think we can move forward."* There are four possible steps you can take to move past this hurdle.

1. Try to respond by confirming their feeling and developing a sense of alignment. "Jim, I understand how you could say (feel) that; it

does seem expensive. Heck, everything seems expensive these days!"

2. Include "others" in your follow-up statement: "You're not alone either; a lot of our customers responded (felt) exactly the same way, before they had the chance to seriously look at the facts."

3. Introduce a pivot statement: "It only seems expensive until you know how much more it will do for you than the cheap ones. What you want is quality, at a fair price."

4. Make your last statement a closing question. "Jim, let's get this done today so we can begin creating the value you are looking for."

A Common Objection during the Initiating Opportunity Phase

As I stated at the beginning of the chapter, there isn't a "right" or "wrong" way to respond to questions, raise concerns, and handle objections. That being said, I've included a few actual options for how you might consider handling an objection when initiating an opportunity; as well as a few you might want to avoid.

Objection: "We're really busy at the moment, could you just send us some literature, and if we're interested, we'll call you back?"

- *Wuss out:* Okay, I'll get that literature right over, and wait to hear from you.

- *Super wuss out:* Just hang up.

- *Smart aleck:* Okay, I'll get that literature right out; and then keep calling you back until hell freezes over. Is that what you really want or can we just set the appointment now?

- *Need new career:* Let's be real. Like that's the first time I've heard that! You're just asking for literature so we can hang up and you will never call me back, right? *Man, I hate you people!*

- *Looking for a fight:* I bet you are too busy losing your ass to try and increase your profits. No? Then you need to see me. All I need is 15 minutes. I'll bring doughnuts.

- *New Yorker:* What, are you going under? I mean, why wouldn't you want to at least know what progressive companies are doing to drive up growth and profits? All I'm asking for is a fifteen-minute meeting next Wednesday. Or, should I have my friend the bankruptcy lawyer give you a call?

- *We hate literature, too:* Hey, I totally understand. I'm happy to hear you're doing so well. Regarding the literature; we did research on what actually happens to the literature we send to our prospects, and we found that either they didn't receive it, or they didn't ever read it, and it eventually ended up in a landfill somewhere. Our goal is to simply introduce our company to you and to explore the ways we work with our customers to improve their operations and profitability. I've got a meeting near you next Wednesday; I'd like to drop by, introduce myself and our company to you. I'll bring some literature, and if you like, we can throw it away together. It won't take more than 15 minutes. I'll plan on it.

- *Genuine:* Look, if you are like me, you hate getting cold calls from strangers. And, if you were me, you'd know I hate making them. Yet this manner of outreach is one of the primary ways we connect with businesses in the community. We work with hundreds of companies that do exactly what you do, and we've helped them to drive up growth and drive down costs. Our only goal right now is to introduce ourselves. I'll be in your town next Thursday, and would just like to meet for a few minutes. Oh, and along with our literature, I'll bring the names of a few of our customers that will be very familiar to you.

The worst way to handle an objection is to *avoid* handling it; so be open to dramatic and repeated failure. Keep pushing on new ideas to stay motivated. Only then will you find your way.

Managing through a Stalled Sale

A stalled sale is a good reason for concern, since stalls usually point toward unresolved objections or questions. We're often called in to rescue stalled sales opportunities at the point when the prospect is no longer returning calls from the salesperson. Sales stall for a myriad of reasons; the late introduction of a competitor, or a prospect's failure to see a compelling value proposition, or his or her distrust in the salesperson's ability to deliver the proposed solution. There might also be internal corporate issues that have nothing to do with your firm or offer. A good starting point for handling a stall is simply bringing it up. If the prospect won't take your call, find a connected colleague who will call them on your behalf.

If a prospect opportunity is stalled for an extended period of time—say, six months or longer—the easiest way to correct the problem is to start the process over with the prospect by creating a list of issues. Ironically—and as is often the case with our personal relationships—the prospect is more likely to take your call after the emotion of breaking up with you has worn off. One option is to make a courtesy call: *"It's been a while since we spoke. I was wondering if you ever solved that backhoe issue? Really—you didn't? Do you mind if I ask what stopped you?"* It is nearly impossible to close through a stalled sale, unless you discount your price to a level so low that it tilts the value proposition in your favor; which you know is called the *drop your pants close.* I don't recommend this practice, although it is widely used in numerous industries.

The "We Don't Want" Needs Analysis Objection

About three months into what would become a very short-term professional relationship, I was scheduled to fly into my sales associate Frank's territory and spend a couple of days making sales calls with him. We reviewed the scheduled calls on the phone several days before the trip. One opportunity looked especially interesting: an electrical firm needing estimating software. Though it wasn't a particularly strong area for our product, the call was scheduled for the day I flew in. Frank informed me that the company had requested a demo and a proposal, and indicated that they didn't want a needs analysis. I suggested that Frank call them back and advise them that we would have to do the needs analysis first; and although he said okay, it wasn't very convincing.

Upon flying in, Frank picked me up at the airport. In the backseat was about 100 pounds worth of computer equipment (this was clearly before the age of the laptop). I asked Frank why he had the equipment in the car. He began explaining that when he called Terry, the electrical firm's owner, he informed Frank that if we didn't bring a computer and be prepared to show them our stuff, that we shouldn't even bother coming. *Interesting.*

Frank remained pretty quiet for the two-hour trip to Terry's office. Upon arriving, we were instructed by the receptionist to set up our computer in the conference room—an offer I politely declined. She looked slightly horrified and walked back into the offices. Soon, Terry himself arrived in the lobby to have a little chat with the computer sales-people. To say that Terry is a big man would be an understatement. He is not only big, but with his attitude he appears even twice as big. I explained briefly to Terry that my job was to actually sell and not merely demonstrate software; and that I had absolutely no chance of selling anything by simply showing him the software without first fully understanding what his company was trying to accomplish. Further, I offered to leave immediately if that wasn't going to be okay with him. I'm not certain, but I suspect Frank may have partially lost control of his bladder at that moment.

By way of offering an olive branch, I offered to have Frank drag the equipment into their office for the full dog and pony show *after* we met to discuss their issues, costs of not solving, and so on. Terry reluctantly agreed. Frank looked squeamish. Once inside their conference room, Terry brought in his estimators—each of whom was bigger than him. If it got ugly, Frank was a goner.

I began the conversation by asking what type of work they did and what they were trying to accomplish. For the next three hours, I learned the facts, beliefs, and emotions behind their issues, problems, and opportunities concerning new estimating software, and the impact to the company by not solving it. Toward the end of the meeting, I did a verbal summary of findings and suggested to Terry and the team that we reconvene in two weeks to walk them through how our solution would help them accomplish their goals. They agreed. The computer gear never left the car.

Two weeks later, after a sixty-minute presentation, they bought the entire solution. Once we signed the paperwork, Terry said, *"I knew you were going to be all right if you had nerve enough to come in here and not get intimidated into doing that demo. Truthfully, we had selected another product, and were just using you to get a third quote because the customer required it. Coming in to the first meeting, you had a 0 percent chance of winning; and if you had shown us the software then, we would have never bought."* Terry's company became one of our best customers. This sales opportunity is indicative of why we have a sales process, and why we develop skills to manage questions, concerns, and objections. When we met, Terry was on a trajectory to buy the wrong solution, because he wasn't aware there was a solution designed to exactly meet their needs. If we had acquiesced to his demand of a demo without a needs analysis, he would have purchased the wrong solution, and his company would have suffered as a result.

WHEN YOU ARE RIGHT, STICK TO YOUR GUNS.

Chapter 15 Recap: Handling Questions, Concerns, and Objections

- Prospects often get nervous when they have to *commit* to something; even when it's something that they want and need. An *objection* may be an underlying psychological desire for the salesperson to reassure us that the purchase is a good idea.

- Three forms of communications malfunctions—*questions, concerns, and objections*—don't only show up when trying to close a sale; they can emerge throughout the entire sales process. They might occur when we're *initiating an opportunity*, putting forth a *value proposition*, or *enabling a decision*.

- There is no *"right way"* to deal with a prospect's objections; there is simply *your way*. Your personality and that of your prospect are hugely important in discerning how to handle communication. You likely get the same questions and objections over and over, so remember: learning how to respond to them is a skill, and one that you can hone and master with practice.

- *Questions* from prospects can sound a lot like *objections*. We can handle these by taking the following steps: (1) *align* (provide reinforcement for asking the question), (2) *clarify* the question to ensure you understand it, (3) *explain* (provide an answer to the question), and (4) *confirm* that the prospect is satisfied with the answer.

- Occasionally, salespeople will receive a request to solve a problem for which they don't have a solution. This will fall into one of three categories: (1) It's no big deal, (2) There is a work-around, and (3) It is a big deal.

- When you cannot work around an issue and it's a big deal for a prospect (situation #3), you'll want to take the following steps: (1) *explain* your position and (2) *complete* your thought with a question. Clients frequently choose options that are not as feature-rich in order to work with companies that they trust. Your willingness to be open and honest about potential weaknesses in your product shows your true intent.

- It's always preferable to hear about a prospect's concerns earlier in the sales process, rather than later. There are often *warning signs* that a sale is in trouble; some of these include a prospect's refusal to return your calls, provide access to important people and information, or follow your process.

- Salespeople typically get less than five objections, and they're most often about a *delay*, a *price issue*, or something *technical* in nature. Prospects are usually reluctant to share their concerns with salespeople; this means that you have to develop a process for helping them speak their minds and share their concerns. You can approach the issue in a nonthreatening way if the prospect isn't bringing it up; use price to get at the real objection, or use a variation of the *feel, felt, found* objection-handling procedure.

- Though there isn't a "right" way to handle objections during the phase of initiating opportunities, tactics such as *honesty and finding common ground* usually work better than other, more aggressive approaches.

- Salespeople experience *stalled sales* for a variety of reasons; the late introduction of a competitor, the prospect's failure to see a compelling value proposition, his or her distrust in the salesperson's ability to deliver the proposed solution, or internal corporate issues that have nothing to do with your firm or offer. If a prospect opportunity is stalled for an extended period of time—say, six months or longer—the easiest way to correct the problem is to start the process over by "checking in" with the prospect and creating a list of issues, perhaps by way of a courtesy phone call.

The Drill
Succeed Every Day

Create Your Super Simple
Sales Success Plan

I t's time to give yourself a big *"Hell, yeah!"* for making it through the first three sections of the book. You've arrived at Section IV, where we discuss the *drill* of selling: the planning, execution, and management of your selling career. This is what you have to do every day, week, month, and year to succeed as a salesperson.

The KYOA Super Simple Sales Plan

If you are ready to sell more than you ever thought possible, then you are going to need a plan by which to mobilize your knowledge, will, and skills into the drill of selling. The components of your sales plan will include a sales goal, key strategies, and specific sales activities that become your daily, weekly, and monthly actions. Keeping the plan simple helps to ensure that you will follow it; in fact, you should be able to fit the plan on a single sheet of paper.

YOU CAN'T MANAGE YOUR RESULTS—ONLY YOUR ACTIVITIES.

Your Selling Success Metrics

You will need to know your key selling metrics to develop a sales plan, because these will serve as the foundation for your *Selling Success Metrics*. In short, you need to know what you actually have to *do* on a daily basis to reach your target. Remember, you can't manage your results—only your activities. You don't control the number of sales you make, just the activities in which you engage that lead to sales. So let's take a look at three metrics that are important to most types of selling. Since there are various types of selling metrics, think about what items make the most sense in your particular industry.

1. *Close ratio:* The first metric you need to know is your *effective close ratio*, which you can calculate by adding up the opportunities you attempted to close in a specific period of time (say 12 months), and then divide by the actual sales closed in the same period. If you don't have exact data, take a guess. It is better to underestimate; by lowering your ratio, you will increase the selling activities required to reach your goal. And you can easily readjust your activities downward later. To calculate your effective close rate, use the following equation: proposals delivered divided by sales closed equals ECR. For example, if you delivered 50 proposals and closed 15 sales, you have a 30 percent close rate.

   Your close ratio is _____ percent.

   Knowing this figure is vital to understanding your overall selling effectiveness. A low close rate signals potential issues in prospecting and qualifying, whereas a close rate that is too high can indicate that you are cherry-picking your opportunities and not taking enough swings at bat. And, unless you are the top rep in the company, you might be known by your coworkers as a *cherry-picking sandbagger*.

2. *Cs to As:* The next data point is the ratio of C prospects you engage that actually become A prospects: *your Cs to As*. For our purposes, we will define a C prospect as one with whom you have had an initial meeting, who is in the matrix, has acknowledged a need or desire, but has not yet made a decision to pursue a purchase. In essence, they are looking. Conversely, an A prospect is one who has made a decision to pursue a solution, for whom you have created a value proposition and presented a summary of

findings, and for whom you believe you have a solution. Your definition may well be different; it could be *lookers to buyers*, or *warm to hot*, or *biting to hooked*. The important data to know is how many "Cs'" you need to get an A; in other words, how many prospects do you have to talk with before you have one that is serious? Is it a 1:1 ratio (100 percent), or 2:1 (50 percent), or 10:1 (10 percent), or 20:1 (5 percent)? Or something entirely different? If you don't know, take a wild guess. You may be closer than you think.

Your C to A ratio is_____percent.

3. *Leads on a silver platter:* The next data point you need to know is how many new initial meetings—or C prospects—are handed to you on a silver platter each year? Does your employer or company create all the leads for you? Or—if you actually have to dig up opportunities on your own—do you get *any* leads handed to you? Hey, if you get all the leads you need, enjoy it. If you ever have to go find your own, it could be quite an unpleasant experience for you.

Number of leads on a silver platter: _____

Putting it All Together

For example, if you are a 10 percent closer and you want to make 14 sales, you will need 140 A leads. If your C to A ratio is 50 percent, you will need 280 C leads. If the big company is handing over 200, you will need to self-generate 80 leads. Won't that be fun?

Goal: At least double quota.

Do the quick math. To reach your sales goal of at least double your quota, how many self-generated leads do you need?

Number of self-generated leads I need to reach double quota. _____ (Note: If you don't have a quota, make one up.)

Selling Metrics of the Backhoe Salesperson

Having a handle on your basic selling metrics lets you know how many *initial meetings* you will need to comfortably exceed your sales goal. Remember when we discussed creating your own ocean of opportunities in Chapter 10? Now we're specifying how big that ocean needs to be. If your type of selling includes creating new customer relationships, the number of initial meetings you hold is the key performance indicator that drives everything. The number of initial meetings you conduct with prospects will ultimately determine your success or failure. Let's take a look at our backhoe salesperson's metrics:

Close ratio: 25 percent

Cs to As: 50 percent

C leads on a silver platter: 400 per year

So if their goal is 100 sales, as a 25 percent closer, they would need to self-generate 400 leads per year. We calculated this using the following formula: 100/25 percent = 400 A prospects. 400 A prospects/50 percent = 800 C leads. 800 C leads – 400 silver platter leads = 400 self-generated leads needed per year to reach the goal of 100 backhoe sales. As you develop your own sales goal and plan, you'll need to know your selling metrics as well.

The Windshield and the Rearview Mirror

As we continue to build your sales success plan, take a moment and reflect back to Chapter 1, specifically the discussion on the origin of New Year's resolutions. Much as the Roman God Janus had a face looking forward and one looking back, an important component of creating a plan is a look at our past performance. While there is a lot to learn from previous experiences, *do not dwell on them*. As we discuss in Chapter 7, remember the relationship between the windshield and the rearview mirror. While it is helpful to look back to find what worked and what didn't, the rearview mirror is roughly 5 percent the size of most windshields—which translates into spending 95 percent of your time looking forward and 5 percent looking backward.

A Quick Look Back

As you begin to your planning process, take a hard look at the effort, activities, and outcomes you've put forth and experienced over the past year. After throwing up, you'll be properly positioned to begin looking forward. If you got the result you deserved for the effort expended, and it wasn't what you would have wished it to be—fear not! This is a new moment. Your destiny is not yet determined. Quickly analyze the difference in your projected versus actual performance, and, if possible, your Selling Success Metrics. Think about what went well, and what could be improved upon. And then, let go of it.

Previous 12 Months: Review

Actual Sales Performance: $ _____, # _____ Other _____

Projected Sales Performance: $ _____, # _____ Other _____

Difference in Performance: $ _____, percent _____ Other _____

Close Ratio percent: _____

C leads self-generated: _____

C leads received: _____

KYOA Focus Questions

16.1. What worked:

_____
_____
_____

16.2. What didn't work:

_____
_____
_____

16.3. Most important lessons:

_____
_____
_____

Now that you've done your 12-month review, forget everything except what you can bring forward.

DWELLING ON PAST FAILURES IS SILLY.

Looking Forward: Setting Your Sales Goal

You begin the process of creating your plan by setting a sales goal—your commitment to yourself and the "what" that you wish to accomplish. Your goal is not your quota, or what someone else wants you to accomplish. In fact, your goal ought to be at least double your quota. Make it as hard or unreachable as you believe you can. But, if you are a *sandbagger*—someone who purposely holds back on goals and commitments—then by all means, triple your goal. The amazing thing about goal-setting is that being serious about it and committing it to paper prompts your brain to start working out the strategies and tactics to achieve it. Thinking about the goal elicits conversations about it; and before long, you begin attracting the outcome you desire.

Your goal will also generate a number of supporting goals; for example, "Sell 100 backhoes this year" breaks down to roughly "Sell two backhoes per week." As we will learn, the "sell two backhoes per week" goal will generate a list of very specific activities that have to take place during every moment of your workday. And that's where you need to be. You must articulate your goal—along with the corresponding activities and key actions—in a single thought. It is your goal elevator pitch; your goal mantra. Simpler is better. Not easier, mind you; but better.

Remember that in Chapter 1 Steve and I set a goal to run up Pikes Peak? The goal was simply a device to remove us from our complacency and bring focus to our lives—and it worked. We did our victory dance upon crossing the finish line at the summit, even though it was 28 degrees, snowing, and we finished firmly in the middle of the pack. We weren't competing with the other 1,798 runners; we were competing against our own personal ruts. And quite frankly, we kicked their asses.

You have to imagine an endpoint when you're beginning your own "race" and discern what is necessary to achieve each component of it. For example, when I'm running a race, I have a finish time in mind before the firing of the gun, which translates into the actual pace I have to maintain each mile. As I'm running—thanks to my Garmin Forerunner 305—I'm able to constantly measure my current pace against the target pace.

Life without Goals

Without a goal, there are no outcomes: There's just existence. You are where and what you are. There is no becoming or personal accountability;

you never get to do a *victory dance*. You never get to overcome obstacles and adversity. There's no gloating with friends and loved ones on achieving a goal—because you didn't set one! The absence of a goal creates, perpetuates, and fosters complacency. We learned in Chapter 6 that many people become complacent because they simply feel powerless to achieve—and therefore stop trying. For others, it's the result of relinquishing what is important in favor of what is convenient. In Chapter 7, we introduced the Potential Process, which is designed to help you change the arc of your potential by setting and achieving goals—something that will energize you and allow you to conquer complacency.

Practice Your Victory Dance

Go ahead right now. *Stand up and practice your victory dance.* Unless, of course, you are reading this on an airplane and the seatbelt light is illuminated. Then, just imagine your victory dance while you wiggle in your seat. As a bonus, seeing you wiggle in your airplane seat will seriously unnerve your seatmate. When they ask what you are reading, tell them about the book; they may want what you've got. By practicing your victory dance, you will begin the essential process of seeing yourself in a new light—one where you set and achieve your goals.

Your Sales Plan

Once you have the goal—the "what" that you want to accomplish—you need the "how" plan to get there. Planning is important; it's a road map with benchmarks designed to provide reinforcement that you are on the right track, or show you just how far off-course you have veered. It's a process that forces you to get your act together, to think through all the activities necessary to fulfill your objectives. That marvelous asset known as your brain—while the brain is not the same as your self or your soul—is an extremely helpful tool in organizing and engaging resources. Planning brings the best of your brain into action and engages it in a positive way. It pushes out the negative internal messaging, thereby increasing your chance of succeeding. Visualizing both the process and the outcome in your brain allows you to work out the challenges before they become *big* challenges.

Your 20 Percent Actions

As you begin thinking about how you will achieve your goal, remember to keep your plan simple. You don't want to schedule more than four activities; it could be as few as two or even just one. Take a cue from Pareto yet again, and concentrate on the 20 percent activities that generate the most return on your investment. As previously mentioned, initial meetings are the key 20 percent action in selling that requires new customer sales to achieve sales goals, Consider how that works. It's totally conceivable that 60 percent of your selling time could be spent creating opportunities. The narrower you make your 20 percent actions, the easier they will be to execute and track.

The Magic of the Refrigerator Door

Undergoing the process of creating a goal and subsequent plan and then relegating the entire document into a desk drawer greatly limits the value. It's like we collectively say, *"Great, I set the goals and built a success plan for the year; and now I can promptly forget them."* My suggestion for you is this: keep your plan as simple as possible—limit it to a single sheet of paper—and put it everywhere, including the refrigerator door. That way, you will see it every day. After all, what good is a road map if you never look at it?

Let's Review

The Pikes Peak Ascent Plan

Goal—Run Pikes Peak Ascent
- Lose 35 to 40 lbs.
- Treadmill workouts at 11 percent grade.
- Long runs of three to four hours.
- Two-hour bridge repeat workouts on Saturdays.

Figure 16.1

Backhoe Salesperson's Annual Sales Plan

Goal: Sell 100 backhoes in the next 12 months.

- Build 10,000 targets in marketing list.
- Send mass communication to introduce market to product.
- Use phone and field canvassing as outreach mechanism.
- Become more active in local construction and agriculture associations

---

Your Sales Goal

Your Projected Sales Performance:
$ _____, # _____ Other _____

Your Annual Sales Plan:
_____
_____
_____

Your Sales Plan Elements:
_____
_____
_____

Your Sales Success Plan Frame

Once you have a goal established and have figured out what basic elements are necessary for sales activities, you need to connect your goal, sales success metrics, and selling activities. Figure 16.2 looks at the performance plan for the backhoe salesperson.

Initial Meeting Generator

The next element of your plan is to design a process to generate your initial meetings. Chapter 10 discusses the various methods salespeople use to create their ocean of opportunities. The examples we examine are referral building, working the phones, public speaking, blasting, and face-to-face cold-calling. For the following backhoe salesperson example, we'll use a three-prong approach of wideband outreach—e-mail and direct mail, working the phones, and face-to-face cold calling. We know how many initial meetings we need; what we don't know is how much activity is

My Goal Calculator

Product or Service	Average Transaction Size	Number per year	Total Annual Revenue	Monthly
Backhoe	$80,000	100	$8,000,000	666,667
Product/Service 2	$0	0	$0	0
Total	$80,000	100	$8,000,000	$666,667

My Performance Planner

My Revenue Goal:	$8,000,000
Average Size Sale:	$80,000
Sales to Reach Goal:	100
Year to Date Revenue:	$0
Gap (+ or -):	-$8,000,000
Actual Sales to Date:	0
My Close Ratio: ⟶	25%
Number of "A" Opportunities to Reach Goal:	400
Conversion Rate - Initial meetings that become A prospects: ⟶	2
Total Initial Meetings Required to Reach Goal:	800
New Initial Meetings Handed to Me on a Silver Platter: ⟶	0
Number of Self-Generated Initial Meetings (Target):	800

Figure 16.2   Backhoe Salesperson Performance Planner

actually required to secure a meeting. Different techniques work for different industries and salespeople. However, for our example, we take a stab at creating metrics:

- For phone work, we establish a ratio of ten dials to one contact;
- For the wideband outreach, we use a ½ percent open rate;
- For the face-to-face cold calling, we use a ratio of four attempts to one meeting.

We create a basic mix of 35 percent phone, 50 percent wideband, and 15 percent face-to-face activities—which means that 15 percent of the leads generated have to come from face-to-face cold calling. Is it totally scientifically accurate? Heck no. Could my numbers and ratios be way off? You bet. So consider your first pass at planning merely as a place to start. Plans are dynamic and meant to be altered as conditions change. For example, you may find the face-to-face to be more effective and enjoyable than phone prospecting, and would therefore want to shift your plan to reflect your preferences. Figure 16.3 shows the tool that's available on the book's web site to help calculate the number of leads you will generate

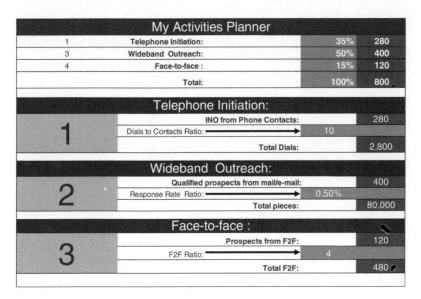

Figure 16.3 Backhoe Salesperson's Activities Planner

from your particular breakdown of activities. It starts with the number of initial meetings you need, and then it calculates the numbers of activities that must be completed to create them.

The final element of developing your activity plan is the *performance recap*, which shows the actual selling activities that have to take place to safely exceed your sales goal. Figure 16.4 shows the performance recap for the backhoe salesperson.

My Performance Plan				
Activity	Annual Goal	Month	Week	Day
Average Size Sale:	$80,000			
Sales to Reach Goal:	100	8		
Year to Date Revenue:	0	0	0	
Gap (+ or −):	−$8,000,000	−666667	−160000	
Actual Sales to Date:	0	0	0	
Telephone Initiation:	2800	233	56	
Customer Referrals:	0	0	0	0
Wideband Outreach:	80000	6667	1600	320
Face-to-face:	480	40	10	2

Figure 16.4 Backhoe Salesperson's Performance Recap

Based on the selling metrics that we discussed, the backhoe salesperson would need the following sales drill each day to comfortable exceed his goal.

- Initiate six new opportunities over the phone daily.
- Send 320 wideband outreach message per day.
- Have two face-to-face meetings daily.

The process of planning your success will bring into sharp focus what actually has to happen to safely exceed your sales goal—or at least double your quota. Creating a goal and subsequently developing a sales activity plan will help confirm you can do it. When broken into small chunks, big goals get achieved. You can *totally* do this. Your goal and plan will look totally different based on your particular industry and product. Use the framework to help create your plan, and don't be afraid to get help if you're struggling! There are a ton of great resources available to help you develop and execute great sales and marketing programs designed to create opportunities that *work*. Visit www.helpingsalespeoplesucceed.com for help and ideas.

Chapter 16 Recap: Create Your Super Simple Sales Success Plan

- The *drill* of selling—the planning, execution, and management—is what you have to do every day, week, month, and year to succeed as a salesperson.
- The components of your *sales plan* will include a sales goal, key strategies, and specific sales activities that become your daily, weekly, and monthly actions. Keep the plan simple; in fact, you should be able to fit it on a single sheet of paper.
- You will need to know your key selling metrics to develop a sales plan, because these will serve as the foundation for your *selling success metrics*. These include your *close ratio* (total opportunities you attempted to close in a specific period divided by the actual sales closed in the same period); your *C to A* ratio (the ratio of C prospects you engage that actually become A prospects); and your *leads on a silver platter* (leads that your company or employer generates for you).
- As you begin your planning process, take a hard look at the effort, activities, and outcomes you've put forth and experienced over

the past year. Compare your *projected to actual* performance; and, if possible, your selling success metrics. Think about what went well and what could be improved upon—then let go of it.

- *You* begin the process of creating your plan by *setting a goal*—your commitment to yourself, and the *"what"* that you wish to accomplish. Committing it to paper prompts your brain to start working out the strategies and tactics to achieve your goal. This elicits conversations about it and, before long, you begin attracting the outcome you desire.

- Your goal will also generate a number of *supporting goals*, which in turn will breed a list of very *specific activities* that have to take place during every moment of your workday.

- Keep your plan simple; try not to schedule more than four activities at a time (it could be as few as one or two). Follow Pareto's rule and concentrate on the *20 percent activities* that generate the most return on your investment. Limit your plan to a single sheet of paper—and put it in every place you will possibly see it on regular basis.

- Once you have a goal established and figured out what basic elements are necessary for sales activities, you need to *connect* your goal, sales success metrics, and your selling activities.

- Then, design a process to *generate your initial meetings*. This can include approaches like wideband outreach (e-mail and direct mail), working the phones, and face-to-face cold calling. You need to discern how much activity is actually required to secure a meeting. Consider your first pass at planning merely as a place to start; plans are dynamic and meant to be altered as conditions change and as you find what works best for you.

- The final element of developing your activity plan is the *performance recap*, which shows the actual selling activities that have to take place to safely exceed your sales goal.

Come Out Swinging

Execute Your Sales Plan Every Day

During a brief hiatus from my sales career, I veered back into a job as the construction coordinator for a customer of mine: a medium-sized production homebuilding company. How I got that job is almost as mysterious as how I got my second sales position. I think that perhaps since I had sold them software designed for homebuilders and was fairly well acquainted with the business end of an Estwing 20 oz. framing hammer, the owner was under the grave misconception I actually knew something about running such a company. The entire experience proved interesting on so many levels that it would be difficult to do them justice in a single book, let alone the introduction to the next to final chapter. Perhaps it could be a new reality television show: *The Misadventures of the Unqualified*. Nevertheless—like many experiences in life—what initially appeared to be devolving into a total career derailment actually proved to be one of the best lessons of my early professional career.

The owner of the company was a smart, demanding entrepreneur with perhaps a slight Napoleonic complex who came to America with his wife to build his financial wealth. He was a lawyer by training, she a certified accountant. After finishing university, the couple went to work for a large homebuilding operation in Europe. Eventually, they accepted an offer to cross the pond to start a joint venture residential construction company. I arrived on the scene shortly after they broke ground on their fifth community, just as they became fully engulfed in operational chaos; hence the need for a "Construction Coordinator."

My role was to handle everything related to building 200-plus homes per year: developing base estimates, estimating change orders and customizations, managing contractor and supplier relationships, working with the field superintendents, assembling preclosing paperwork, managing production schedules, tracking inspections, handling warranty work, dealing with unhappy customers, coordinating subcontractors and employees, refereeing fights between husband and wife, creating and approving change orders, verifying and approving invoices, and so on. Within the first two weeks, I was buried in a mountain of work with no chance of ever catching up.

I dealt with this hardship by refusing to admit my predicament and keeping my troubles to myself. I couldn't admit to my boss, myself, or anyone else what I perceived to be utter failure less than one month into a new job. My ego simply wouldn't allow it. However, working in a position that requires juggling a thousand balls at once—in a company with eight employees—makes it difficult to hide turmoil, chaos, and screw-ups. And when the balls started falling, my manager started screaming . . . for good reasons, too.

To showcase a couple of the more glamorous screw-ups we experienced: In one instance, a field superintendent accidentally framed up an entire house five feet too close to the road. (This was only important in that the city inspector required us to move it back five feet.) Another memorable incident occurred when a brand-new superintendent, fearful of running behind schedule, ordered the entire lumber package for a home to be delivered on a Friday, so that the framers could work over the weekend. When the framers actually arrived on the scene Monday morning, the lumber was entirely gone. Ix-nay on the lumber package-ay. In our newly updated org chart, the construction coordinator was responsible for all screw-ups. In the bosse's world, nothing was ever his fault, and whoever was at fault was paying for it.

It wasn't too long before I became completely overwhelmed with activity and unable to accomplish anything. Everything became an urgent issue that required an immediate response. Soon after realizing that the job was unmanageable, my manager and I sat down for a little talk. Instead of attacking, he changed my professional career, and helped me realize that *achieving your goals requires executing your plan every day.*

To begin, we had a conversation about my job requirements and performance. He wasn't blaming or punishing me; rather, he was looking at the situation's facts. I explained that I was unprepared to handle the amount of work, and wasn't getting anything accomplished as a result. He agreed that it was a lot to handle and offered to work together to create a more structured plan and schedule in the hope that it would improve my performance.

Did I Miss the Memo?

We created the following personal activity and time management process, which was a game changer for me. Am I the only one who missed the memo on "how to manage time and organize yourself?" If you struggle with organization and execution as well, I hope the lessons I learned help you, too. While this experience was with a construction company, the actual planning and execution construct is nearly identical to the requirements for most sales functions. In fact, I've taught this methodology to salespeople and their managers for years. My goal in sharing this with you is to encourage you to find your way of managing your execution.

Step 1: Organize Your Current Work

First, we made a list outlining all outstanding issues—tasks, commitments, activities—regardless of condition, priority, or percentage of completion. We then prioritized the list and created a time-sensitive plan for addressing each item. It is very easy to become paralyzed amidst chaos, making it nearly impossible to accomplish anything. Organizing these tasks into doable chunks took a huge amount of anxiety off my shoulders. I improved my outlook on everything, simply by creating an actual list of stuff to do with corresponding target completion dates. I was no longer drowning in anxiety; I was confident that I could actually complete it. As we reviewed each task and discussed relevant issues it became apparent that some were being inappropriately prioritized as "urgent and important."

Now it's your turn—give it a try.

1. Make a list of all your outstanding tasks, meetings, to-do items, and so on.
2. Prioritize the list.

3. Create an action plan to complete each item, or kick it off the list.

4. Schedule time to complete each item on your calendar.

Step 2: Create a List of Your Work Activities

Our second task was develop a list of every on-going job-related activity, task, or meeting for which I was responsible—including conservative estimates for how much time per day or week each activity should take, and what (if any) deadlines there were for each. Activities differed in frequency and regularity; while some occurred every day, some—like field meetings with superintendents, for example—were scheduled for specific days and times each week, and still others were periodic in nature. We included all of that in the list along with firefighting, since we needed to allocate a good bit of time to handle in-bound questions from superintendents, repair requests from homeowners, or change order requests from real estate agents. When things like these aren't scheduled, they stop any forward momentum on anything else. Calling "firefighting" a task allowed us to schedule it and meet our goal of cataloging every responsibility that was necessary for successful execution of the job.

The particular items on your list will depend on the specific type of selling you do. You may work with existing relationships exclusively over the phone, or manage a huge geographical territory and travel. Regardless of how or what you sell, it is possible to create a fairly accurate register of activities. While many (if not most) selling activities don't occur on a set schedule, we learned in the previous chapter that you can usually predict the number of meetings or phone calls that have to happen in a day or week. Therefore, you can pinpoint when these meetings should take place. For example, I always preferred to do presentation and closing meetings Tuesday through Thursday mornings; so while I couldn't schedule the exact events, I knew when I wanted them to occur. Additionally, I needed to set aside specific times each day to do initial outreach prospecting. Finally, I always include work and personal activities on my list. Both are important, and both have to happen—and we have to schedule both to make sure that one doesn't always take a backseat to the other.

Now it's your turn—give it a try yourself.

Create a list of your work activities by using the following categories and time periods as guidelines.

Daily: prospecting, initial meetings, self-education, physical exercise, face-to-face meetings, time with family or friends

Weekly: sales or other company meetings, civic involvement, reports due from or to me, updates to sales charts, dates or special time with family and friends, volunteer and community work

Monthly: monthly performance review, review and update annual plan and adjust as necessary, monthly company and industry meetings, specific goal setting and review, volunteer and community work

Quarterly: quarterly performance review, update annual plan and adjust as necessary, special meetings, and so on

Annually: review previous annual performance, create annual sales and success plan; vacations, family outings, continuing education, mission trips, and so on.

Prioritize Your Activities

It is helpful as you develop your list of activities to assign priority levels to tasks in terms of importance and the need to complete them within the specified timeframe. When assigning priority, consider these four basic descriptions of priority.

1. Important and time sensitive (your 20 percent activities)
2. Important and not time sensitive
3. Not important and not time sensitive
4. Not important and not time sensitive, but personally interesting

Assign a Time to Complete the Task

Decide upon a point in time when the task should begin and end. (For example, your annual sales planning should begin in October and be complete in early December.) Note dependencies of the task, others who are required to be involved, and so on.

Step 3: Build a Calendar

The third thing we did was to establish a daily, weekly, and monthly schedule of activities, events, due dates, and meetings, which we were able to build from our prioritized list of activities. We grouped each activity into its appropriate class—daily, weekly, monthly—and then, starting with important and urgent activities such as meetings, we blocked out time for the actual meeting as well as prep time before. From there, we added other, less time-sensitive activities, and so on. I knew everything I had to do and when I was going to do it—which made it much less stressful to handle all those urgent issues, and made a once unmanageable job entirely manageable. I realized that not all tasks had equal importance, and that not every request had to be handled immediately.

Now, this process might seem somewhat constrictive and uncomfortable for you gunslingers out there who prefer to "just wing it in terms of personal time management," but it's just the opposite. If you want to improve your performance, knowing what you have to do and when you are going to do it is actually quite liberating. It's a paradox: the more structured and organized you are, the more freedom and success you will enjoy, and the less you will procrastinate. Not knowing what to do, when to do it, or how to get it done—a lack of knowledge and planning— is a significant reason that people put off completing important tasks. However, when you assess your current level of productivity, you will likely find vast gaps of actual productive work spent doing things like surfing the Internet, organizing your e-mail, cleaning out filing cabinets, and so on. Having a structured plan really helps; I know this from experience.

Step 4: Track Your Progress

The fourth thing to do is to build and update a daily log of your 20 percent activities—those critical endeavors that have to happen each and every day for you to safely exceed your goals. Tracking your activity is helpful for a number of reasons: first, making the commitment to document your commitments will ensure that you actually keep them. Second, the data you monitor will help you refine your selling metrics. A log is simple to create and maintain, and takes less than a minute per day to update. Though the mechanics of how to track progress can vary, Act! software— an essential tool for anyone in sales—is a great place to keep your data.

Hell or High Water Commitments

As we discussed earlier, not all tasks are urgent and important. However, there are a few key 20 percent actions you must take each day to ensure your forward momentum. Making a commitment to complete your 20 percenters and to track your daily progress is not always a fun experience; frankly, there are days when having to report that nothing happened is painful. But despite the occasional difficulty, pledging to yourself to complete and measure your key activities goes a long way to ensure you'll actually change the arc of your potential. These commitments, your 20 percent actions, are what I call "hell or high water" commitments because you declare that no matter what happens, you're doing to do X, Y, and Z by a given time. These types of commitments are the ones you are unwilling to break. This isn't only for work. In fact, of the five key HOHW commitments I make each day, only a couple are work related.

Make Tomorrow Less Stressful

It's also a good idea to make sure you are tactically and mentally prepared for the next day while you are still at your desk at the end of the day. It's an easy habit to add, and looking at your calendar before leaving for the evening increases the likelihood you will actually complete tomorrow's tasks. Feeling unprepared can add to your anxiety, which is unproductive.

Executing your sales plan is essential, and completing your 20 percent activities each day will work. If you are struggling, review Chapter 7 and work with your mentor to correct this. In addition, try implementing a super simple sales execution methodology; it will help you realize that there are really just a few actual activities that are absolutely necessary for success. Recall our discussion of the four elements of selling—prospecting, qualifying, presenting, and enabling a decision—and when prioritizing your activities, focus 80 percent of your effort on prospecting and qualifying.

Selling is a simple enterprise. Our collective challenge is staying on task and avoiding distractions that take us away from our goal. By meeting this challenge, you can become more focused on the right activities and—when your focus is combined with knowledge, will, and the necessary skills—you can improve. I did, and soon you will, too.

Chapter 17 Recap: Come Out Swinging: Execute Your Sales Plan Every Day

- Achieving your goal requires that you execute your plan every day. Creating a structured time-management plan in which you itemize and prioritize your responsibilities can vastly improve your performance.

- The first step of the plan is to organize your current work by outlining all outstanding issues—tasks, commitments, activities—regardless of condition, priority, or percentage of completion. Then prioritize this list, and create a time-sensitive plan for addressing each item. You may soon realize that not all items that you've labeled "urgent" are really so.

- The second step is to create a list of your work activities by constructing a list of every on-going job-related activity, task, or meeting for which you are responsible. Include conservative estimates for how much time per day or week each activity should take, and what (if any deadlines) there are for each. Since you can usually predict the number of meetings or phone calls that have to happen in a day or week, you can probably pinpoint when these meetings should take place.

- Include both personal and professional events in this list, and break it down by daily, weekly, monthly, quarterly, and annual activities. Assign priority using the following system:

  1. Important and time sensitive (your 20 percent activities)

  2. Important and not time sensitive

  3. Not important and not time sensitive

  4. Not important and not time sensitive, but personally interesting

- The next step is to build a calendar using your daily, weekly, and monthly schedule of activities, events, due dates, and meetings. Group activities by category, and then discern how much actual and prep time is needed for each. You'll find that the more structured and organized you are, the more freedom and success you will enjoy, and the less you will procrastinate.

- The final step is to track your progress by building and updating a daily log of your 20 percent activities—those critical endeavors that have to happen each and every day for you to safely exceed your goals. This log will ensure that you actually keep your commitments, and the data you monitor will help you refine your selling metrics.

- Whatever system you decide to use, the only thing that matters is that it works for you and that you actually *use* it. Make a "hell or high water" pledge to get certain items done no matter what happens. You can become more focused on the right activities and—when your focus is combined with knowledge, will, and the necessary skills—you can improve.

Intensity, Velocity, and Mentorship

Spin Up the Arc of Your Potential

M astering the will, skill, and drill of selling will help you sell more than you thought possible. It's a simple fact: If you create more opportunities, and execute those opportunities more effectively, more prospects will become your customers. By improving your will, skill, and drill, you will enable more prospects and customers to make good decisions—in most cases working with you. The single greatest obstacle to greater selling success is more often will-related fears manifesting in procrastination or avoidance than a lack of actual skills. This book is intended to give you the tools to help you change the arc of your potential by engaging your will, honing your skills, and executing the drill of selling better than before. Regardless of where you are, you *can* improve your sales performance—and your life. Your enhanced ability and accomplishment will create a new reality from which you can begin the process of changing the arc of your potential yet again. The faster you spin up the arc of your potential, the higher it becomes.

To reflect briefly: In Chapter 1, you learn that each of our lives is on a trajectory, and that you're likely to stay on your current course without a significant interruption. However, you can change this course if you choose—and sell and achieve more than you ever thought possible. Chapter 2 introduces the idea that *"your raise becomes effective when you do"*—a harsh but valuable lesson that you—and *you alone*—are responsible for creating success in your life. In Chapter 3, we explore the concept that skills alone don't guarantee success; that, in fact, success requires an integrated approach of the will, skill, and drill of selling. Additionally, we learn the importance of passion in selling. Passion sparks drive, and drive ignites energy, and energy drives performance. In Chapter 4, you learn how important the four areas of knowledge—product, industry, competition, and sales skills—are to creating a foundation of success. By becoming an expert, you become a valuable resource to your industry and customers. This, in turn, attracts more customers to you, since we all want to work with experts and specialists.

Engage Your Will

The "will" section discusses how different personality styles can impact sales performance. Contrary to what many think, there is no single "sales" personality. Committing energy and drive opens greater success to every personality type. Chapter 6 focuses on how core issues can manifest in resulting behaviors, which can derail a sales career and flatten the arc of your potential. We look at the primary behaviors that plague salespeople the most. In Chapter 7, we introduce the Potential Process: a personal goal-setting change management process designed to assist in regrooving your neural pathways to anticipate success instead of failure. Your life moves in the direction of your most dominant thought; so if it is positive, the arc of your potential rises. The more you believe you can achieve, the more you will. Your will becomes the gas pedal to meaningful, sustained superior performance and satisfaction—which will bring you more enjoyment and satisfaction in life.

Hone Your Skills

We move from the foundations of knowledge and will into the skill section, where we focus on learning the few skills that can have the most dramatic impact on your career. We examine ways to create a sales process and an ocean of opportunities; develop trust and intent; listen effectively;

develop a value proposition; enable a decision; and handle questions, concerns, and objections. We learn that the buying process relies on a logical argument to support a decision, and an emotional connection with the solution and the seller. Without either component, the likelihood of a successful transaction is diminished.

We know that selling is a skill-based enterprise, and that the most important sales skill is trust. As defined by Stephen M. R. Covey, your prospect must trust your intent and your competence. The second most important sales skill is listening: Without effective listening skills and trust-based relationships, you will struggle to develop a compelling value proposition and your prospects will resist exploring their issues in a fear-based environment. In that situation, prospects confine their communication to clichés and bare facts and avoid the vulnerabilities of sharing beliefs and emotions—resulting in an inordinate percentage of opportunities heavily discounted to close, or sales lost to competitors or to "no decision." The good news is that skills are not unchangeable personality characteristics; like learning the piano or a foreign language, they can be developed and polished. Regardless of past performance, you *can* improve your skills. How good could you be if you practiced each skill 1,000 times? *Wicked, scary, good.*

The Daily Drill

In the drill section, we discuss the importance of creating a goal and a plan to reach it. We also discuss a methodology for building a daily sales execution procedure to ensure that you safely exceed your goal—at least double your quota. We emphasize how important it is to execute and track your 20 percent activities. Making a *"hell or high water"* commitment on your part makes the likelihood of you changing the arc of your potential a near certainty.

Now—if you are ready to change your arc, and spin up your potential, there are a few keys to consider.

This first of these is your *intensity.* The next time you're at the gym in January, look at the legion of people working out on treadmills and elliptical trainers. Some are hitting it harder than others. I personally don't know how a person can actually read a paper while doing a serious cardiovascular workout. I mean—you just can't. Why not install a beer tap and ashtray and call it a bar stool. However, I constantly see people engrossed in some kind of reading material while gyrating on an elliptical machine; which seems silly. Yes, they get to check the "workout" box on their HOHW list; but they derive almost no benefit from doing it. Why bother?

GREATER INTENSITY OF EFFORT PRODUCES GREATER OUTCOMES.

In another intensity example, a popular TV workout infomercial sells a workout system that uses a concept known as "muscle confusion" as a core element of their program. The theory is that muscles experience diminishing benefit by doing the same thing over and over. Their program is based on changing up both the type of workout and the intensity of the workout. Real muscle growth comes from changing the pattern and intensity of the workout.

Selling is the same. You need to create your own "sales confusion" by varying your activity level and intensity. Something you believe to be impossible to achieve today will be a no-brainer after you push through your wall. For example, plan a week in which to double your normal activity level. By changing your intensity, you build your sales muscle. More output for the same effort changes the arc of your potential, and your performance. If you are going to spend your valuable time doing prospecting, make it count. Be very prepared. Be protective of your time, and don't share it. Be upbeat on the phone. Be willing to get repeatedly rejected. Be focused. Learn from your rejections. Set hard-to-achieve goals. Flex your sales muscle. Kick your own ass—over and over again.

VARIABLE INTENSITY OF EFFORT CREATES BIGGER SALES MUSCLES, FASTER.

The second thing to do is to change the *velocity* of your sales process. This is what takes place in the absence of fear and allows you to move with greater confidence. You overcome rejection instantly and move forward to the next opportunity. You ratchet up the speed of the transaction. The less fear you operate under, the more you do. Your clients will recognize your cadence and move at your pace. Velocity translates into urgency in the buying and selling process; and greater urgency improves your close rate. An easy way to ratchet up your velocity is to build deadlines and impending events into your transactions. Placing impossible-to-meet deadlines on activities and projects creates urgency in everything you do. Your prospects will sense your urgency and efficiency, and will modulate their behavior to meet it.

The result of increasing your intensity in execution and the velocity of your sales process is *momentum*. Momentum is the compound interest of selling; the more you sell, the more people are drawn to you, which results in more sales. It's hard to build, but even harder to stop.

Become a Mentor

If you want to fully change the arc of your potential and create sustainable success in your career, then become a mentor to other salespeople in your life. The best way to learn is to consistently teach. Selling is a tough career choice and requires help and reinforcement in order to succeed. One of the best things you can do for yourself and others is to help others on the journey.

This book is a framework for changing the arc of your potential, and your mentorship will help others on their journey. Be open to sharing your struggles and triumphs with others, and you will change the arc of yours. For more information on how to mentor others on their journey, visit the web site, www.helpingsalespeoplesucceed.com.

Results or Excuses

The boss who informed me that "Your raise becomes effective when you do" had another special phrase he used frequently: "Rob, there are only two things: 'results' or 'excuses.' You either hit your goals, or you create excuses for why you didn't." He certainly had a colorful way with words. Normally, this little ditty only came out when the results we (he) desired were somewhat in doubt. As usual, he was correct; we live our lives achieving results or creating excuses for why we didn't. Some people get so beat down they just stop trying. They give up on setting goals because they are tired of having to create excuses for why they didn't hit them.

If you have struggled to achieve the results you desire, it simply means you haven't found the right path yet. Remember: you are not a failure un-til you fail to try. I can't tell you how true that has been in my life—

because frankly, it would take too long. Many times along the journey, my only visible asset was my unwillingness to quit. I hope that *Kick Your Own Ass* will provide the path for you to engage your true potential; to see yourself in a new light, and to embrace your unlimited potential. Now, quit whining, and go kick your own ass into gear. Then, go kick your competitor's ass.

Enjoy the uphill run.

God bless and good selling.

ABOUT THE AUTHOR

Robert Early Johnson has helped thousands of salespeople and businesses change the arc of their potential and the trajectory of their careers. A veteran of 25 years' worth of sales, sales management, and sales training, he personally understands the struggles that salespeople face in their pursuit of success, as his journey has often been arduous. His experience is the foundation of his expertise at helping his students overcome their issues. He is a transformative figure in helping students overcome their obstacles and master the *will* to sell, the *skill* to sell, and the daily *drill* to sell more than they thought possible. An engaging public speaker, Mr. Johnson leaves audiences laughing and thinking at the same time. A long-time employee of Sage—the world's leading provider of enterprise resource planning (ERP) and customer relationship management (CRM) solutions for small and medium-sized businesses—Mr. Johnson helps his fellow employees and company partners to improve their sales performance. He lives in Jacksonville, Florida, with his wife Anita and their children. His interests include running, reading, music, and spending quality time at the local hardware store. For more information, visit www.RobertEarlyJohnson.com.

INDEX

experience
customers for life

Getting—and keeping—customers is a necessity for every business. With **Customer Relationship Management (CRM) solutions** from Sage, you gain a complete view of customer interactions so you can make the most of every opportunity.

- Access detailed account and contact information in one place
- Track opportunities from lead through close
- Manage team calendars and activities
- Monitor, forecast, and report on sales activity and revenue
- Customize and automate your sales processes

Achieve stronger sales and a more successful business, now and into the future.

Go to www.sagecrmsolutions.com

Sage offers CRM solutions to meet your unique needs:

ACT! by Sage
Sage SalesLogix
SageCRM

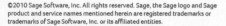